IMAGES
of America

Schaefferstown and Heidelberg Township, Lebanon County

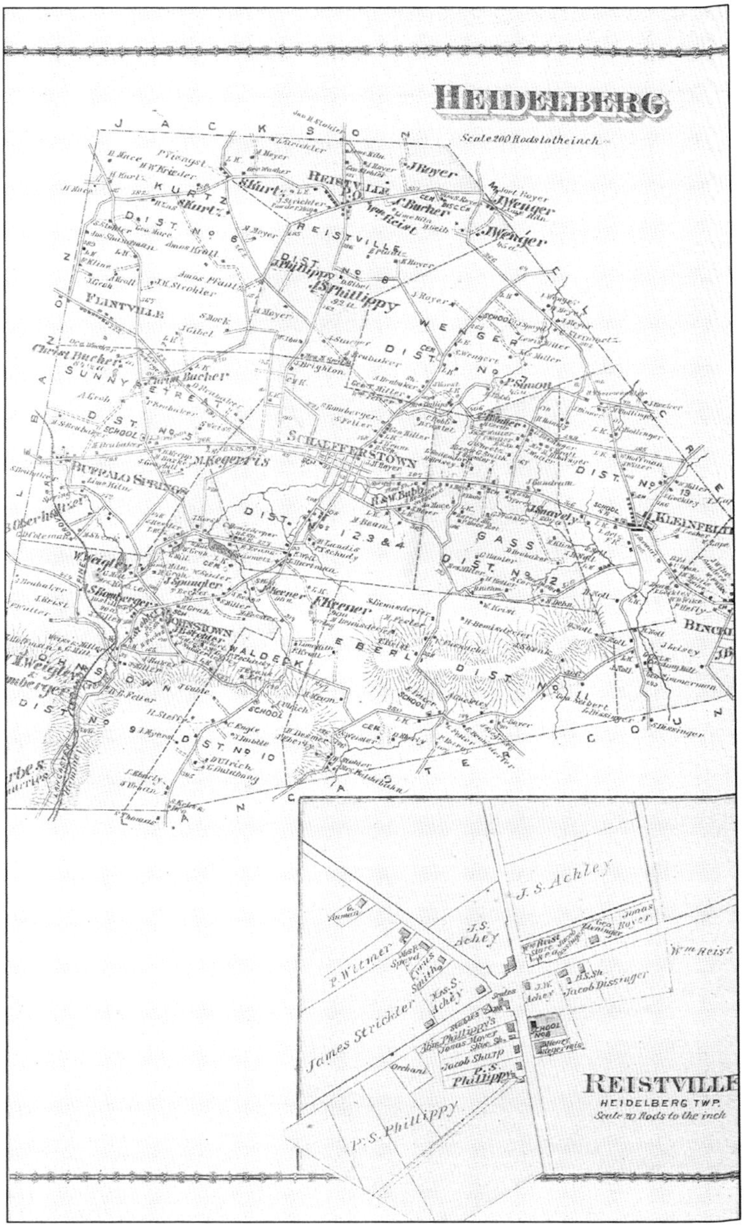

A treasure for researchers and historical enthusiasts, F.W. Beers's 1875 *County Atlas of Lebanon Pennsylvania* map of Heidelberg Township includes not only roads and towns but also locations of landowners, schools, and some businesses. One example is the powder magazine located near the little village of Reistville (on main map). The map is especially useful in locating township landowners listed on the 1870 and 1880 US federal censuses. (Courtesy of Historic Schaefferstown.)

On the Cover: Men and boys lined the front porch of the Franklin House, on the Schaefferstown square, for this turn-of-the-century photograph. Alexander Schaeffer built this iconic structure in the mid-18th century, but the exact date is not clear, since the date stone was removed years ago. Schaeffer operated a tavern and store here; it remains a busy bar and restaurant. (Courtesy of Dona Nye.)

IMAGES
of America

SCHAEFFERSTOWN AND HEIDELBERG TOWNSHIP, LEBANON COUNTY

Diane Wenger and Jan Taylor

ARCADIA
PUBLISHING

ISBN 978-1-4671-2084-5

Published by Arcadia Publishing
Charleston, South Carolina

Printed in the United States of America

Library of Congress Control Number: 2013943174

For all general information, please contact Arcadia Publishing:
Telephone 843-853-2070
Fax 843-853-0044
E-mail sales@arcadiapublishing.com
For customer service and orders:
Toll-Free 1-888-313-2665

Visit us on the Internet at www.arcadiapublishing.com

This book is dedicated to residents of Schaefferstown and Heidelberg Township, past and present.

CONTENTS

ACKNOWLEDGMENTS

This project began in 2012, when Arcadia acquisitions editor Abby Henry contacted Candie Johnson, who was then the Heidelberg Township zoning officer, to ask whether anyone in the area was interested in writing a history of the township. Candie contacted Diane, Diane called Jan, and soon, we were off and running. The archives of Historic Schaefferstown, Inc. (HSI), proved to be a rich resource, and unless otherwise noted, images in this volume appear courtesy of HSI. As time went on, the project became a community one. A number of township residents and former residents generously offered their recollections about the pictures we had found and lent us their own photographs for scanning. We thank local residents Carol Fetter, Walter Heisey, Ray Horst, Bob Krall, Lyle and Loretta Krall, Raynor Seltzer Leed, Robert Martin, Rita Mock, Betsy Nolt, Dona Nye, Susan Horst Kerschner, JoAnn Hartman Rager, Mary Smith, Susan Verhoek, and Glenn Wolgemuth, as well as Frank Summers of Park Ridge, Illinois, Diana Wike Castor of Horseheads, New York, and Merle Glime of Vista, California, for sharing their memories and photographs with us. Thanks, too, to the congregations of Zion United Methodist and St. Paul's United Church of Christ. Also, we are grateful to Donald R. Brown, founder of the Institute of American Deltiology, for allowing us access to his collection and for helping us understand real-photo postcards a bit better. Our only regret is that space did not permit us to use every single one of the wonderful images this project yielded.

INTRODUCTION

Schaefferstown is located in Lebanon County, in South Central Pennsylvania, just north of Lancaster, midway between Reading and Hershey. It is the largest town in Heidelberg Township. Visitors to Schaefferstown today take delight in the somewhat sleepy village, which retains so much 18th-century character, including its early public waterworks. This appearance is somewhat deceiving, however, because in the 18th and early 19th centuries, Schaefferstown was a busy commercial center and a hub for wagon freight lines. It was situated at the intersection of two major roads, and the town square was ringed by stores and taverns that served the steady stream of traffic that flowed through the town. A market house sat prominently on the square, and mountain springwater flowed continuously through underground pipes into two troughs on the square. Because Schaefferstown was close to a number of iron plantations, workers driving wagonloads of ore were regular customers at its business places. Freight companies with lines that ran to Philadelphia eventually established offices here, and craftsmen, including coopers, weavers, hat makers, and carpenters, worked in their shops throughout the village. A tannery and a brewery operated on the edge of town. The countryside was dotted with farms characterized by massive barns and limestone farmhouses; mills of various types harnessed water power along streams to grind grain or power other equipment. Lime kilns, in which native limestone was burned to produce lime, were a common sight along rural roads.

Heidelberg Township, when incorporated in 1757, was much larger than its present 24 square miles. Then, it was part of Lancaster County, one of the three original counties in the state. It became part of Dauphin County in 1786, when that entity was carved out of Lancaster County. Still more changes occurred in 1813, as Lebanon County was created out of Dauphin and Jackson Township split off from Heidelberg. The township took on its present size in 1844, when Millcreek Township was formed from portions of Heidelberg and Jackson.

In addition to Schaefferstown, Kleinfeltersville and Reistville are Heidelberg Township's main towns. The township also takes in a number of smaller settlements, including Buffalo Springs, Flintville, and Waldeck.

The first European settlers in the area were German and Swiss, arriving during the 1720s. These people often traveled to America in family or village groups, and, unlike the Scots-Irish, they tended to stay put once they reached a favorable place. They found such a place in the fertile farmland of the Lebanon Valley. These settlers spoke an informal German dialect that became known as Pennsylvania "Dutch" or Pennsylvania German, although they used standard German for their worship services. The migrants included two "church" groups: Lutherans and German Reformed. Other migrants were Mennonites and Amish, "plain" groups who worshiped in homes rather than in church buildings. Among the earliest landowners in the area were John and Katherine Meily and Durst and Margareth Thoma. Some of these early arrivals, including members of the Thoma family, moved to the Ephrata Cloister to join the religious community there.

Following on the heels of the Meily and Thoma families was another early immigrant who would leave much more of a mark on the area: Alexander Schaeffer. Schaeffer and his family emigrated from Schriescheim, near Heidelberg, Germany. In 1738, they arrived in Philadelphia and then made their way west to the Lebanon Valley. Schaeffer, who was somewhat of an entrepreneur, eventually bought some 700 acres in the area. This land included a 100-acre plantation now known as the Alexander Schaeffer Farm and several larger pieces of land on which, in 1758, he laid out a town. He called the town "Heidelberg," but it was commonly referred to as "Schaeffer's Town," and before long, this became its official name.

Schaeffer sold lots in the town for five shillings each, and he collected an annual ground rent of two to three shillings from each purchaser. He kept a prime spot on the square for himself, and there he built a large limestone hotel in which he also ran a general store. Period records suggest that Schaeffer lived at the hotel and used his farm to provide supplies, including whiskey, for his business.

Persistent folklore holds that Jewish traders were among the earliest settlers in Schaefferstown and that they were numerous enough to have established a synagogue and burial ground. If the existence of such a sizable settlement could be confirmed, it would be a significant example of an early American Jewish community. Primary sources do show that Jewish merchants with ties to Lancaster and Philadelphia operated stores here in the mid-18th century, however, and this is further evidence of the area's commercial importance.

Reistville, situated two miles north of Schaefferstown, was known as Achey's Corner in the early 1800s; like Schaefferstown, it was also once a busy commercial center. Members of the Achey family ran a hotel and store at various places on the Reistville square. The last known Reistville hotel, however, was the Farmer's and Drover's, operated by livestock dealer Isaac Phillippy. He brought in western horses and cattle and held auctions every two weeks in the summer and fall; he also sold horses as far away as New York. In addition to the livestock trade, Reistville was known for the sizable business in butter and eggs conducted by Samuel Achey, George Spayd, and Samuel Phillippy. The three men bought these products locally and shipped them to distant markets in New York and elsewhere. The present name came into use when William Reist, who ran a general store here in the 1880s, applied for and received a US post office under the name of Reistville. The post office closed in 1905.

Kleinfeltersville lies a few miles east of Schaefferstown. It is best known for its association with Jacob Albright, founder of the Evangelical Church, and in 1850, a memorial chapel was erected in his honor. The town is named for John R. Kleinfelter, a traveling Evangelical minister whose circuit brought him through the spot that would eventually bear his name. In 1823, Kleinfelter married local resident Catherine Becker, daughter of John George Becker, who was a staunch Evangelical Church member. Kleinfelter bought property in the area, including the Becker farm in 1824 and a 49-acre tract of land he purchased in 1844. He divided this latter plot into lots and sold them to his son-in-law, his six daughters, and his son. The town that grew up here became known as Kleinfeltersville. It is said to have the longest name of any US post office.

In the late 19th century, both Schaefferstown and Kleinfeltersville were home to a flourishing tobacco industry. Many small factories employed men and women in processing tobacco and rolling it into cigars. Other trades carried on in the area at the end of the century included blacksmithing, tinsmithing, cabinetmaking and undertaking, saddlery and harness making, photography, cigar-box manufacturing, tailoring, shoemaking, wheelwright work, chair-making, house painting, masonry, butchering, watchmaking, carriage painting, and baking. In the Reistville area, low-grade iron ore was mined in open pits and then taken by the wagonload to furnaces in Lebanon, Sheridan, and Robesonia. When the iron pits were abandoned, they became farm ponds.

The late 19th century also saw a flurry of construction. In the 1880s, hotel owners in Schaefferstown and Kleinfeltersville enlarged their buildings by adding a third floor to accommodate more guests and community activities. Prosperous businessmen and professional men such as William M. Weigley built large sandstone mansions in the latest fashion. As the United States looked forward with pride to celebrating its centennial in 1876, Schaefferstown musicians did their part by forming a town band. In 1879, the Washington Camp of the Patriotic Order Sons of America (POS of A) was instituted in Schaefferstown, and, in 1909, the camp erected its own building on North Market Street. Kleinfeltersville also had its own patriotic lodge group.

Because the area showed so much potential for development, it was a disappointment to local citizens that major transportation routes, including the Union Canal and, more significantly, rail lines, bypassed them. And so it was quite exciting when the Ephrata & Lebanon trolley line came through Reistville, Schaefferstown, and Kleinfeltersville in 1914. However, the increasing popularity of automobiles and the construction of better roads soon made the trolley obsolete; the lines were sold for scrap in 1931. Around World War II, as taste in tobacco products changed, the cigar factories closed. They were replaced in some cases by sewing plants, which also ran their course as more and more of this kind of work moved overseas.

In 1963, Schaefferstown residents came together to celebrate the 200th anniversary of their town water system. A few years later, locals and interested parties from outside the area formed Historic Schaefferstown, Inc., a nonprofit educational organization dedicated to preserving and disseminating information on Pennsylvania German culture and local history. One of its first acts was to purchase the Alexander Schaeffer Farm and hold folk festivals there. As it began to collect artifacts and memorabilia related to Schaefferstown and the surrounding area, HSI needed a display space, so in 1969, it acquired the former POS of A hall, which now houses HSI's office and the Thomas R. Brendle Museum. In 1987, HSI purchased the historic Gemberling-Rex House.

In 1973, the Middle Creek Wildlife Management Area, a 5,000-acre refuge for waterfowl and other wildlife, was established on the eastern edge of the township, extending into adjacent Lancaster County. In the creation of this site, 63 families were displaced and many early homes were destroyed. The site has become a popular hunting and recreation area.

The township's population by 2013 was about 3,800, and in that year, still more dramatic changes took place. After many years of sometimes contentious discussion, construction started on the Route 501 bypass around Schaefferstown. At the same time, work began to install a sanitary sewer system for Schaefferstown and Kleinfeltersville. In addition, township supervisors passed an ordinance to change some street names. Route 501 was renamed Stiegel Pike, and Main Street in Schaefferstown became Heidelberg Avenue, ending 200 years of tradition but making it easier for emergency workers to locate addresses through global positioning systems.

Despite inevitable evolution, changing technology, and sometimes disruptive change, the towns, villages, and surrounding farmland of the township retain much of their old-time character and charm. Reminders of the area's Germanic roots are everywhere. Local residents appreciate the history of their land and their houses, many of them early log, stone, or even rare half-timbered structures. Farming remains an important way of life for many families, and in the summer months, the area abounds with fresh produce stands. The Pennsylvania German dialect can still be heard, spoken by older residents and by Amish people of all ages, and residents continue to enjoy scrapple, pig stomach, pot pie flavored with saffron, and other traditional foods that reflect the area's heritage. Springwater still flows to the fountain on the Schaefferstown square, where Schaeffer's hotel, known today as the Franklin House, continues the tradition of welcoming travelers as well as locals to the tavern and restaurant.

The pages that follow offer a pictorial trip back in time, a glimpse into the rich history of Schaefferstown and Heidelberg Township. Enjoy your visit!

One

Town and Country Scenes

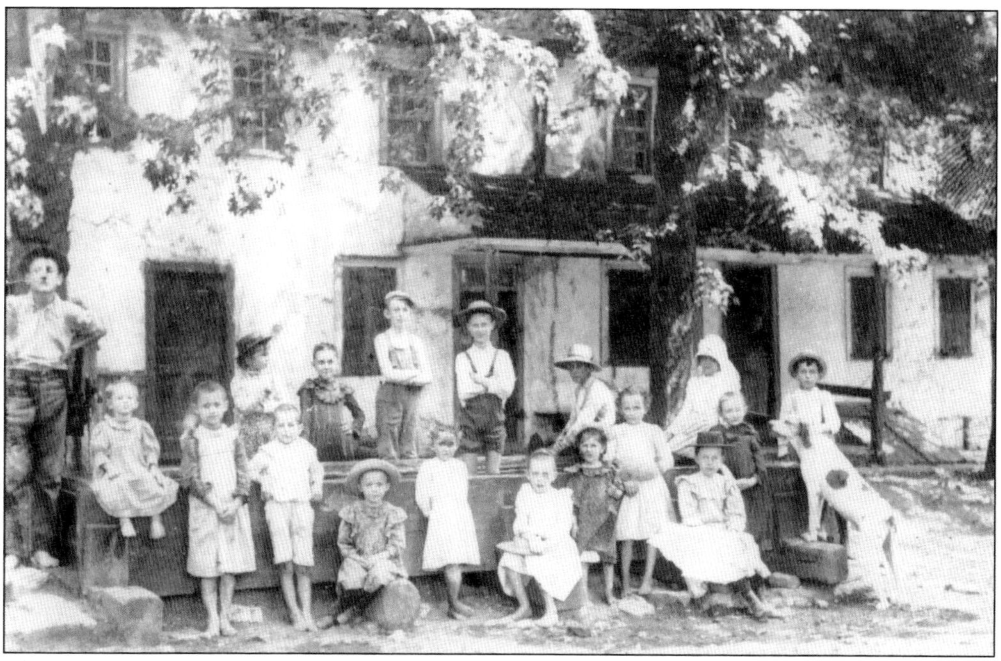

The trough on South Market Street, Schaefferstown, was a popular gathering place for the town's youngsters in 1900. Shown here are, from left to right, (first row) Landis Bachman, Dewey Hartman, Mabel Hartman, Paul Hartman, Norma Hickernell Leib, Florence Snyder, Edna Houser Borrell, Beulah Plasterer, Mabel Snyder Boltz, Annie Hickernell Weaver, and Anna Keath Moyer; (second row) Marie Zerbe Winneshek, Elizabeth Hartman, James Keath Jr., Ray Beamesderfer, Paul Wike, Mabel Becker Mentzer, and Taylor Zerbe, with his dog, Bang.

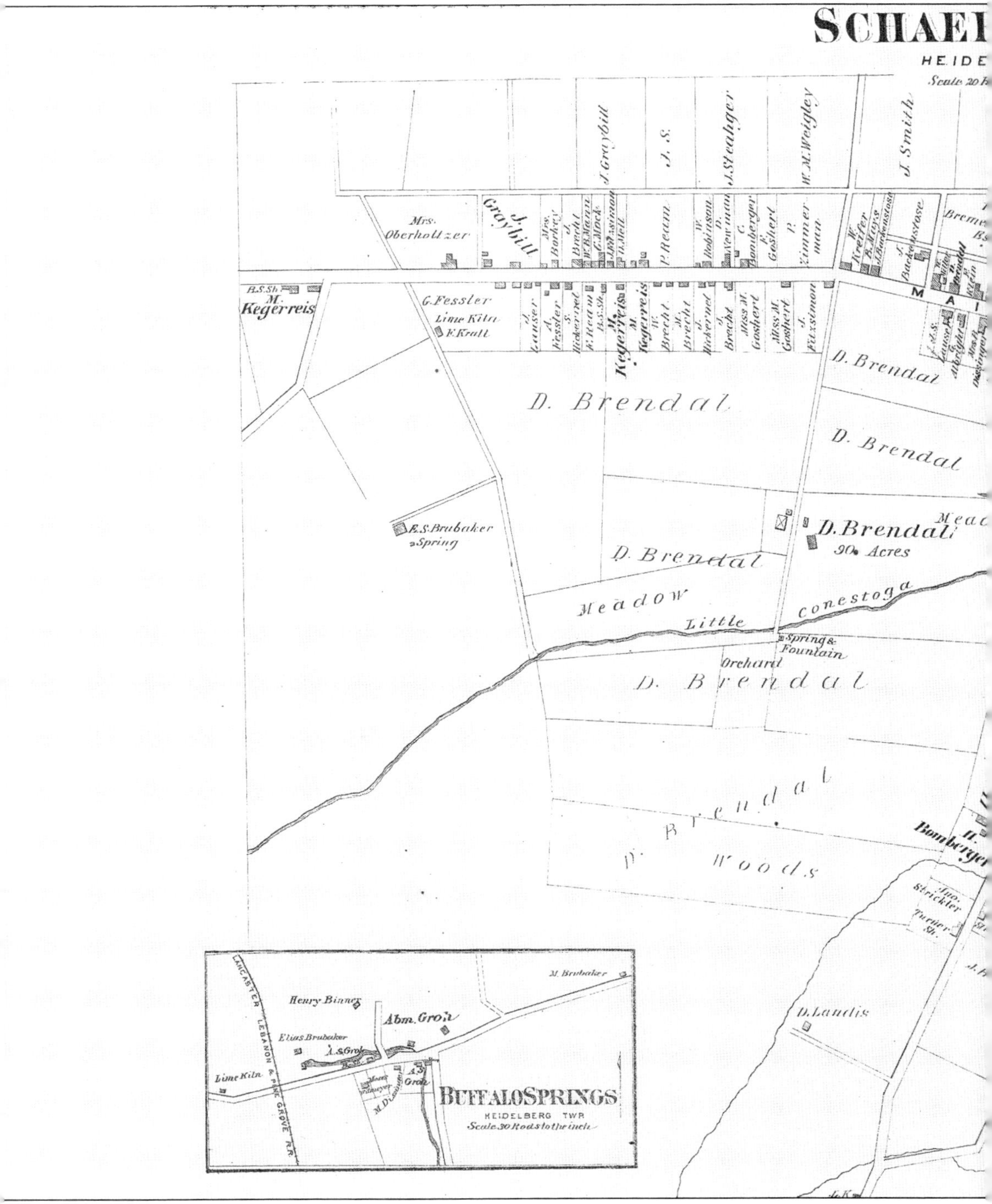

The companion to the 1875 Lebanon County atlas map of Heidelberg Township is the two-page detailed map of Schaefferstown proper, which also includes insets for the smaller communities of Buffalo Springs, Kleinfeltersville, and Flintville. These maps are a valuable tool for researchers, showing names of landowners (larger landholders are labeled with larger font), lots, houses and outbuildings, roads and waterways, churches, cemeteries, stores, blacksmith shops (Bs Sh.), and

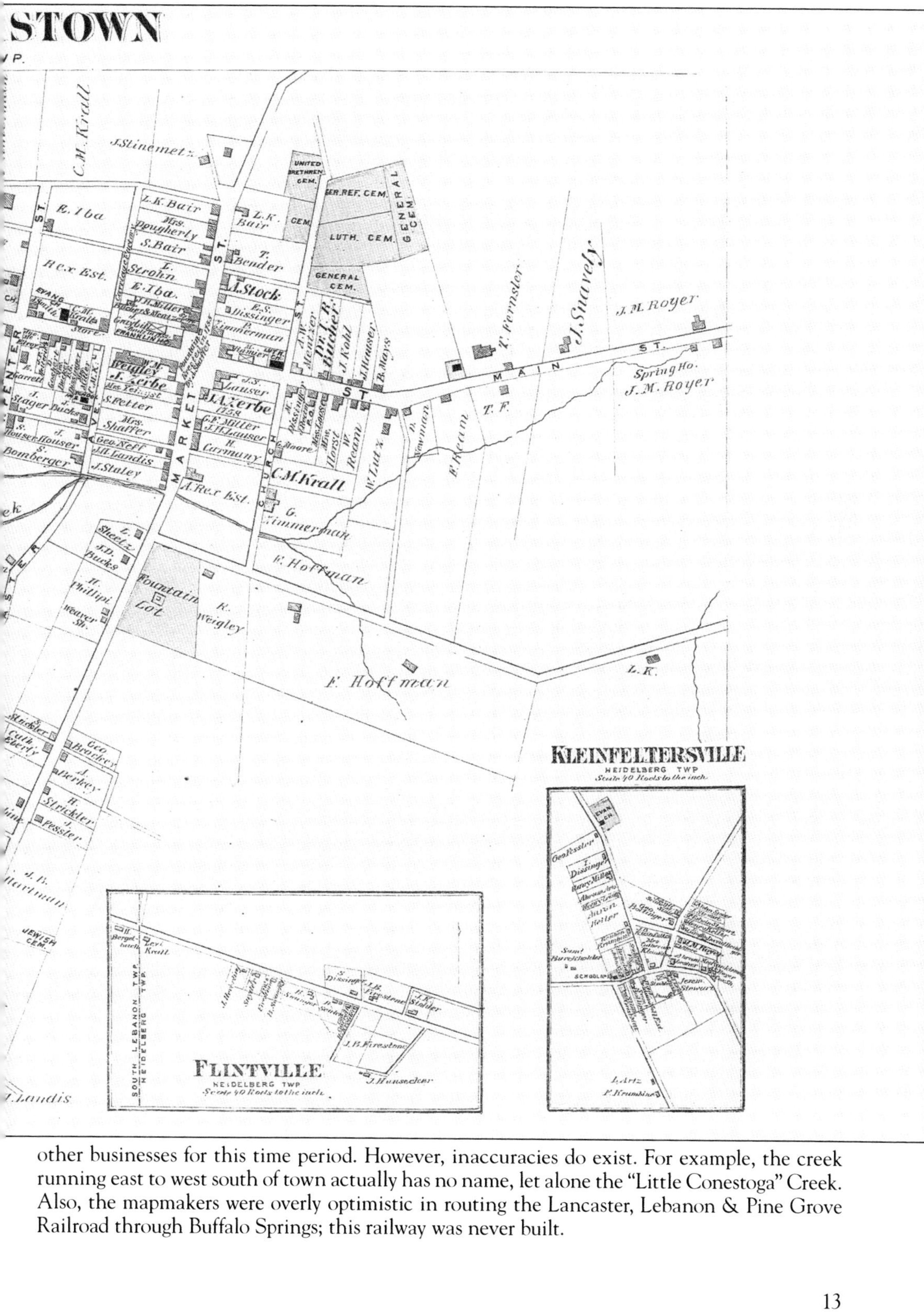

other businesses for this time period. However, inaccuracies do exist. For example, the creek running east to west south of town actually has no name, let alone the "Little Conestoga" Creek. Also, the mapmakers were overly optimistic in routing the Lancaster, Lebanon & Pine Grove Railroad through Buffalo Springs; this railway was never built.

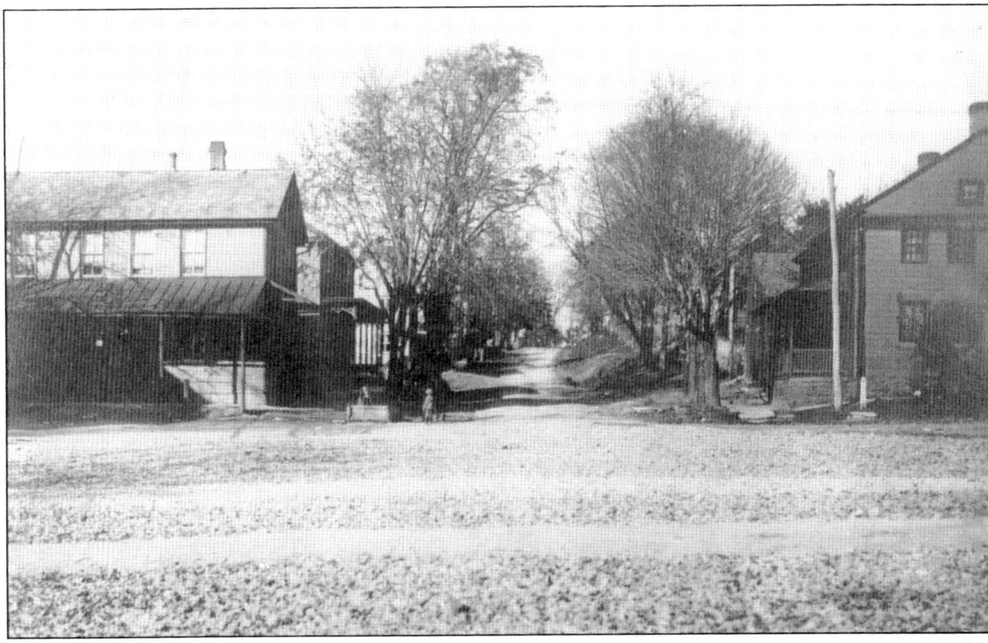

This photograph is of Schaefferstown square, looking north. Until about 1850, an open-sided market pavilion stood here; markets were never held, but the pavilion was used during the annual cherry fair. The building on the left is Carpenter's Hall, built by Fred Carpenter, proprietor of the Franklin House. It was at various times a clothing store, jewelry shop, soda fountain and restaurant, cigar factory, and dentist shop.

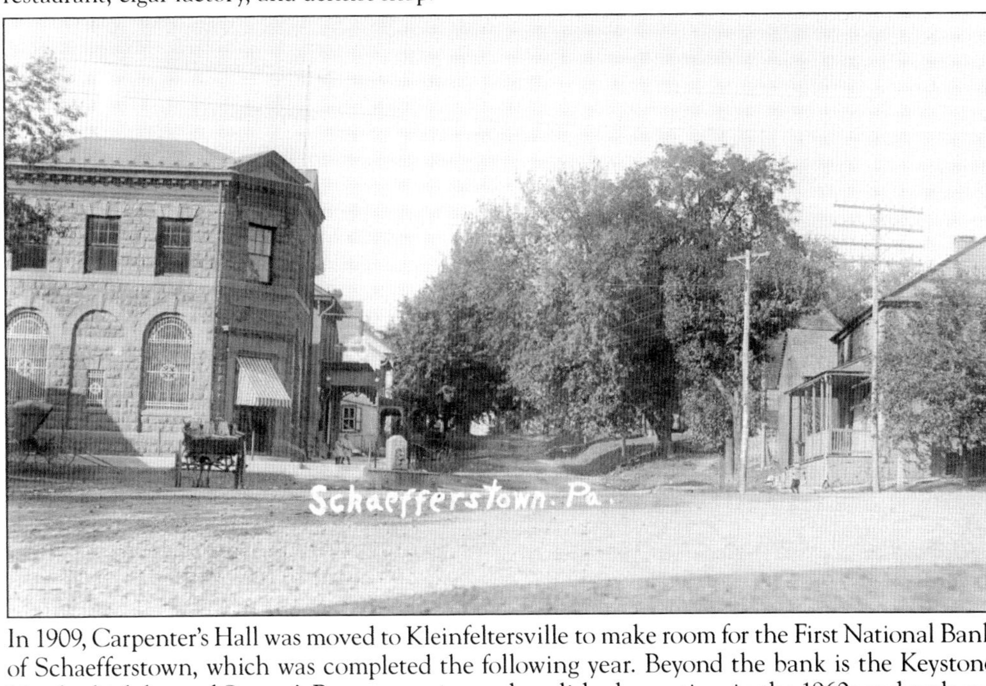

In 1909, Carpenter's Hall was moved to Kleinfeltersville to make room for the First National Bank of Schaefferstown, which was completed the following year. Beyond the bank is the Keystone Hotel, which housed Speece's Restaurant; it was demolished sometime in the 1960s and replaced by a parking lot. Note the gable-roofed building next to the Gemberling-Rex House on the right. (Courtesy of the Institute of American Deltiology.)

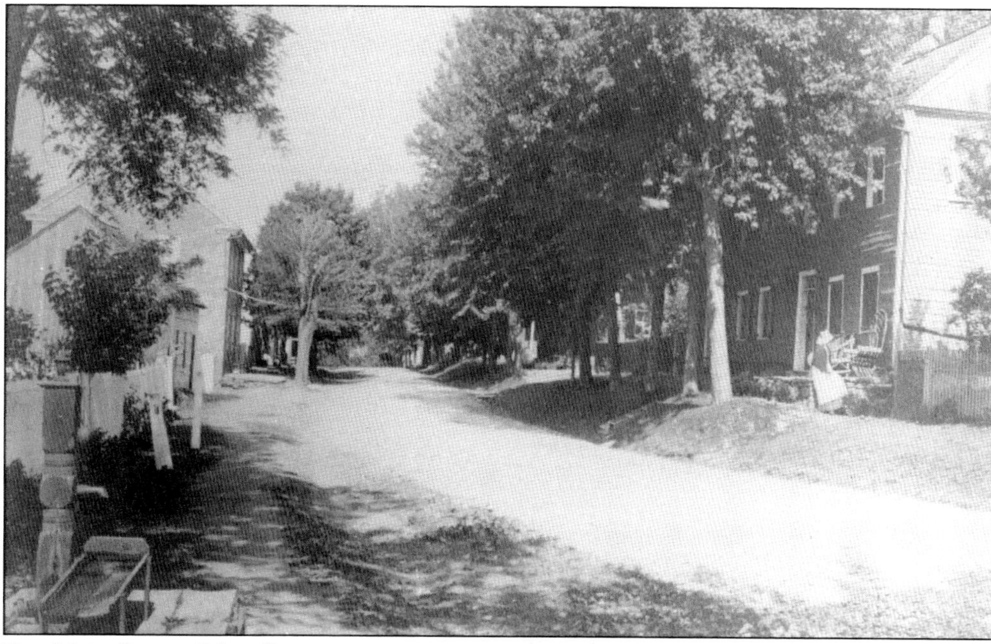

East Main Street, Schaefferstown, was narrow and tree-lined when this photograph was taken, looking west, in the early 20th century. The house on the right is made of logs and covered with clapboards. The attached shop (where the woman is sitting) has since been removed. The building at one time was Benjamin Mace's carpentry shop and, later, George F. Miller's general store.

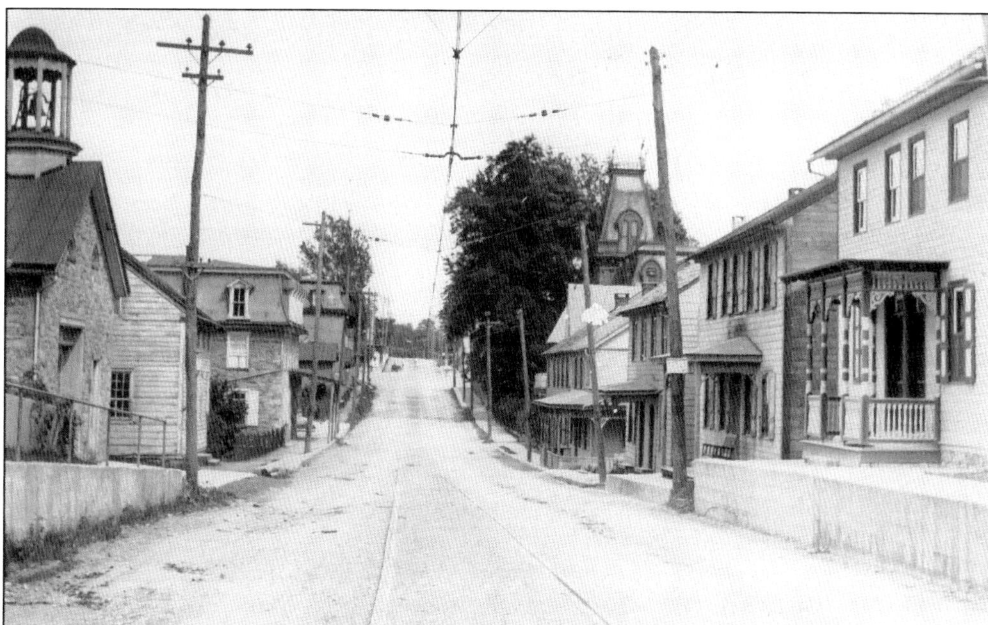

The trolley tracks and overhead lines in this photograph of West Main Street, looking east, indicate that it was taken sometime between 1914, when the lines were installed, and 1931, when they were removed. Note the elevated sidewalks and the Weigley Mansion tower, visible in the background. (Courtesy of Diana Wike Castor.)

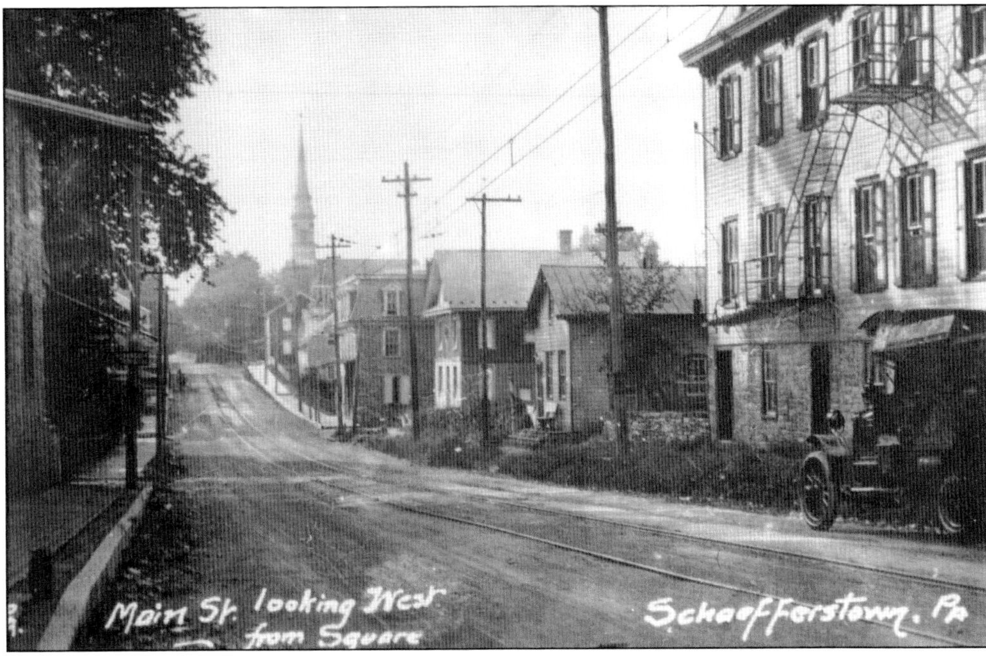

Residents of Schaefferstown today could wish for a view such as this of Main Street on a lazy summer afternoon. Aside from a distant horse-drawn vehicle, there is no traffic. This peaceful scene includes the Reformed (UCC) Church steeple, Evangelical Church bell tower, the mansard-roofed Cyrus M. Krall Store, and the post office (left of Franklin House). (Courtesy of the Institute of American Deltiology.)

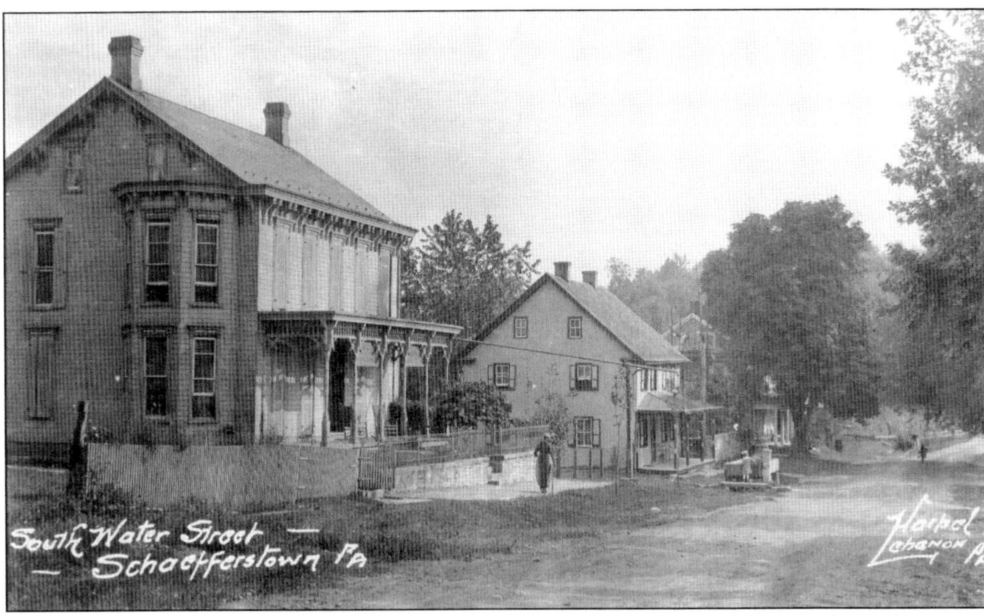

Postmarked January 17, 1919, this Harpel photo postcard shows homes along South Market Street as well as the lower fountain as viewed from the square. Take note of the drainpipe leading from the front porch of the left-hand house, over the sidewalk to above the road. Even today, rainwater from gutters empties onto the street in this way. (Courtesy of Rita Mock.)

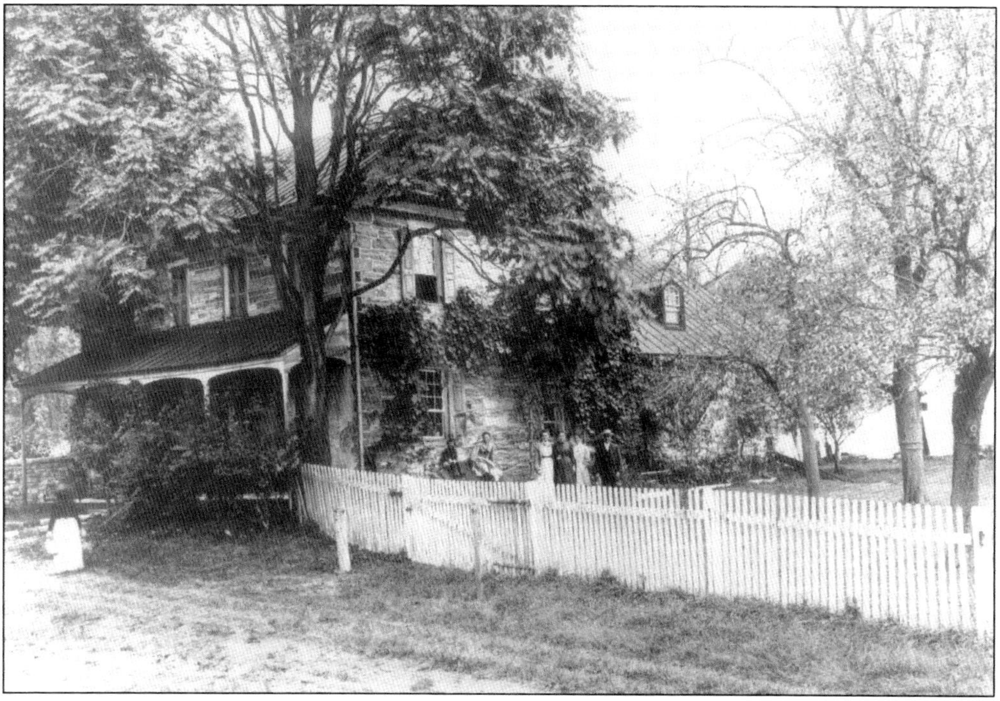

Philip Erpff (1724–1803) and his wife, Susanna Magdalena (1724–1798), came to America as redemptioners and worked "along the Muhlbach" to pay their passage. This was a typical path for many Germans who could not afford the voyage. Later, Erpff purchased land on South Market Street, Schaefferstown, and built this impressive limestone house. The people shown here may be the Keath family, who lived in the house at the turn of the century.

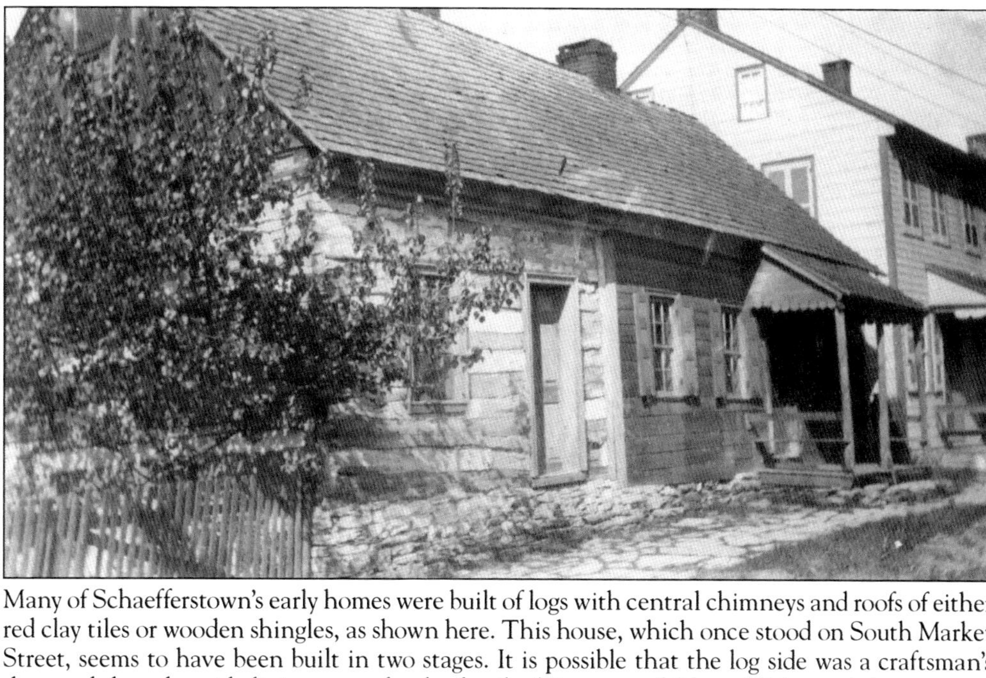

Many of Schaefferstown's early homes were built of logs with central chimneys and roofs of either red clay tiles or wooden shingles, as shown here. This house, which once stood on South Market Street, seems to have been built in two stages. It is possible that the log side was a craftsman's shop and the other side living space for the family. (Courtesy of Glenn Wolgemuth.)

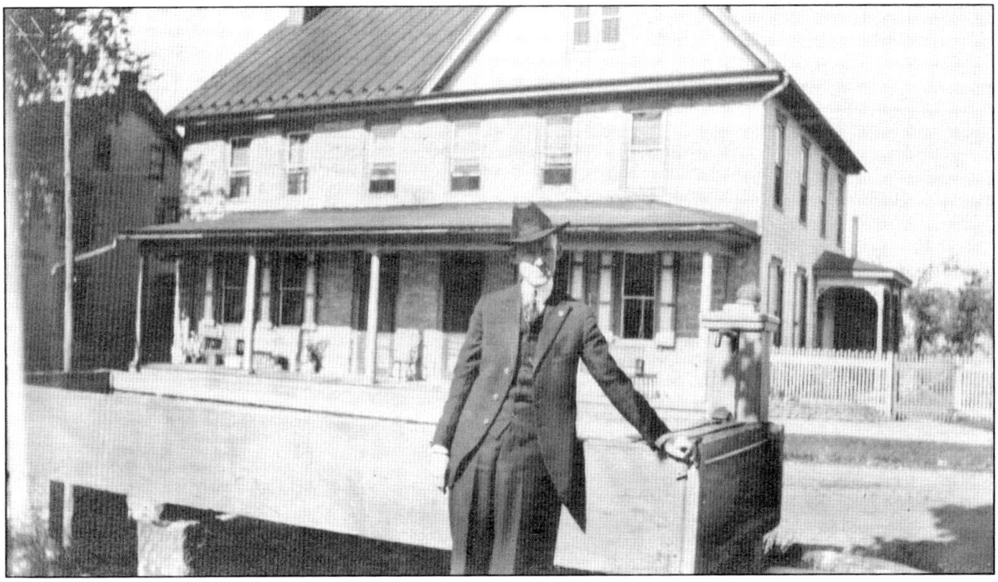

Charles Zerbe (1885–1973) posed for this photograph sometime before 1936. It was taken on South Market Street, Schaefferstown, near his family's home (shown below). Behind him is the Mock family home; built in the mid-18th century, it once served as a store and tavern. The large addition on the right side of the house was built in the 19th century.

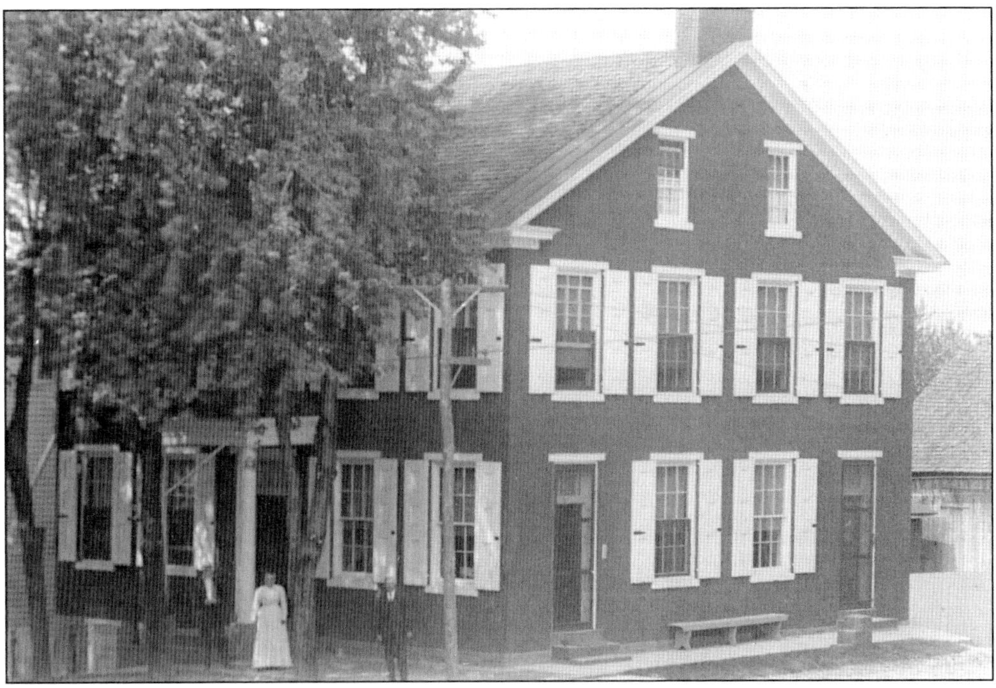

This brick house, on the corner of South Market Street and Schaefferstown square, was the home of Dr. B. Frank Zerbe (1853–1915). Note the stone mounting block, which provided an easy step into a carriage. Zerbe practiced medicine with his brother Thomas, who lived across the street. In 1883, the brothers began manufacturing cigars, and the business was so successful that they eventually gave up medicine. (Courtesy of Dona Nye.)

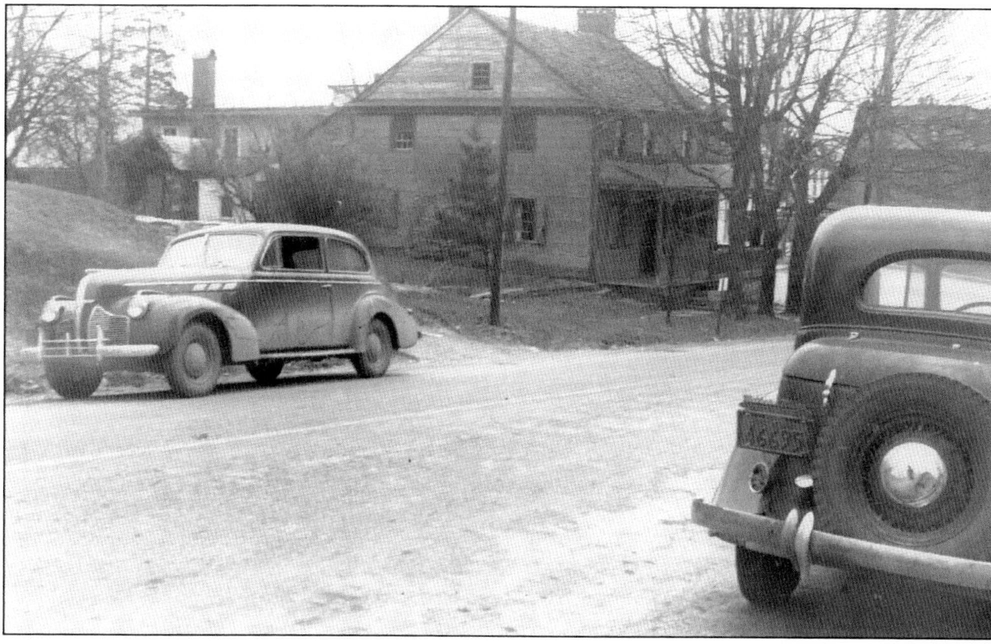

The Gemberling-Rex House, on the northeast corner of Schaefferstown's square, was built around 1758 by tavern keeper Paul Gemberling. It is one of several half-timbered structures remaining in the town. The rear stone addition was built before 1798. The building was a tavern until 1807; then, storekeeper Samuel Rex and his wife, Mary, made it their home. It remained in family hands until the 1970s.

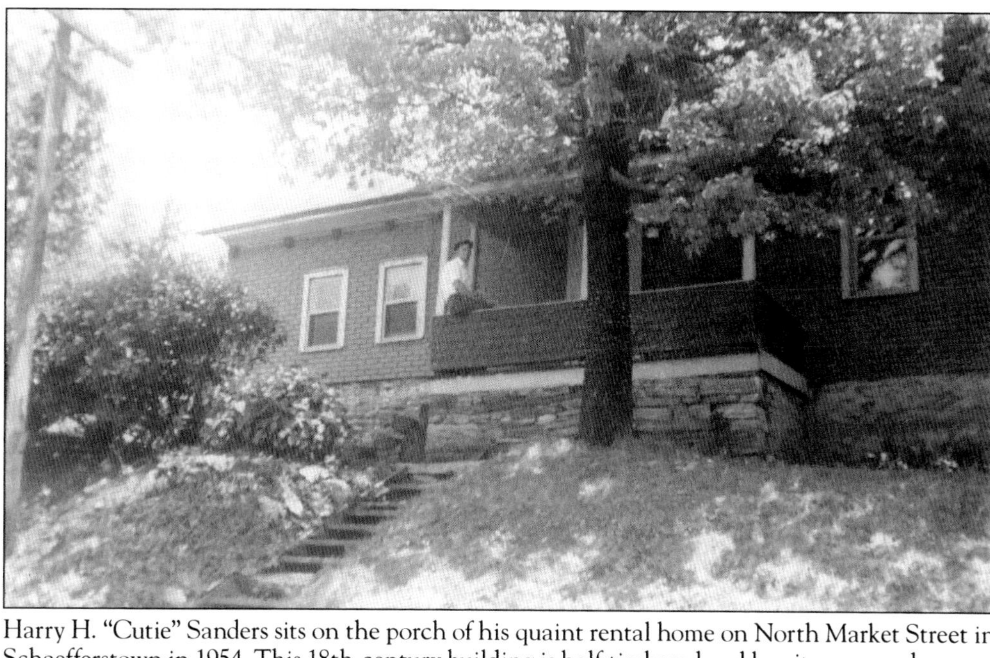

Harry H. "Cutie" Sanders sits on the porch of his quaint rental home on North Market Street in Schaefferstown in 1954. This 18th-century building is half-timbered and log; it was once home to Dorothea and Anthony Stiegel, mother and brother of ill-fated ironmaster Henry Stiegel. After Stiegel was released from debtor's prison in 1774, he taught school in Schaefferstown and lived here with his brother. (Courtesy of Carol Fetter.)

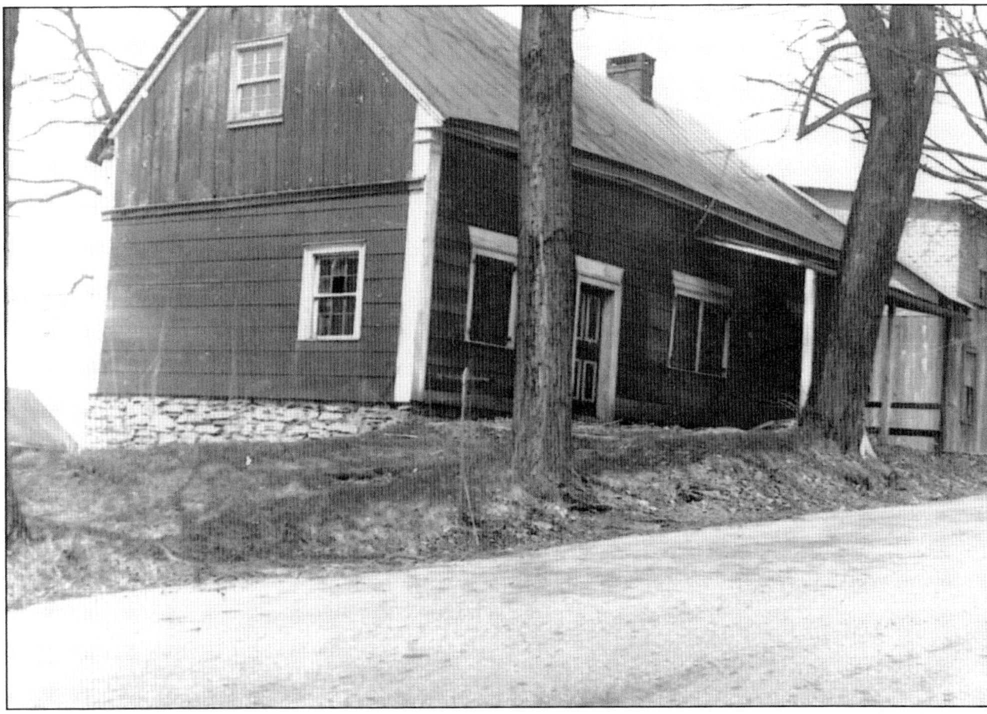

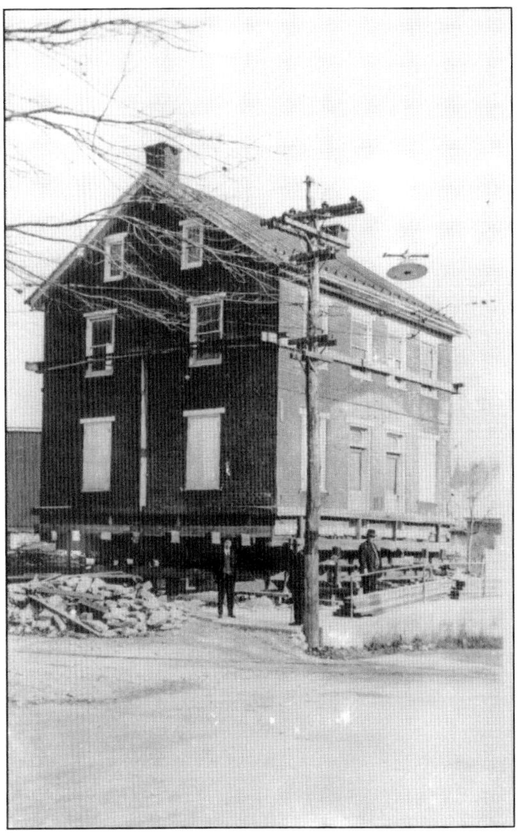

Absalom Daugherty (1799–1872), a local gunsmith, lived in this log home with his wife, Sarah, and family. Sarah was the daughter of Henry and Barbara Iba, who once owned this lot on the west side of North Market Street. The house was torn down, but the foundation stone was reused in the foundation for the small Cape Cod–style house standing there today. (Courtesy of Ray Horst.)

Uriah Brubaker Horst owned this house originally located on the northeast corner of Main and Carpenter Streets. He also owned the vacant lot next door. When Horst wanted to build a new home on the corner lot, he sold this two-story house to the Sanders family and engaged a contractor to move the house. The contractor fell through, so Horst moved the house himself. (Courtesy of Glenn Wolgemuth.)

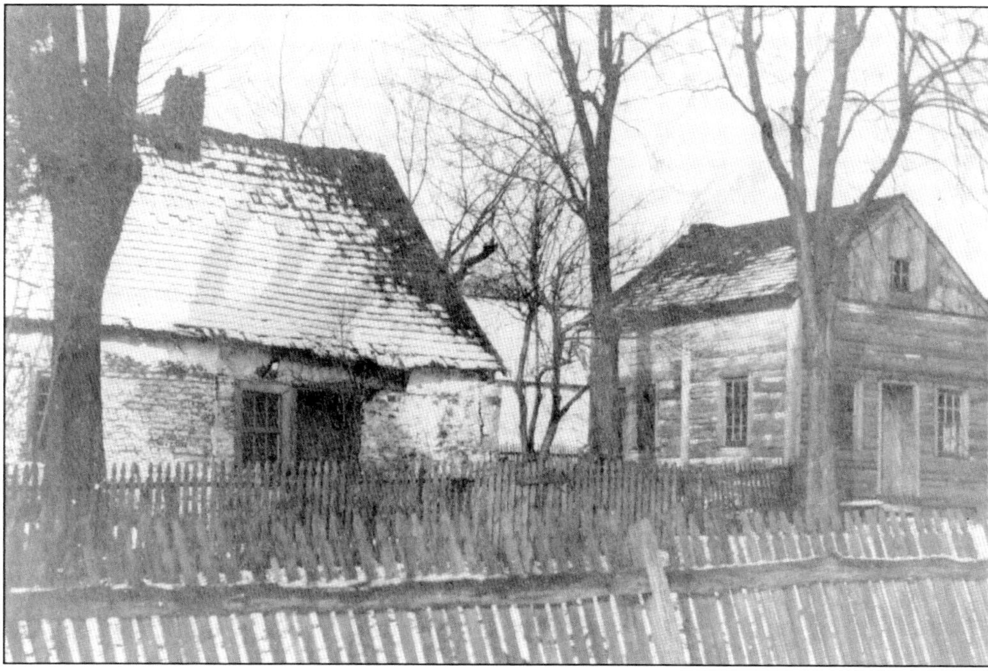

Isaac Sheiner, his wife, Sophia, and their family lived in this small log home on the west side of South Carpenter Street just north of the creek. The structure to the left is built of brick and may have served as a barn or workshop. Note the characteristic picket fence, so common with homes "in town."

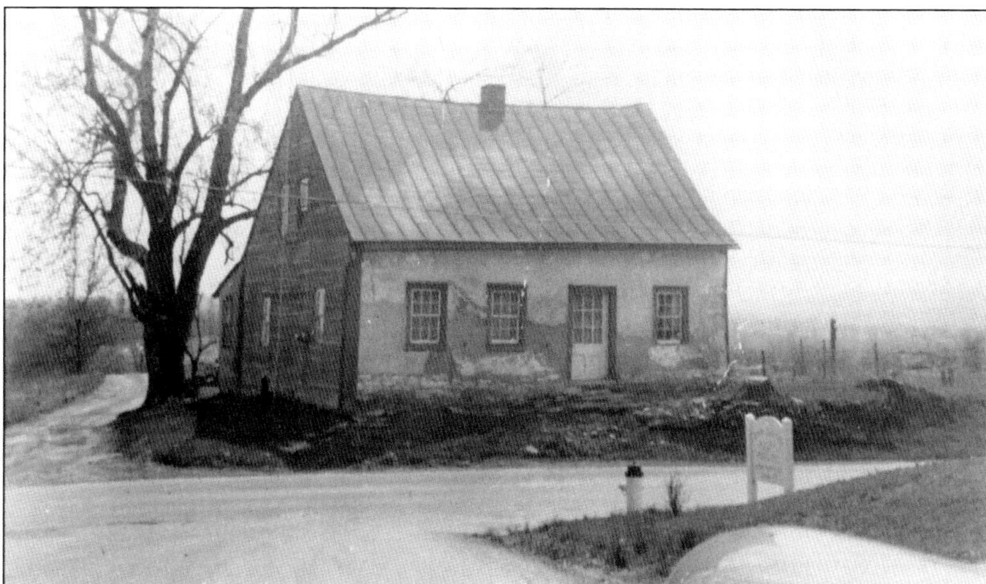

Schaefferstown resident Peter Ream once lived in this log home on West Main Street opposite Locust Street. The lane to the left leads down to the Brendle farm, now Historic Schaefferstown's Alexander Schaeffer Farm. Just to the right of this view was Frank Horst's limestone quarry, where stone for the United Brethren Church and the Patriotic Order Sons of America Hall was quarried.

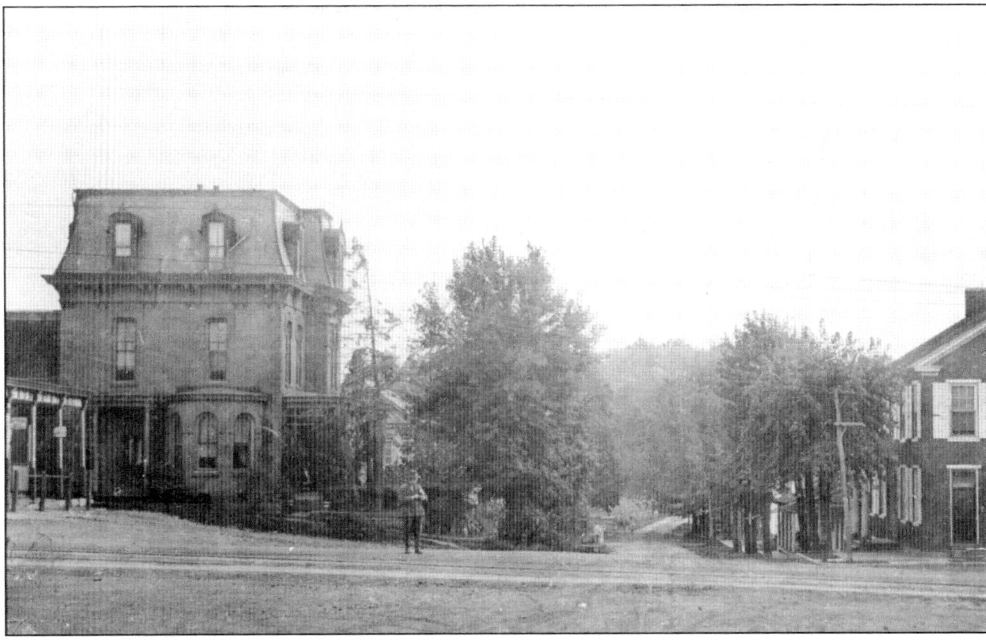

Dr. Thomas T. Zerbe (1846–1920) built this imposing brown sandstone home with mansard roof on the southeast corner of the Schaefferstown square about 1880. A.S. Brendle, writing in 1901, noted that the mansion was built on the site of the 1758 Mathias Albright house, and he observed that "the town may pride itself" on handsome residences such as this and the Weigley Mansion.

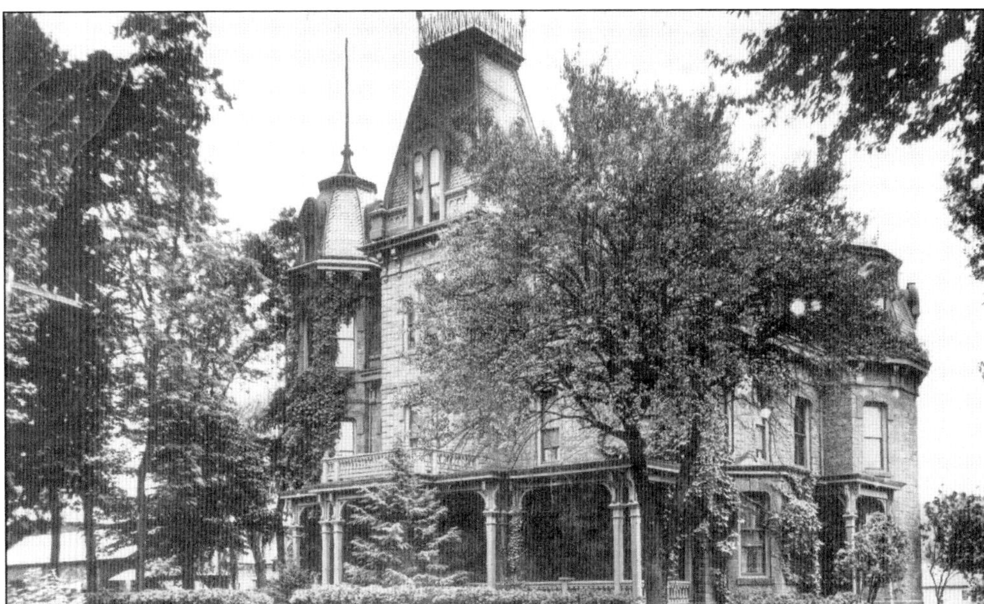

In 1883, William M. Weigley built this sandstone mansion behind his store, facing Main Street. Weigley died in 1887; his widow, Anna Rex Weigley, lived here until her death in 1900. Their son, Rex Weigley, operated a watch and jewelry shop in the mansion. Subsequently, Ralph and Anna Miller purchased the building for a home and jewelry shop. (Courtesy of Rita Mock.)

GODEY'S LADY'S BOOK AND MAGAZINE.

SUBURBAN RESIDENCE.

Drawn expressly for Godey's Lady's Book, by ISAAC H. HOBBS & SON, *Architects, 804 North Eighth Street formerly of 809 and 811 Chestnut Street, Philadelphia.*

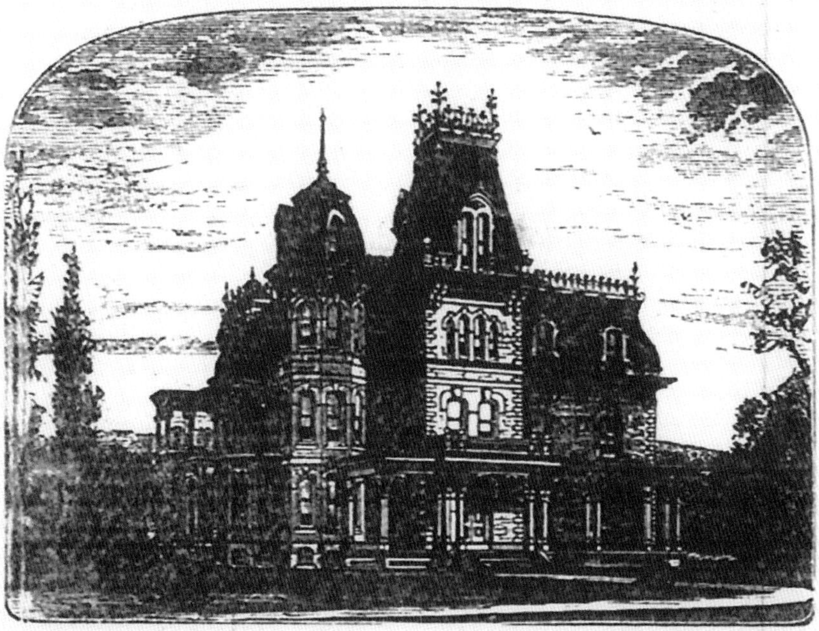

THE above design is an evolution of the ovo laws of proportion, with a Mansard roof. The design of the structure, with its symmetrical appearance, must render it obvious to all that it will be, when built, beautiful. It is being erected by William M. Weigley, in Shaefferstown, Lebanon County, Pennsylvania, of a very fine toned brown stone from the quarry of William M. Weigley. There is a very fine ridge of the stone running through his lands, of a peculiarly rich reddish-brown color. The work will be rock face range work with draughted base course, and other dressings of picked centres. All of the stone work will be very fine. The building is to be finely finished interiorly with hard, natural wood. The situation of the house rendered it of advantage to

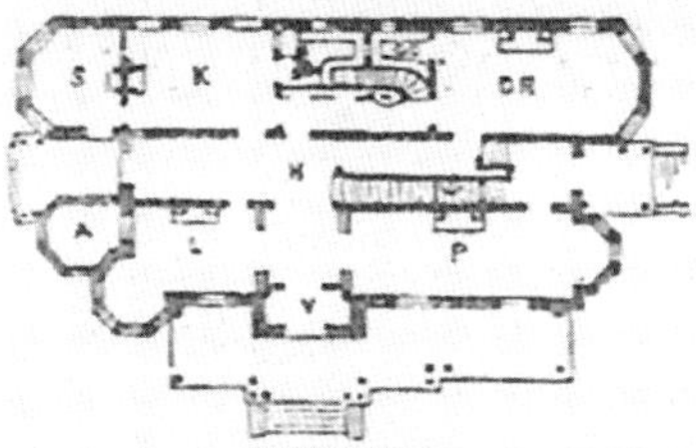

FIRST STORY.

have a broad front and not to be deep. So much depends upon the lay and shape of grounds for the plan of a house to be effective upon them, that original designs becomes necessary to successful operations. The building will cost $22,000. It is rarely indeed that you see houses of such appearance costing less than $50,000; so much must be credited for architecture and proportion. The interior arrangements are as follows:—

First Story.—V vestibule, 6 by 12 feet; H stair hall, 10 feet wide, connecting main hall, 10 feet, separated by an ornamental arch connection; P parlor, 15 feet wide, 30 feet long; L library and sitting-room, 15 by 15 feet wide; an octagonal corner room 10 feet diameter forming an alcove of beautiful proportions; A is a conservatory connecting library and side porch by windows down to the floor; DR dining-room 15 by 25 feet long; K kitchen, 15 by 17 feet; S scullery, 15 by 16 feet. This story is provided with ample store-room, butlery, pantry, and a lavatory under main stair, also a lift from cellar to this story.

The *Second Story* contains four fine chambers marked C, all of which are 15 feet wide, and of the following length: one with octagonal projecting tower alcove 15 by 15 feet; alcove 10 feet; two, 15 by 25 feet; one, 15 by 17 feet 4 inches. This story also

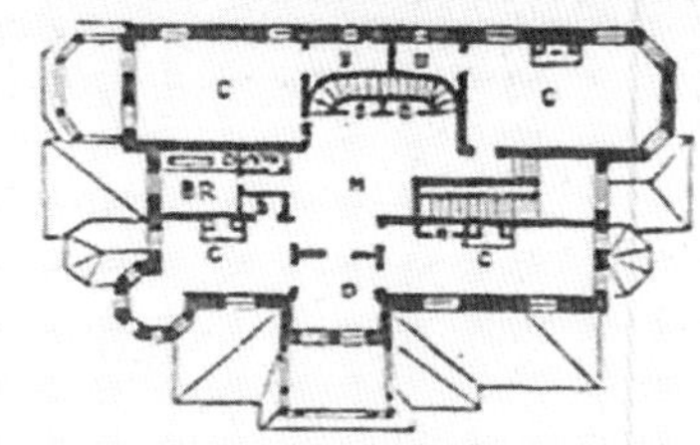

SECOND STORY.

contains a dressing-room or boudoir, 11 by 13 feet; a bath-room, 11 by 10 feet, with ample linen and other closets. There is a veranda in front, and a covered veranda upon its side.

The *Third Story* will contain the same number of finely-ventilated rooms and accommodations as described for the second story.

CIVILITY attracts the regard of men.

THE eyes of other people are the eyes that ruin us, not our own.

In 1875, *Godey's Ladies' Book*, a popular magazine of the time, ran this piece praising the handsome "suburban residence" that William M. Weigley planned to erect in Schaefferstown, using stone from his own quarry. The writer estimated it would cost $22,000, but after it was completed, A.S. Brendle put the price at $30,000. It remains a private, single-family residence.

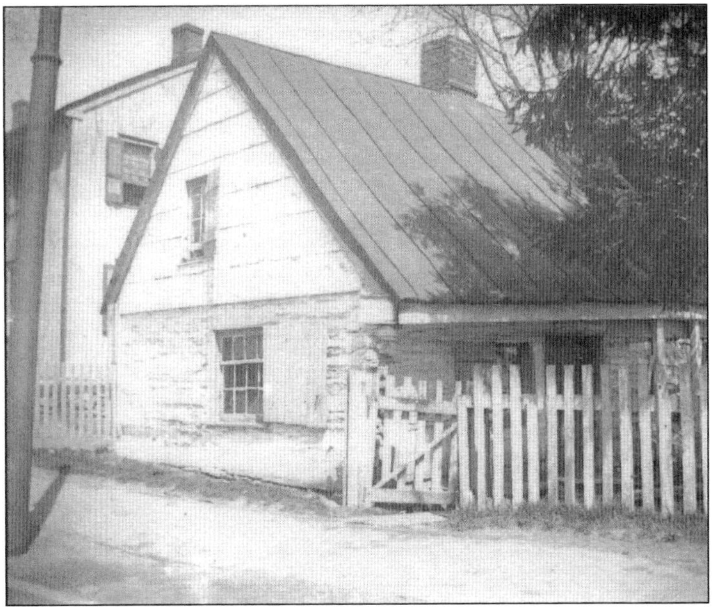

This photograph was incorrectly labeled on the back as the home of Schaefferstown resident Kitty Plaster. Built in 1743, the house stood at the northeast corner of Germantown Avenue and Mermaid Lane in Germantown, Pennsylvania, until it was demolished in 1911. Nevertheless, its log construction, steep roof with "kick" at the eaves, and center chimney are typical of many early Germanic houses in Schaefferstown and Heidelberg Township.

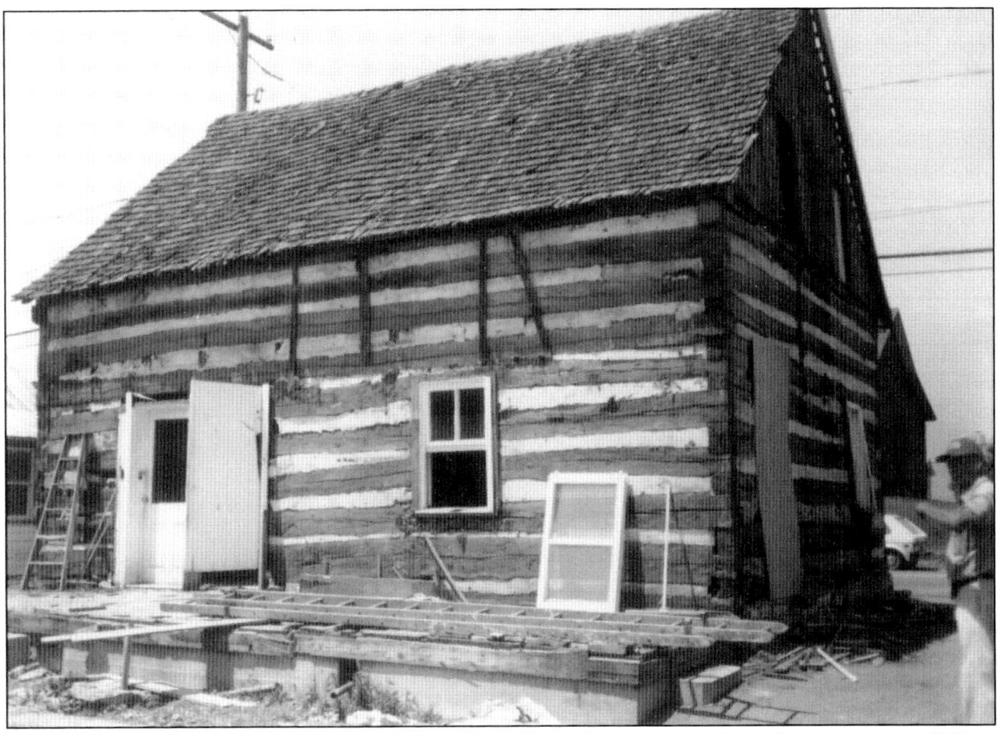

This one-and-a-half-story log structure, seen here from the rear, stood on the south side of West Main Street, Schaefferstown. It is typical of many homes built by Pennsylvania Germans in the 18th and early 19th centuries. Its last owners, the Samuel Netzley family, operated a grocery store next door in what is now Caruso's Pizzeria. The house was dismantled in 1976 to create space for the pizzeria's parking lot. (Courtesy of Diane Wenger.)

The well-kept garden in the front yard accentuates this Pennsylvania "four (rooms) over four (rooms)" house with two front doors. One door provides access to the working side of the home, while the other welcomes guests into the neat parlor for Sunday visits. Many homes of this style can still be found in Pennsylvania German areas today.

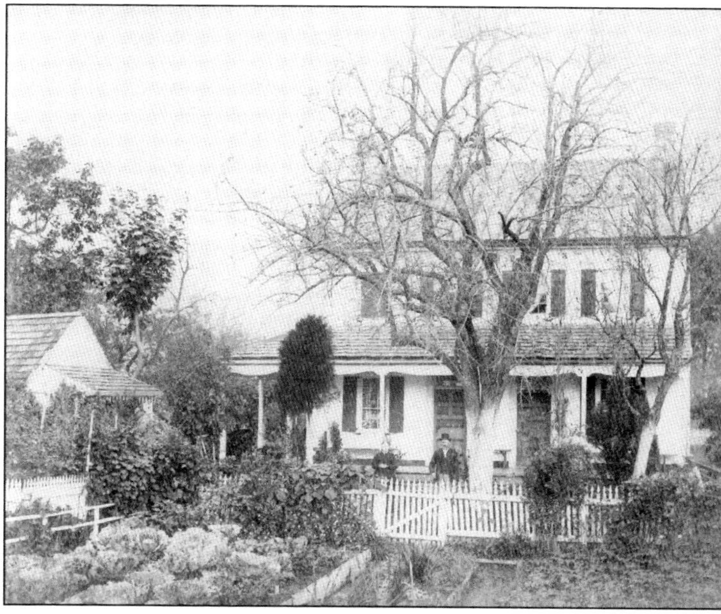

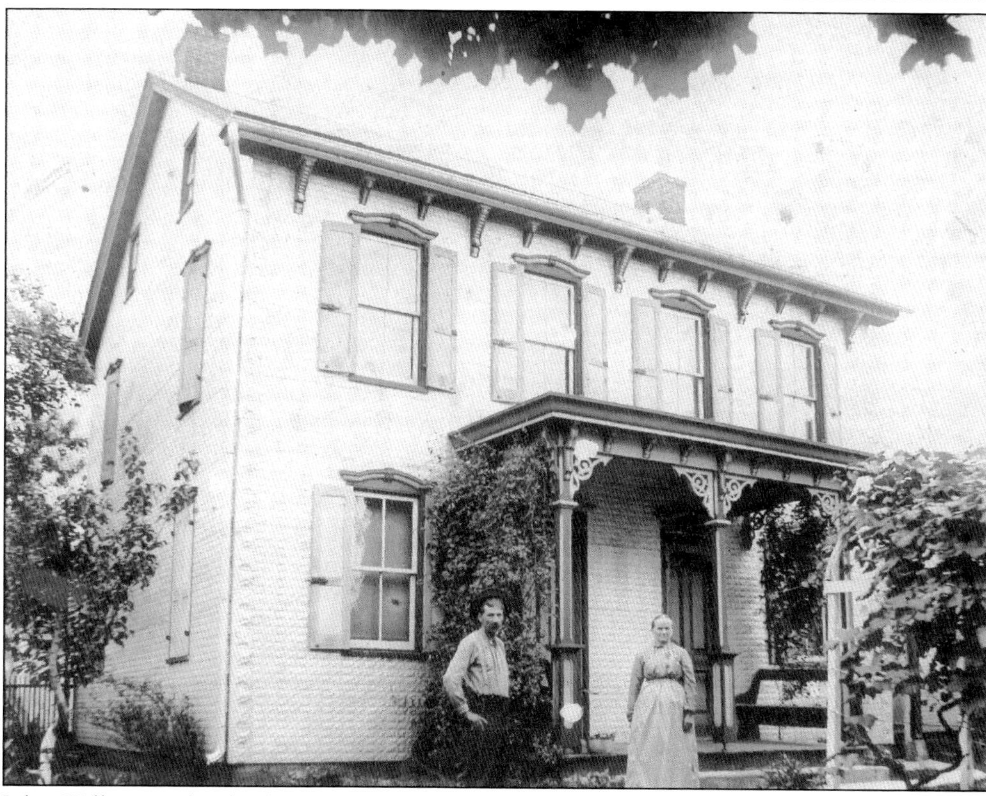

John William and Salinda Hauck Binkley stand in front of their house with unusual pressed-metal siding southeast of Kleinfeltersville. John, son of landowner Jacob Binkley, inherited this large farm. Family members recall the red sandstone soil was known for growing excellent watermelons. Today, this land is part of Middle Creek Wildlife Management Area. (Courtesy of Diana Wike Castor.)

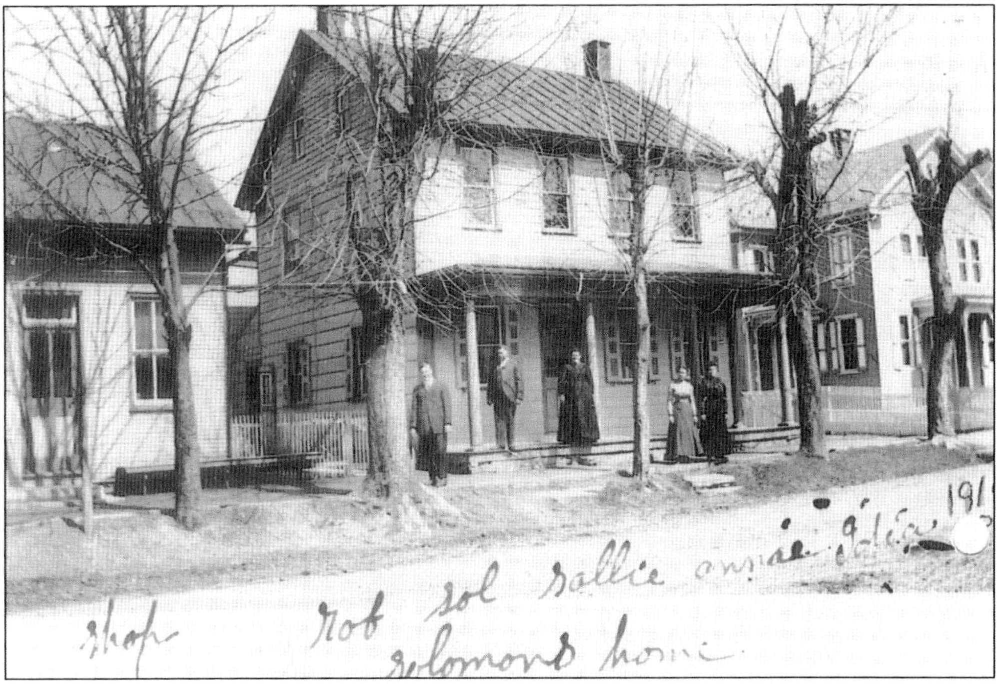

The Solomon Beamesderfer family poses in front of their home opposite the United Brethren Church on Main Street in Schaefferstown in this early-1900s photograph. "Sol" and Sallie (Wenger) stand on the porch with their children, from left to right, Rob, Annie, and Ida, in front. The small building to the left was Beamesderfer's tinsmith shop, where he also sold potbellied and kitchen wood stoves. (Courtesy of Frank Summers.)

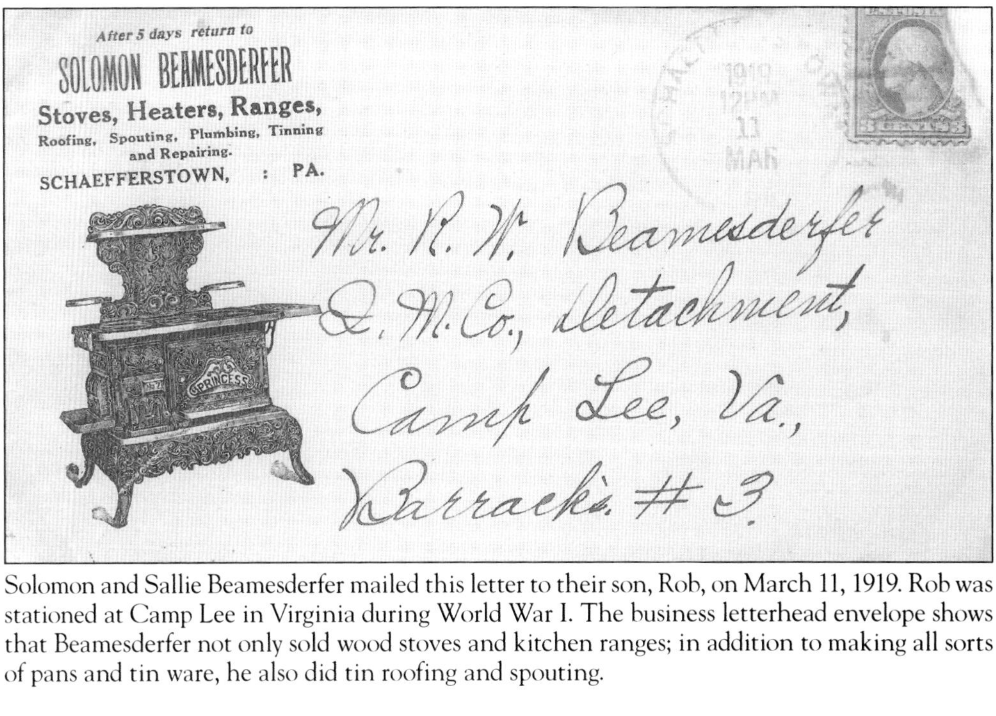

Solomon and Sallie Beamesderfer mailed this letter to their son, Rob, on March 11, 1919. Rob was stationed at Camp Lee in Virginia during World War I. The business letterhead envelope shows that Beamesderfer not only sold wood stoves and kitchen ranges; in addition to making all sorts of pans and tin ware, he also did tin roofing and spouting.

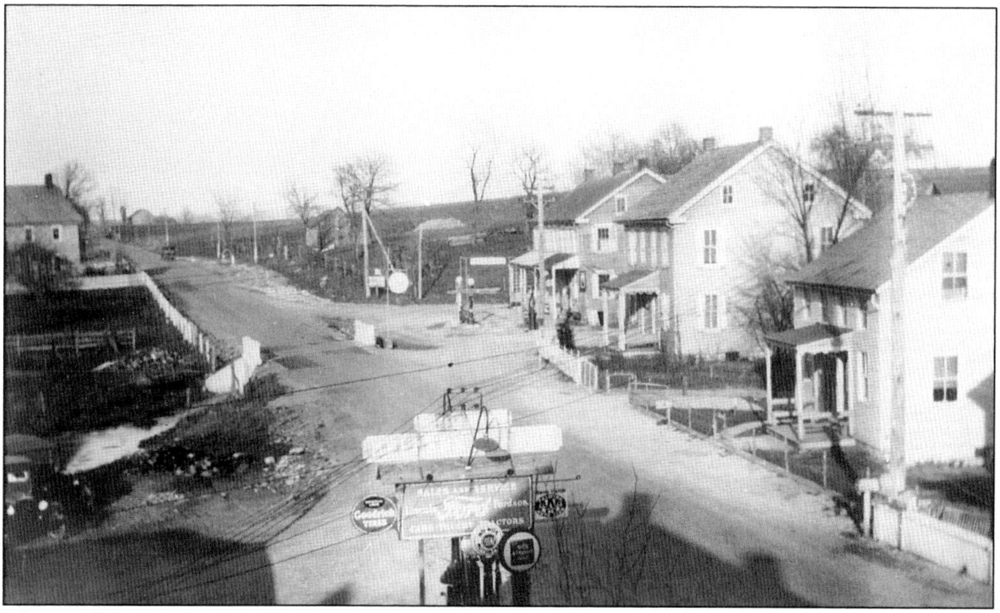

This mid-1920s photograph shows the small community of Buffalo Springs at the intersection of Route 419 with Distillery Road. In addition to Keller Brothers Ford, the gas pumps at Groh's Store on the opposite side of the road indicate the automobile age was here to stay. Local lore says Buffalo Springs was named for eastern buffalo sighted in the area. (Courtesy of the Institute of American Deltiology.)

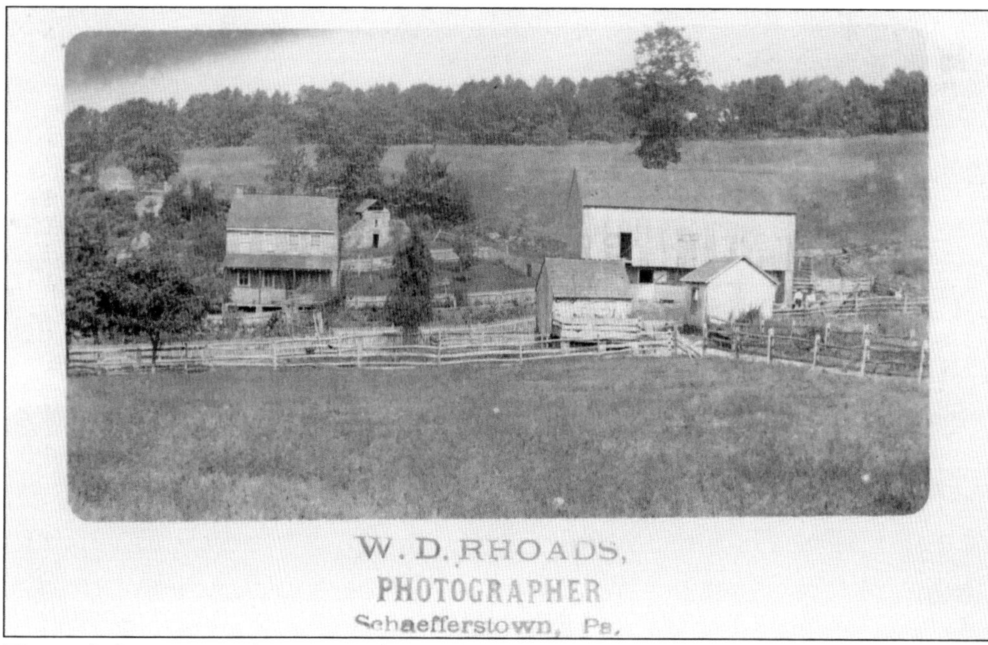

This real-photo postcard appears to be an advertisement for the photographer, W.H. Rhoads of Schaefferstown. Rhoads may have been one of many small town photography enthusiasts, armed with an affordable pocket camera and home dark-room, swept up in the national postcard craze around 1905 to 1910. Unfortunately, this photograph is unlabeled, and the location of this farm is unknown. (Courtesy of the Institute of American Deltiology.)

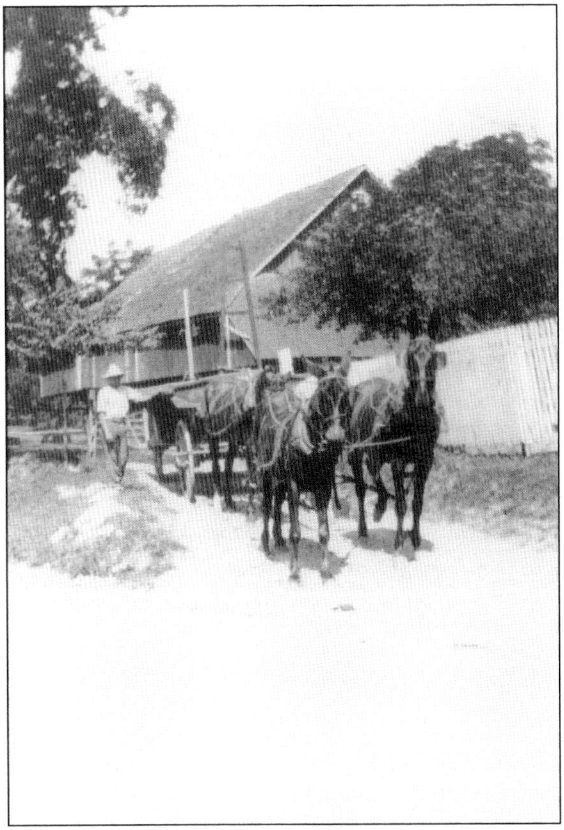

Victor Krall (1909–1989) is pictured at left in front of the barn on his family's farm just east of Schaefferstown. The double crib log barn with two threshing floors was built in the late 1700s. It measured 36 feet by 72 feet and was typical of barns built by settlers in the area, although few such structures survive. In 2007, new owners of the farm donated the barn to local historical groups, who then raised funds to have it professionally dismantled. Lebanon County Historical Society plans to have the barn erected at the Union Canal Tunnel Park in Lebanon. The farmhouse is still standing, but the springhouse in the foreground below was removed years ago.

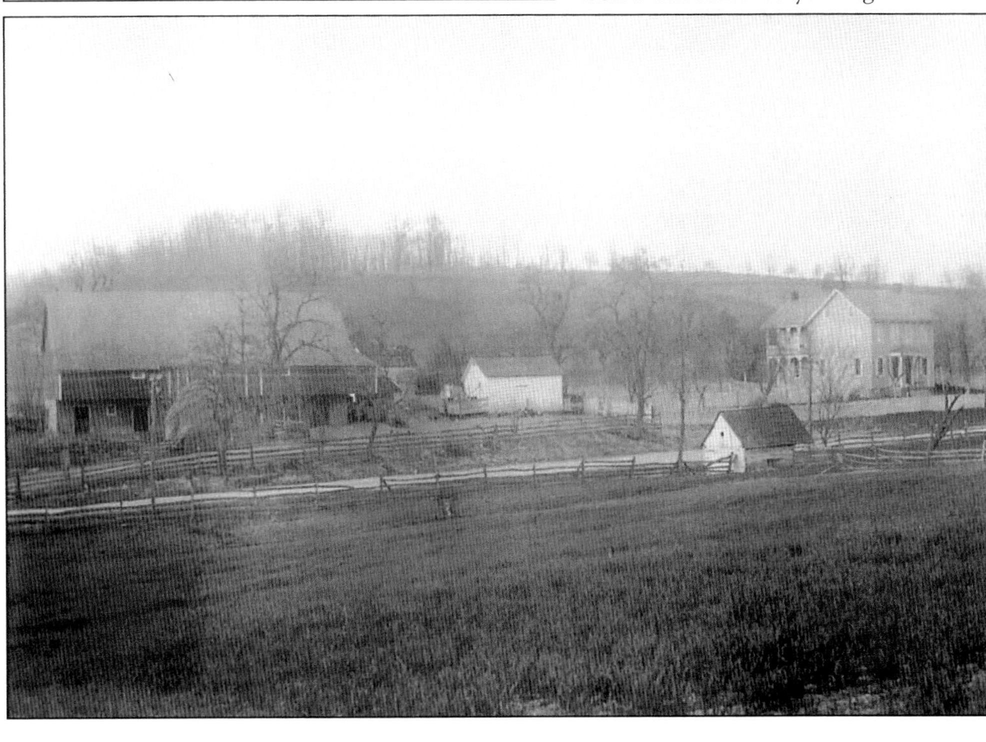

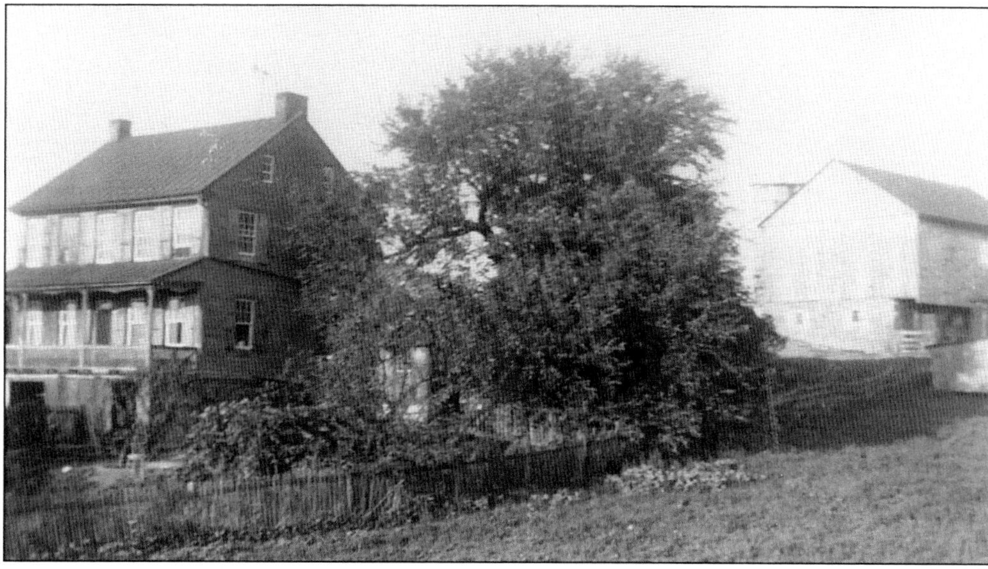

Located on a lane off Sheep Hill Road in Schaefferstown, this Georgian-style home overlooked the valley that contained the Krall farm. A barn with silo and various outbuildings are visible to the right. Screened by the large tree in the side yard is a small square building with a window; this may have been the family's outhouse, not an uncommon sight here even into the 1940s. (Courtesy of Carol Fetter.)

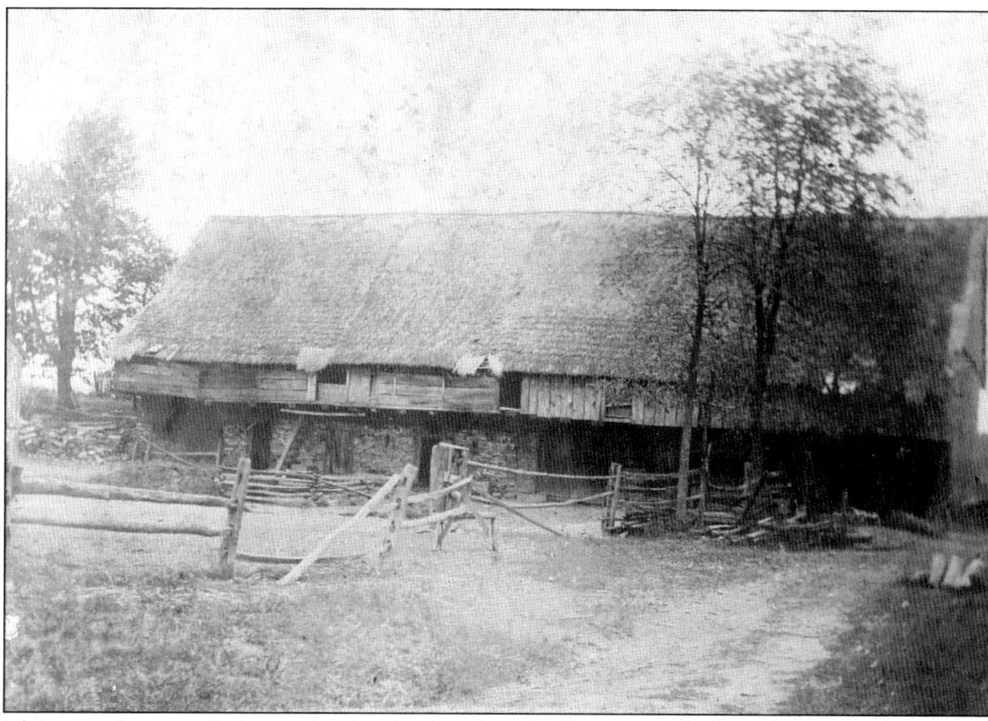

This rare photograph shows the thatched roof on the Henry Landis barn. Very early barns were roofed with rye straw. Later, this material was replaced with long wooden shingles, side and end lapped, or with locally made clay roofing tiles. Even later, tin roofs were common. Henry Landis and his family farmed the land on South Market Street, south of Schaefferstown.

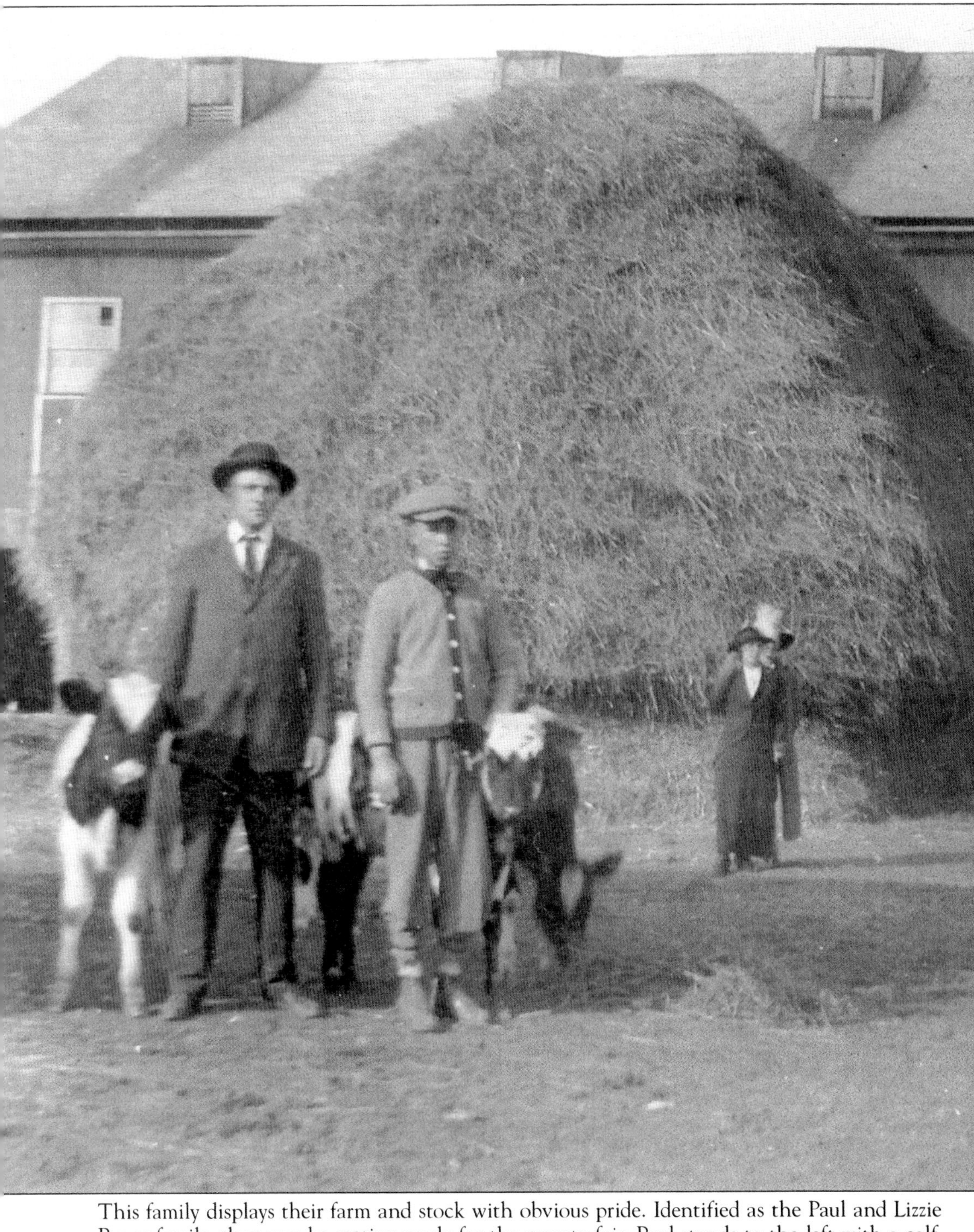

This family displays their farm and stock with obvious pride. Identified as the Paul and Lizzie Royer family, they may be getting ready for the county fair. Paul stands to the left with a calf, Lizzie shows off a handsome horse at right, and daughter Mabel has the dog. Paul's brother John M. Royer holds two mules. The other young man and three ladies in traveling costume may be other family members. The large Pennsylvania barn with typical forebay (a ground-level area

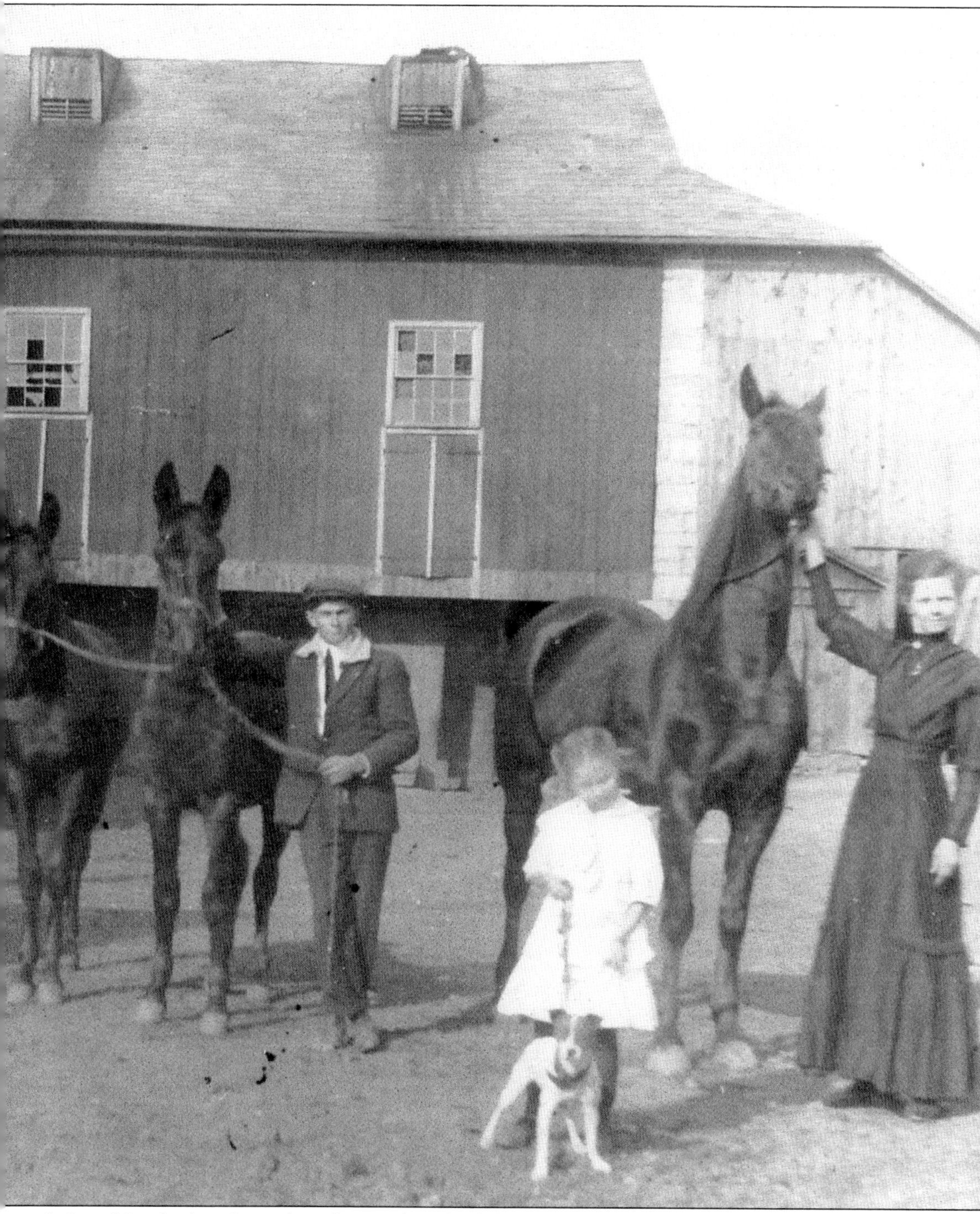

sheltered by the barn's overhang) provides a backdrop to this photograph, taken around 1912. A huge straw stack almost dwarfs the barn. This wonderful barn and homestead still exist on a lane off Route 419, opposite the intersection with Reistville Road. It continues to be one of many working farms in Heidelberg Township. (Courtesy of Carol Fetter.)

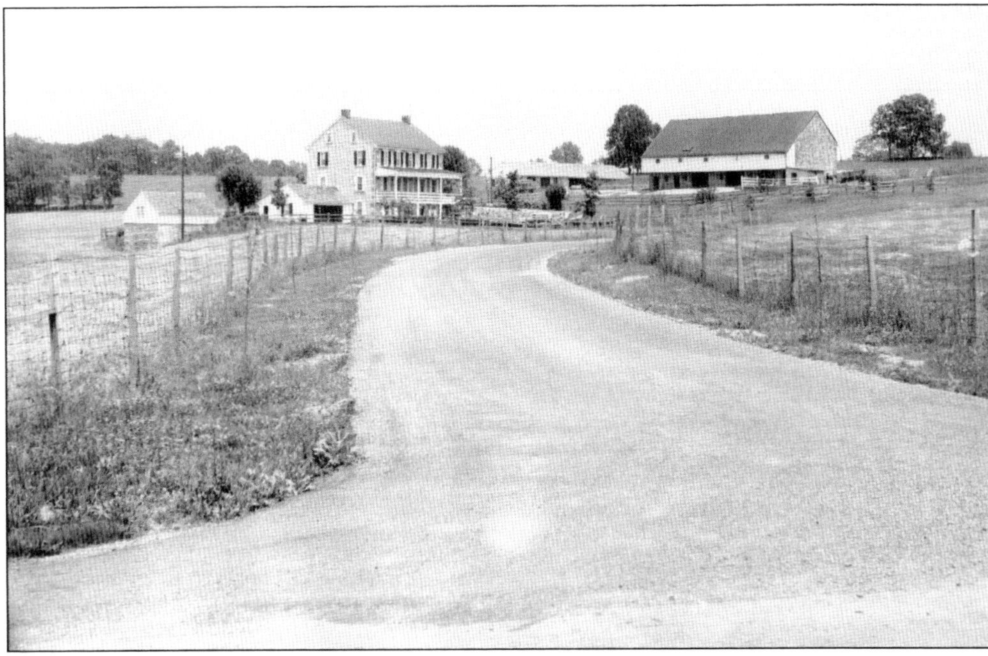

All the requirements of a good farm are visible in this 1950s photograph of the George Binner farm: a sturdy farmhouse built of limestone with decorative sandstone quoins, a limestone bank barn with forebay facing south, a stone springhouse that may be combined with a summer kitchen, and several outbuildings. This farm is located on Distillery Road just south of its junction with Old Mill Road.

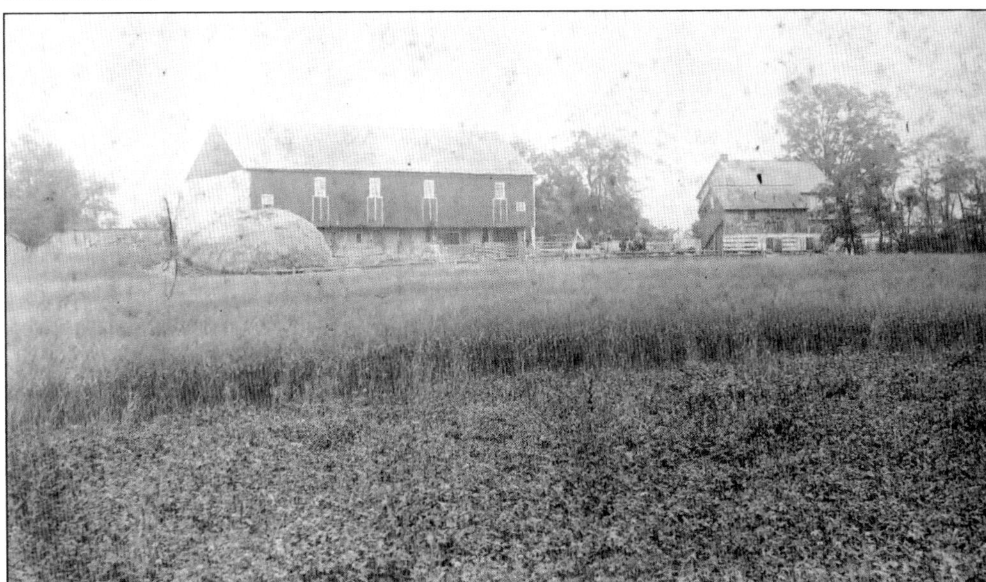

In 1895, Joseph S. and Mary Brubaker Horst deeded land to each of their four sons. Franklin Brubaker Horst's share included this farm off Horst Road north of Schaefferstown. Grandson Ray Horst remembers living here as a boy and riding the trolley into Schaefferstown from the farm to run errands or visit grandparents Franklin B. and Jennie Beckley Horst, who by then lived in town. (Courtesy of Ray Horst.)

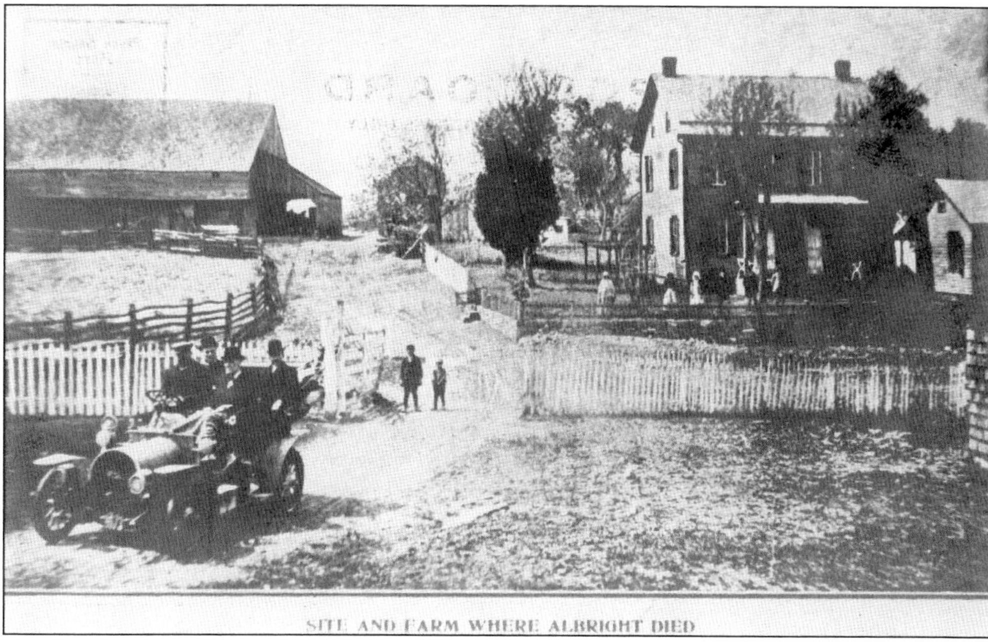

The caption on this postcard refers to the Reverend Jacob Albright (1759–1808), who founded the Evangelical Church. Albright was born near Pottstown and later lived in Lancaster County, but he took a special interest in preaching in the Schaefferstown area. The George Becker family, who lived near Kleinfeltersville, was among Albright's early converts. When he became ill while traveling nearby, companions brought him to the Becker farm, where he died.

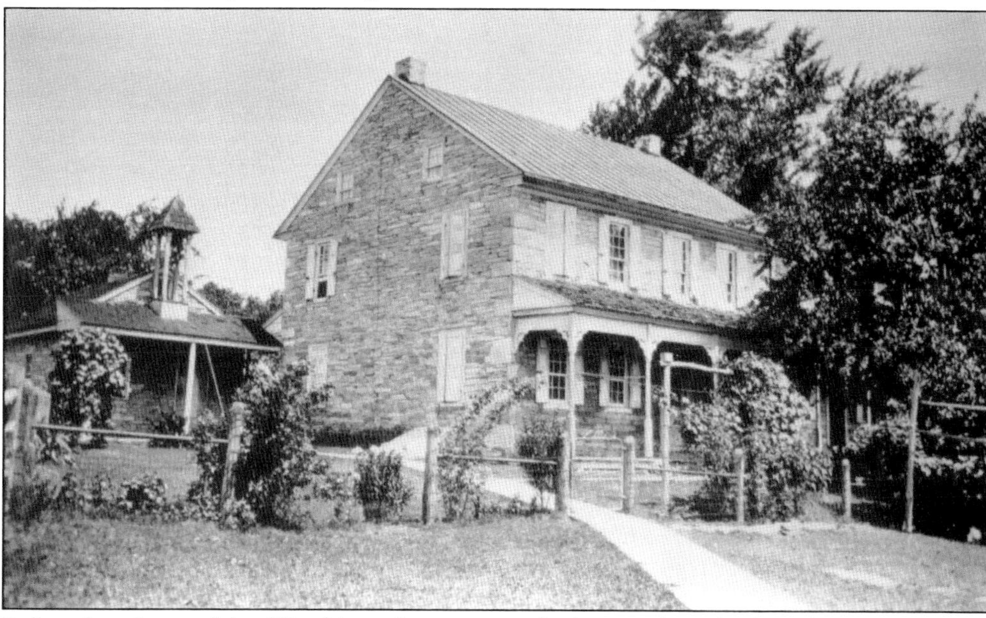

Before the advent of the 911 address designation, which was adopted relatively recently (1999), roads tended to acquire the name of the major landowner living near or on that road. Such was the case with Gibble Road. This large limestone farmhouse belonged to John Gibble. It is located on a long lane off of Gibble Road, northwest of its intersection with Route 897. (Courtesy of the Institute of American Deltiology.)

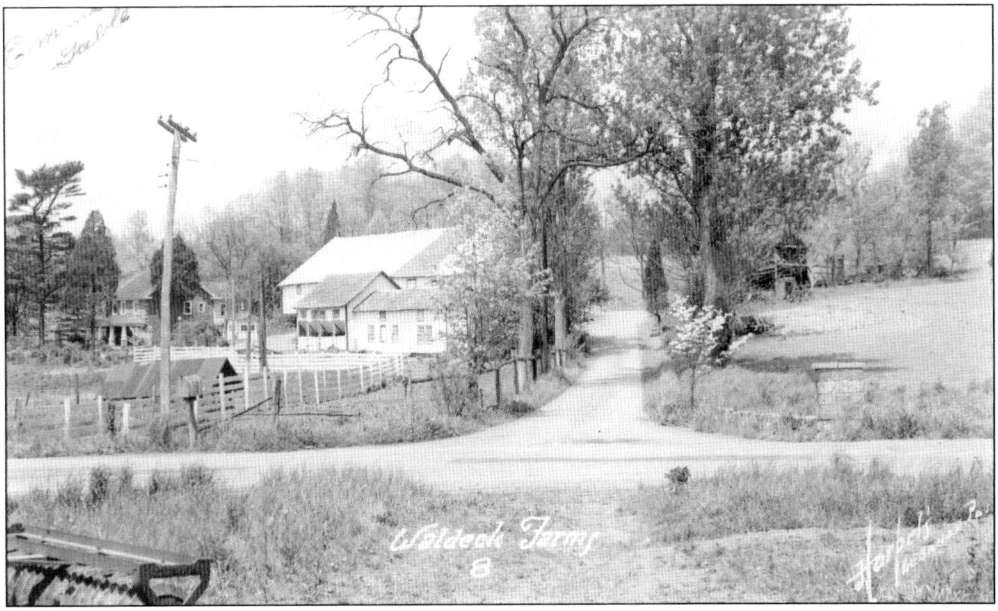

A view up this lane shows the handsome farm owned by John F. Gable (1850–1921) in Waldeck on the road to Lancaster, south of Schaefferstown. Gable's father bought this land in 1860. John farmed this land with his father and later inherited it. He also operated Weigley's Mill, during which time it was called Locust Grove Flour and Grist Mill. (Courtesy of Rita Mock.)

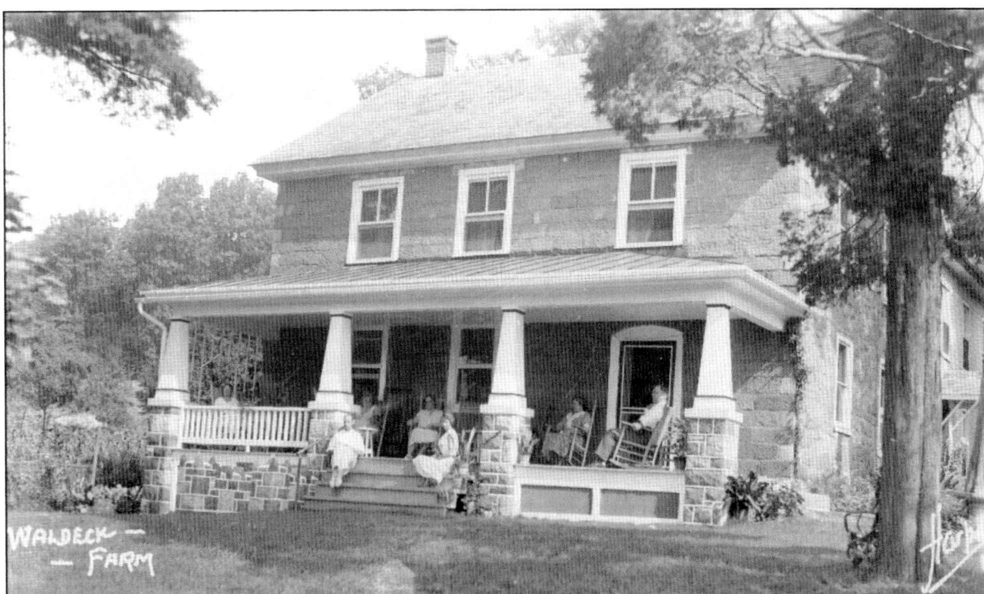

Guests relax on the porch of the 1749 Waldeck farmhouse, hoping to catch a summer breeze. Mollie, Mary, and Charlotte, daughters of John F. and Clara Bennetch Gable, served Sunday dinner to the public by reservation. The small community of Waldeck, so reminiscent of the Black Forest area of Germany, provides a wonderful view even today. (Courtesy of the Institute of American Deltiology.)

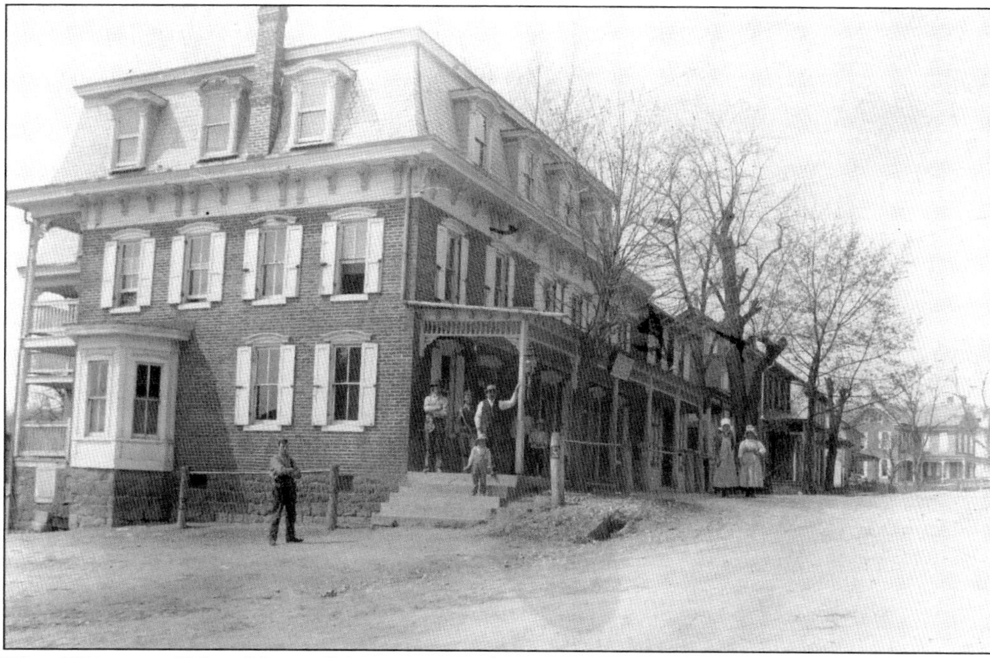

This 1911 view of Kleinfeltersville's main street features the Kleinfeltersville Hotel, owned by A.L. Spayd. Kleinfeltersville, Heidelberg Township, was founded in 1848 by Evangelical minister Rev. John R. Kleinfelter, who bought the 200-acre Becker farm (where Evangelical Church founder Jacob Albright died) and also the 49-acre Trostle homestead. He later laid out the town into lots. (Courtesy of Rita Mock.)

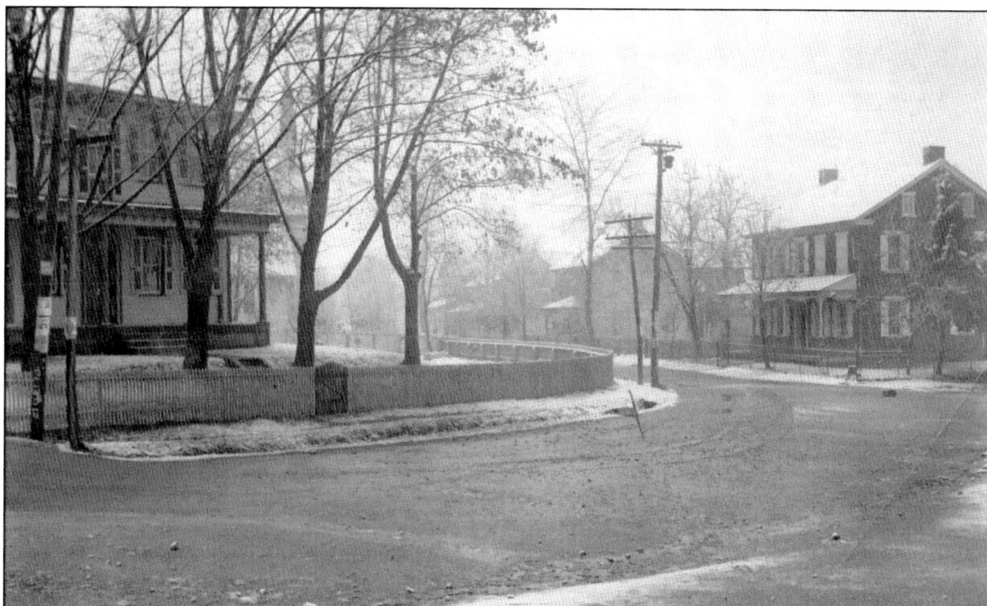

Snow has fallen, and the road is quiet in Kleinfeltersville in this 1912 photograph of the intersection of Route 897 and Millbach Road, facing north. It is labeled "first snow." The fence is gone from the house on the left, as is the porch from the home on the right, but the rest of the scene is remarkably unchanged 100 years later. (Courtesy of Rita Mock.)

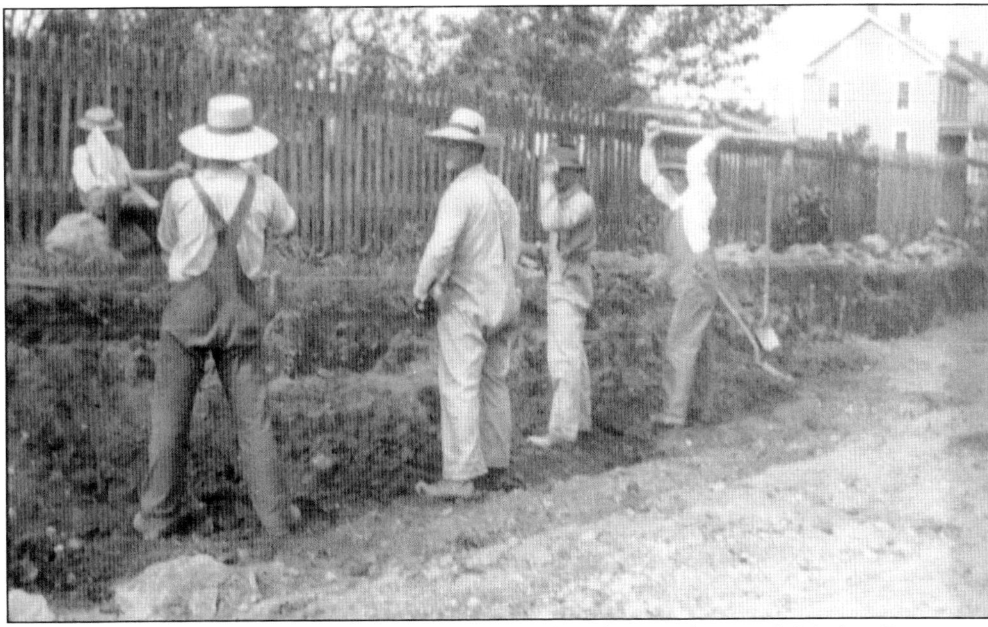

A number of men are working with pick and shovel to deepen the South Market Street road cut through Tower Hill, where local lore places William Henry Stiegel's "tower." Stiegel's 75-foot pyramidal wooden tower was built in 1769, supposedly marking a halfway point between his other properties. This view looks north on South Market Street near its intersection with Sportsman Lane. (Courtesy of Rita Mock.)

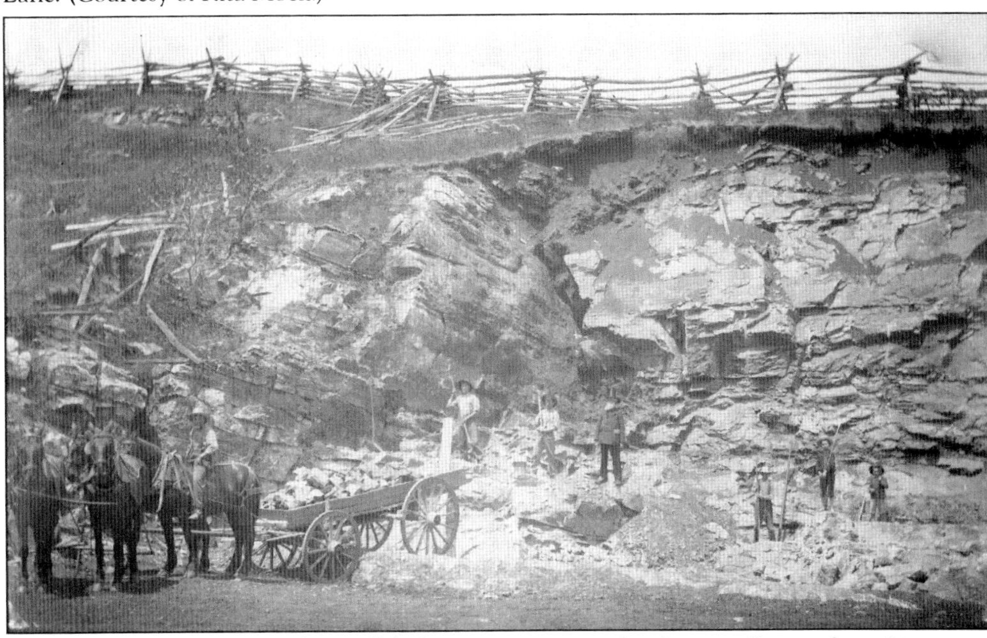

Men break up limestone in this Buffalo Springs quarry on the Ammon Binner farm. Limestone was important for "sweetening" acidic soils on local farms. First the limestone was quarried, then it was loaded into wagons and taken to a lime kiln, where the stone was burned with wood and charcoal. The resulting lime ash was then suitable for spreading on the fields before planting. Note the loaded wagon ready to go.

Two

Posing for the Camera

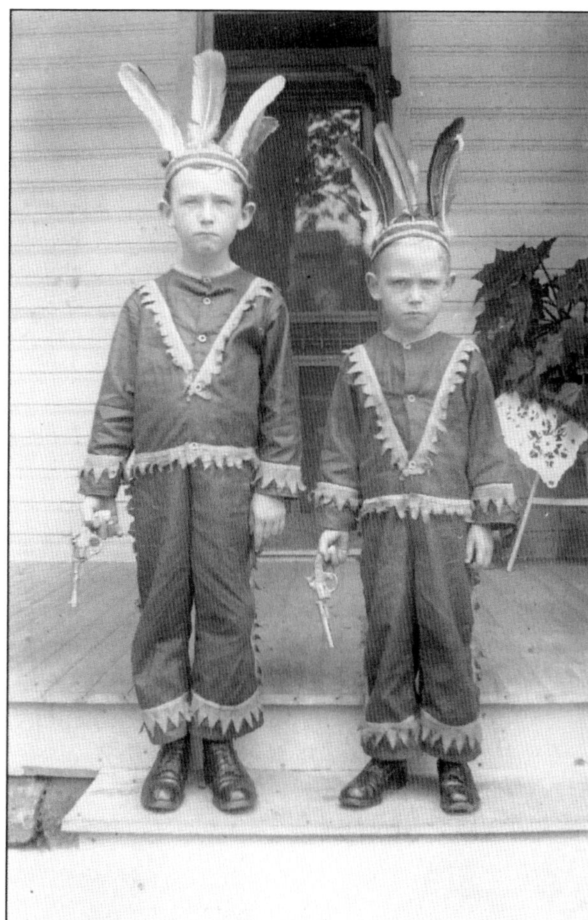

Russell (left) and Roy Weik are dressed for Halloween or for playing "cowboys and Indians." The boys grew up in Kleinfeltersville and did what boys the world over did for play before the computer age: make believe. Russell Weik was one of three Heidelberg Township residents who made the ultimate sacrifice during World War II. (Courtesy of Rita Mock.)

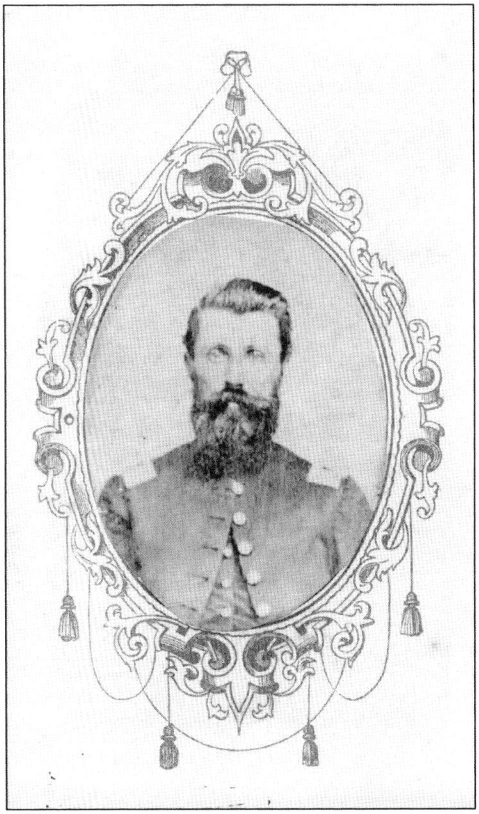

William B. Iba, a Heidelberg Township farmer who lived near Reistville, was one of many township men who served in the Civil War. His portrait shows him in his uniform as captain of Company I, 173rd Regiment, Pennsylvania Infantry. Captain Iba's uniform and some of his possessions are in Historic Schaefferstown, Inc.'s, Thomas Brendle Museum.

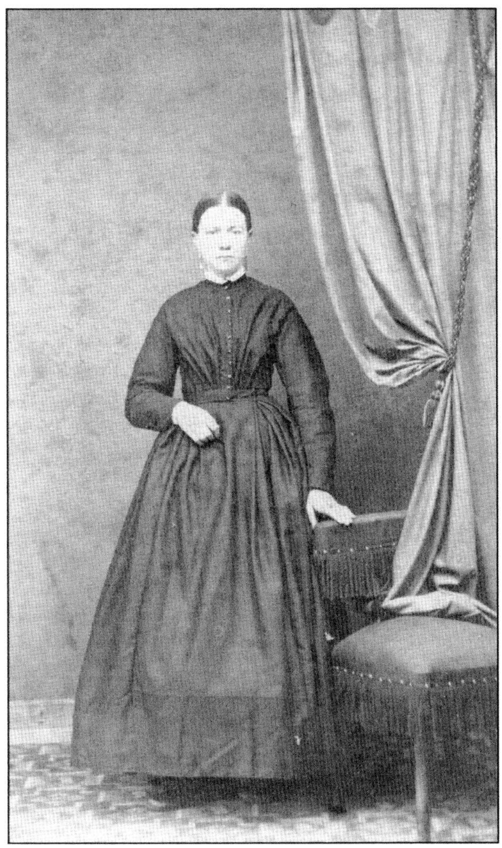

This photograph was taken by Levi K. Bair at his "Excelsior Photograph Car." The woman's plain black dress is typical of mourning attire and may indicate that the photograph was taken during the Civil War or after Pres. Abraham Lincoln was assassinated in 1865. The lack of identification is a reminder to all of the importance of labeling!

Jacob Souder poses in his Civil War uniform at "Daily's Excelsior Gallery, in C. Henry's New Building, Lebanon Pa." Souder served with Company K, 142nd Pennsylvania Volunteers, a unit consisting largely of Heidelberg Township men. This regiment fought in the Battle of Fredericksburg and served until the end of the war. Souder achieved the rank of captain.

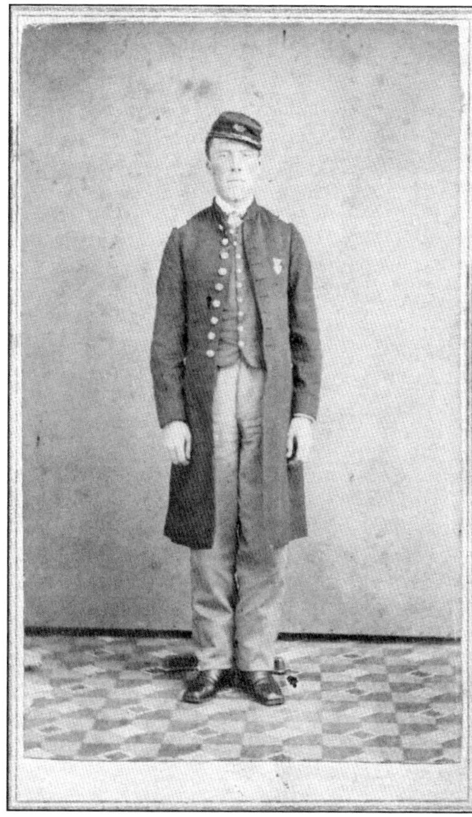

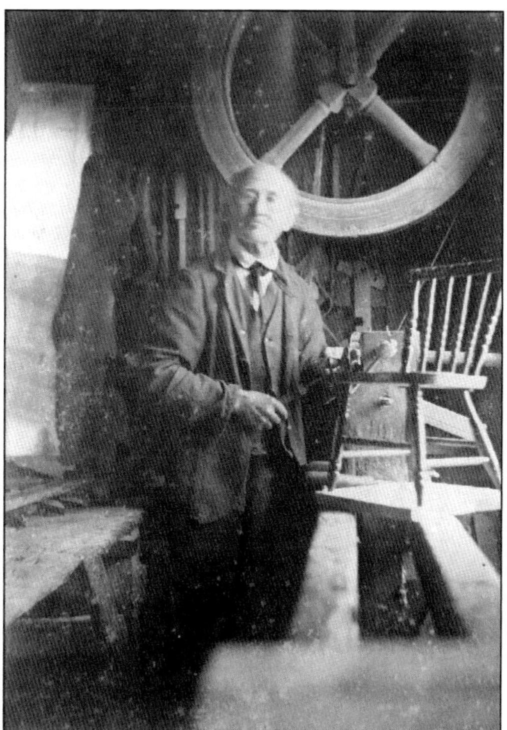

Schaefferstown resident John B. Strickler (1813–1900) is pictured in his turner shop on South Lancaster Avenue. He is surrounded by the tools and products of his trade. At age 18, he learned the trade of turning from Lititz craftsman Adam Brossman. Strickler made spinning wheels and especially excelled at chair making, for which he was well known in the area.

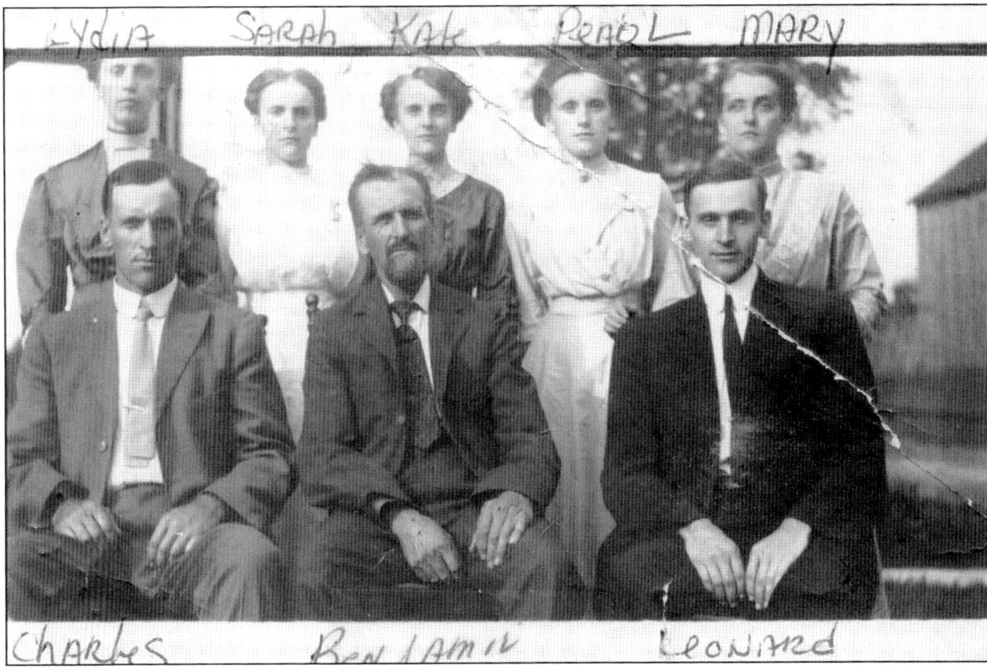

Benjamin Hartman, shown here in the first row, center, surrounded by his family, was a well-known cabinetmaker, cigar-box manufacturer, and building contractor who lived in the Canada area of South Market Street, Schaefferstown. He is best remembered for building the Patriotic Order Sons of America Hall and Schaefferstown United Brethren Church, now known as Zion United Methodist Church. (Courtesy of JoAnn Hartman Rager.)

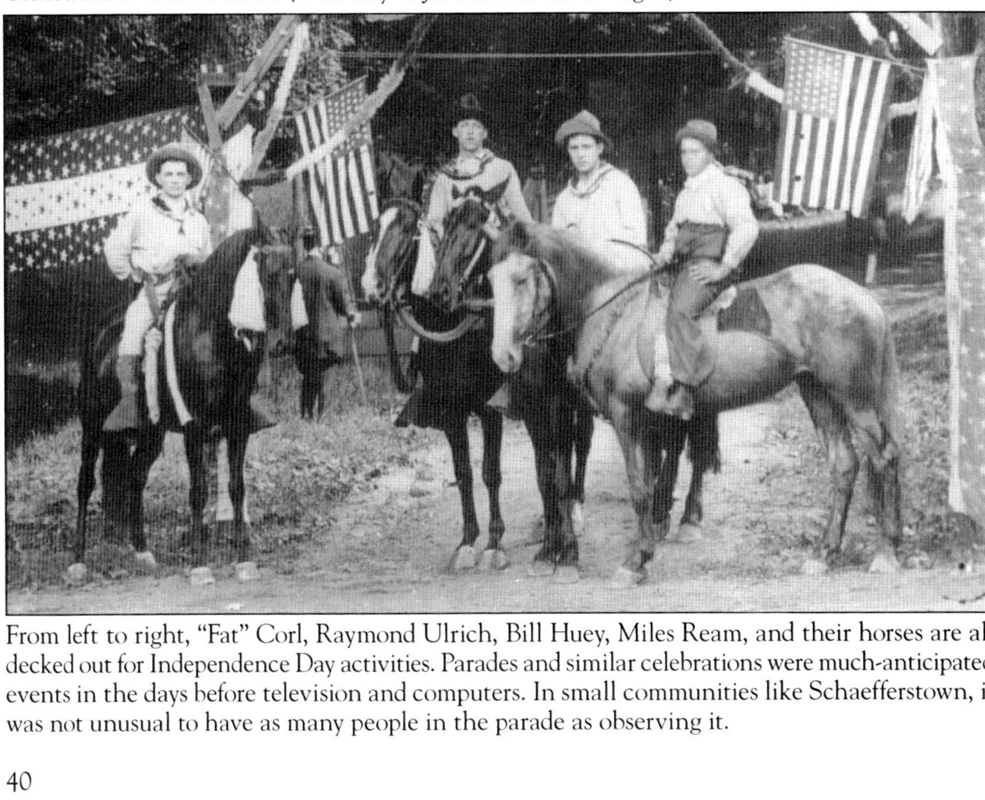

From left to right, "Fat" Corl, Raymond Ulrich, Bill Huey, Miles Ream, and their horses are all decked out for Independence Day activities. Parades and similar celebrations were much-anticipated events in the days before television and computers. In small communities like Schaefferstown, it was not unusual to have as many people in the parade as observing it.

Daniel Mell (1829–1901) was a mason by trade. In 1852, he and his wife, Mary (1827–1883), bought a two-story house on West Main Street, Schaefferstown, from Jacob Hartman. In March 1881, Swiss immigrant and itinerant artist Ferdinand A. Brader (1833–1901?) rendered the large and quite detailed pencil drawing below of the Mell residence and associated buildings. Brader lived in Berks County but traveled from place to place, trading drawings for room and board. By 1884, he had left Pennsylvania for Northern Ohio. Brader disappeared without a trace in 1896 just after receiving word of a bequest from his brother in Switzerland, and he was declared dead in 1901. An exhibit of Brader's work is planned for December 4, 2014, through March 15, 2015, at the Canton (Ohio) Museum of Art.

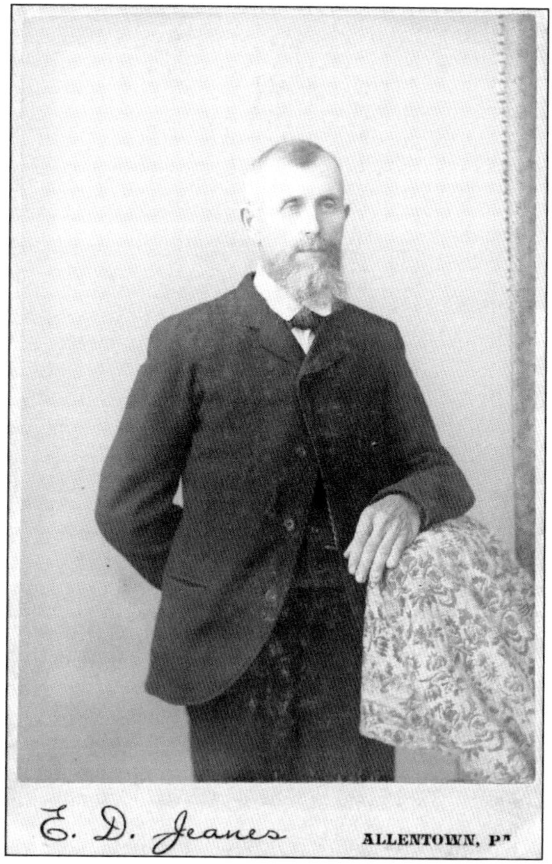

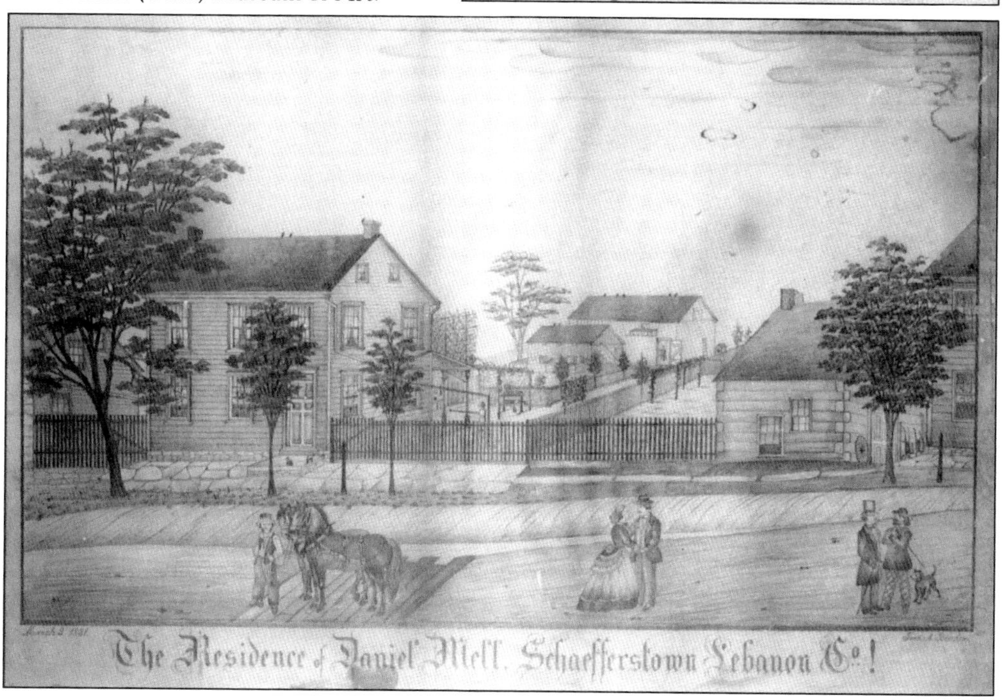

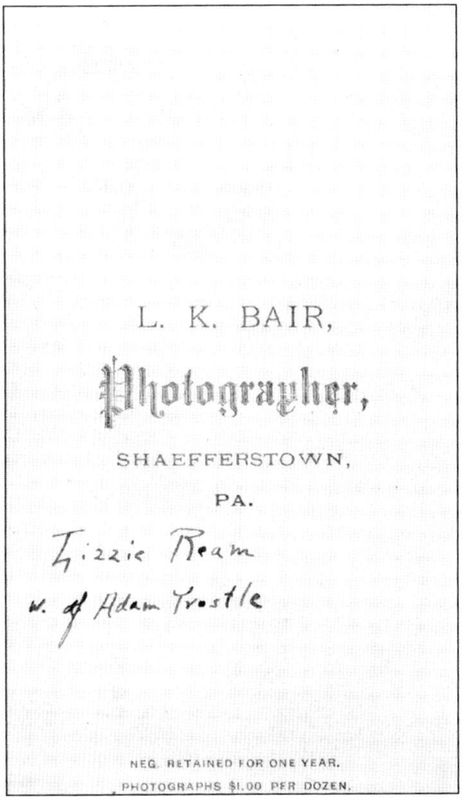

Photographer Levi K. Bair (1843–1918), who was also a coach maker and taxidermist, had his studio on North Market Street in Schaefferstown. He combined two of his professions by creating a mobile photography unit. If clients could not come into town to have their photographs taken, he took his camera, portable screens, and chairs, in a wagon he built himself, to their homes. Bair reportedly carried two mirrors with him, one rectangular and one oval, so that customers could look at themselves and decide the shape for their photograph. By 1896, Bair's son, Staley (1873–1958), had joined him in the business. A number of Bair photographs survive, but not all are identified. The below photograph is of Lizzie Ream, who married Adam Trostle.

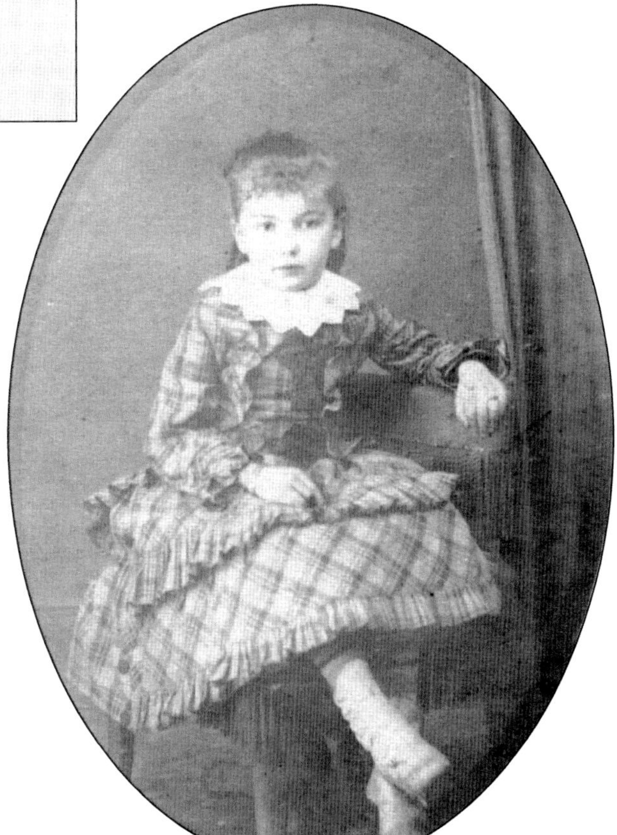

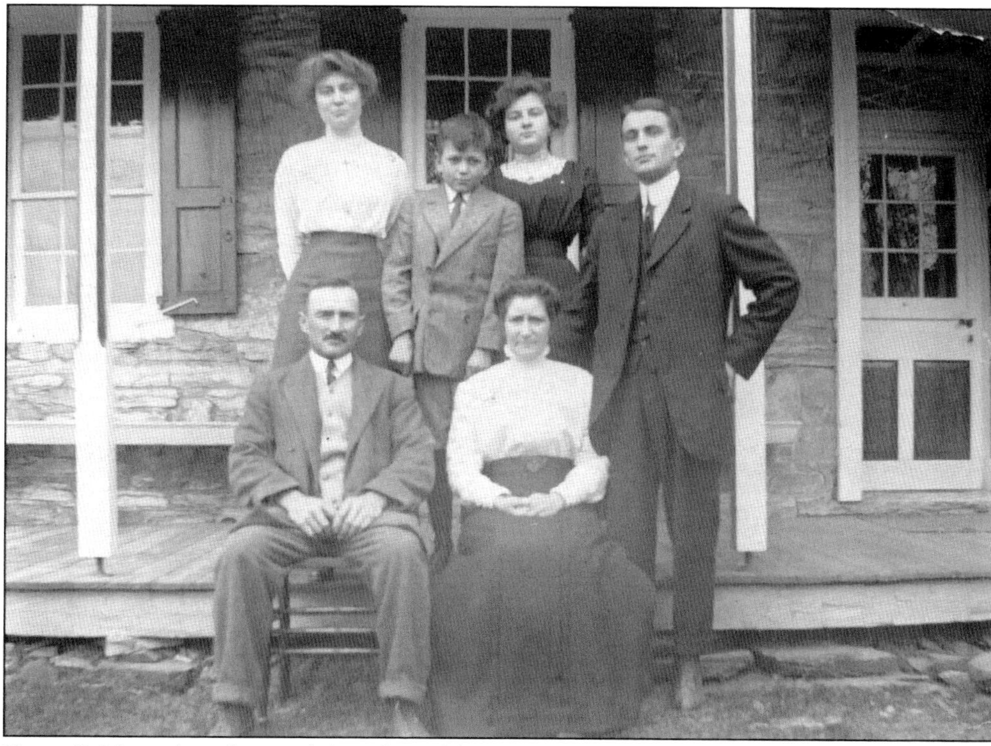

Harry C. Moyer (standing, right) graduated from West Chester Normal School in 1910; he served as principal of Heidelberg School and later on as superintendent of Lebanon County Schools. He married Anna Keath (James W. Keath's daughter) about 1917. In this photograph, Harry poses with his parents, Robinson and Salinda Moyer, who are seated. Behind them, from left to right, are his siblings Katherine C. Moyer, John Moyer, and Elizabeth Moyer.

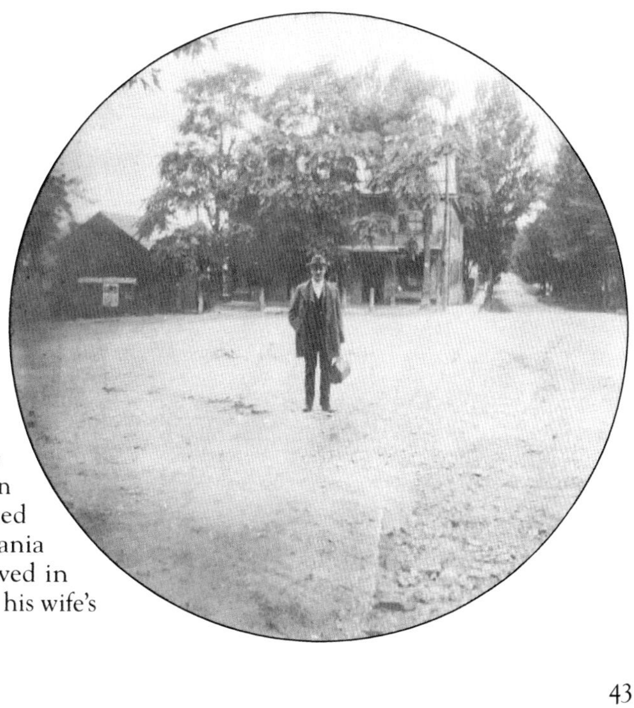

James W. Keath (1855–1910), shown here on the town square, was one of Schaefferstown's doctors. While still in his teens, he lived and studied with local physician I. Reilly Bucher. Keath graduated from the University of Pennsylvania in 1876. Keath and his family lived in the former Erpff house, which was his wife's family home.

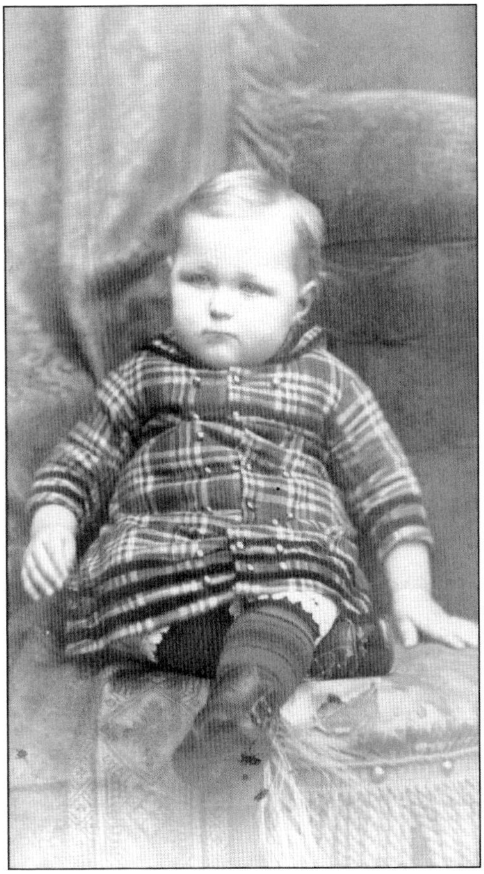

This infant is believed to be a young boy, Mase Hoke. In the 19th and early 20th centuries, the common practice was to dress both boys and girls in dresses until the age of five or six. This was done for ease of diapering and toilet training as well as for the convenience of altering the garment and handing it down to the next child. (Courtesy of Mary Smith.)

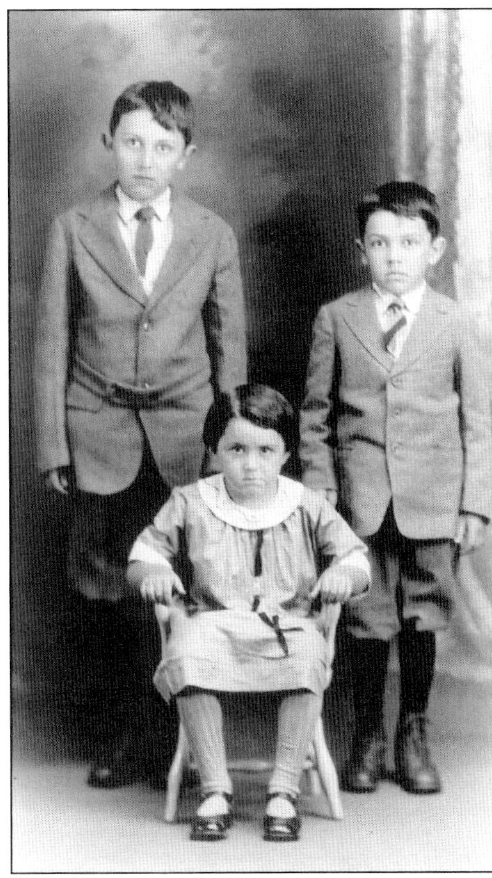

Sylvan (left), Arnetta (sitting), and Winfred Royer pose for the camera in their Sunday best. Sylvan and Winfred wear wool knickers and jackets, typical boys' clothing of the 1920s. Arnetta wears a simple dress with rounded collar. The fashions of the day were not made for comfort, as evidenced by the grim expressions on these children's faces. (Courtesy of Carol Fetter.)

Kleinfeltersville resident George Ream proudly displays his dogs and the skins of opossums and skunks from hunting endeavors in this 1912 photograph taken by Eden S. Noll. Ream was the town barber and lived just east of the present-day Kleinfeltersville post office. In his spare time, he enjoyed the benefits of Heidelberg Township woodlands. (Courtesy of Rita Mock.)

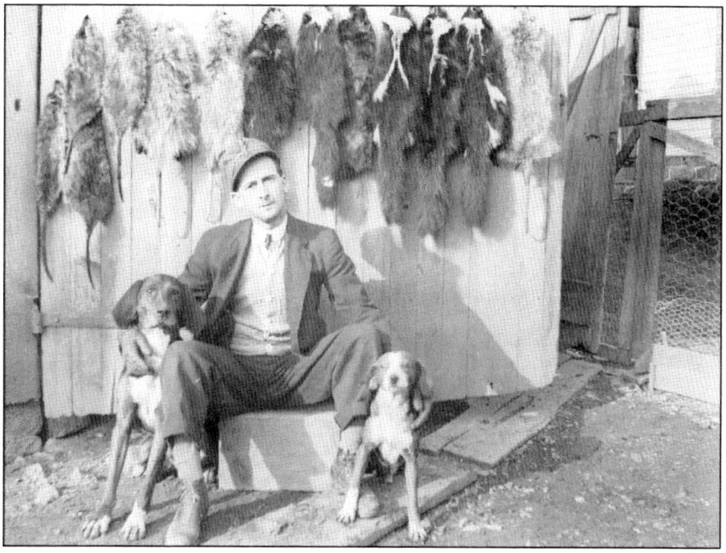

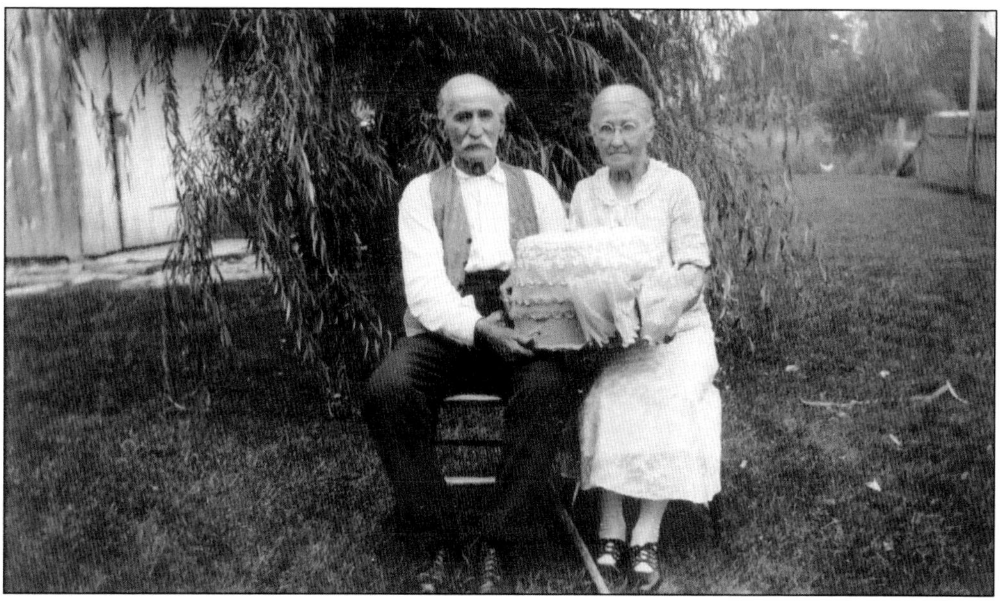

Franklin and Amanda Noll appear to be celebrating a major wedding anniversary at their home on East Main Street, Schaefferstown. The Nolls farmed the property later bought by Victor Krall, which included the Krall barn. Water for the barn was piped from springs on the hillside above. This aquifer remains an important part of Schaefferstown's water supply today. (Courtesy of Rita Mock.)

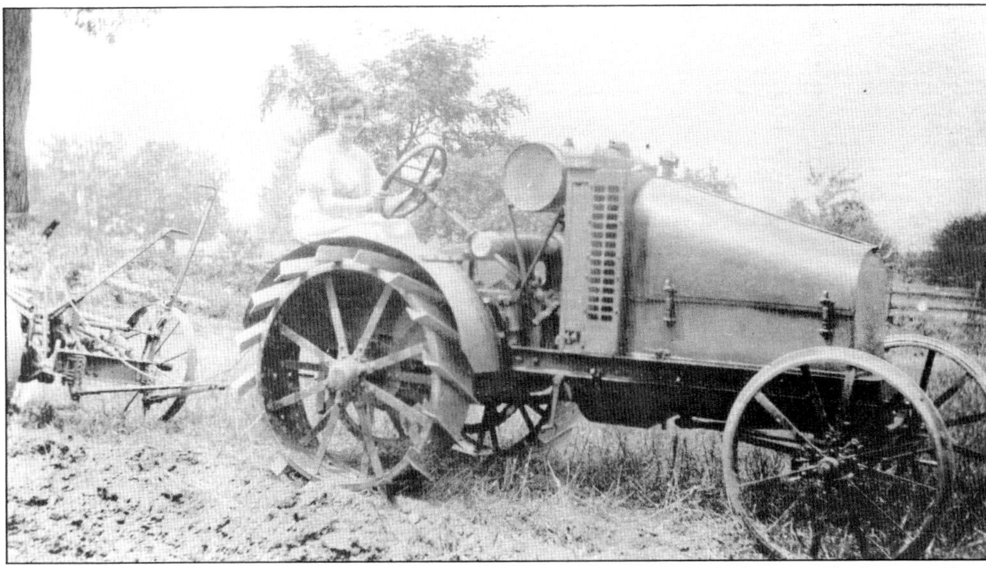

Farm work was not exclusive to men, as this real-photo postcard shows. Ella Dierwechter Horst, wife of Lloyd Horst, drives an early tractor on the Horst Farm, located on North Market Street, a mile north of the square. Originally about 244 acres, this farm had the distinction of remaining in the same family from 1801 until 2012. It continues to be a working farm. (Courtesy of Glenn Wolgemuth.)

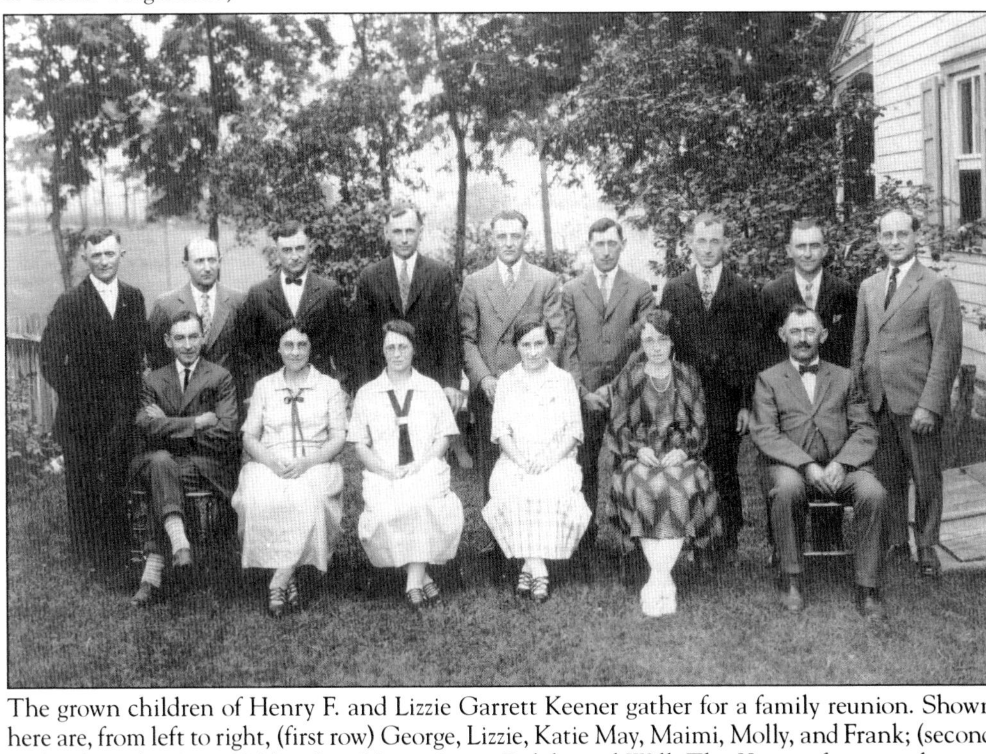

The grown children of Henry F. and Lizzie Garrett Keener gather for a family reunion. Shown here are, from left to right, (first row) George, Lizzie, Katie May, Maimi, Molly, and Frank; (second row) Al, Paul, Wayne, Miles, Jim, Harry, Leon, Ralph, and Will. The Keener farm was located between Schaefferstown and Waldeck, at the southern end of what is now known as Sinclair Road. (Courtesy of Ray Horst.)

Mamie Beamesderfer Miller (1892–1978) and great-niece Kathy Glime are shown during a family visit to the Miller home in 1972. Miller, whose right hand was disfigured as a result of an accident sustained on a carnival ride, lived on South Market Street. Her husband, Nathan (1887–1969), played tuba in the Schaefferstown Band. (Courtesy of Merle Glime.)

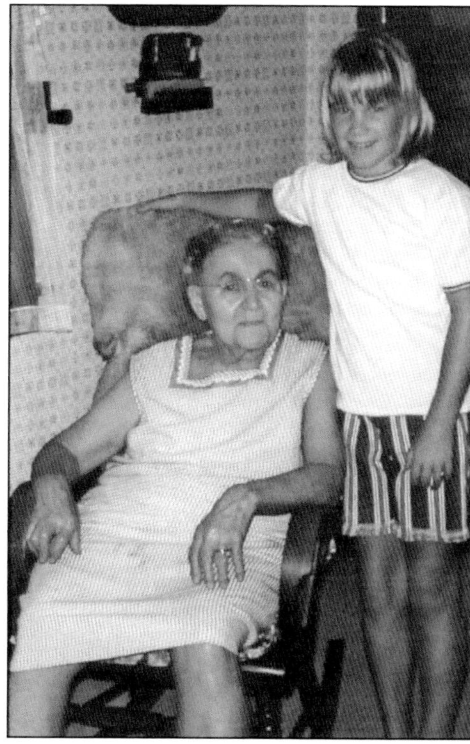

The Schaefferstown Band members pose in costume in 1935 at the Harry C. Moyer residence. Galen Funck is seated on the ground in front. The others are, from left to right, (first row) Harry Rhoades, Gerald Jackson, Guy Kreider, Hayden Kurtz, and Art Strohman; (second row) Nathan Miller, Bill Bahney, Franklin Zimmerman II, George Horst, Walter Steckbeck, Russell Hardy, and George Boltz.

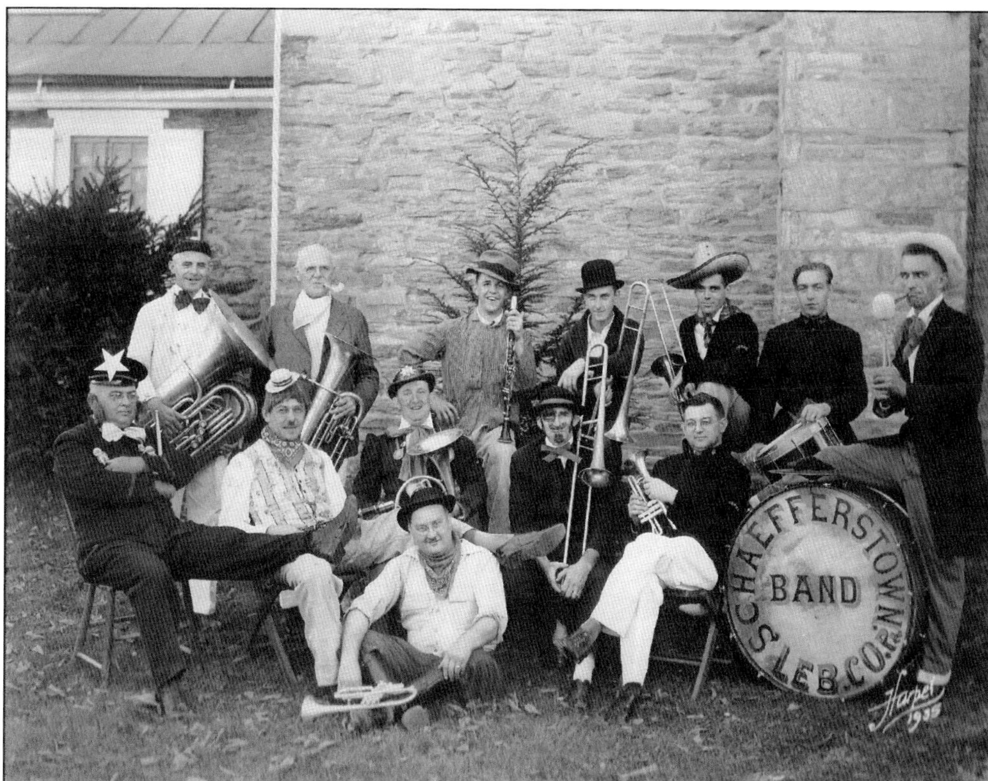

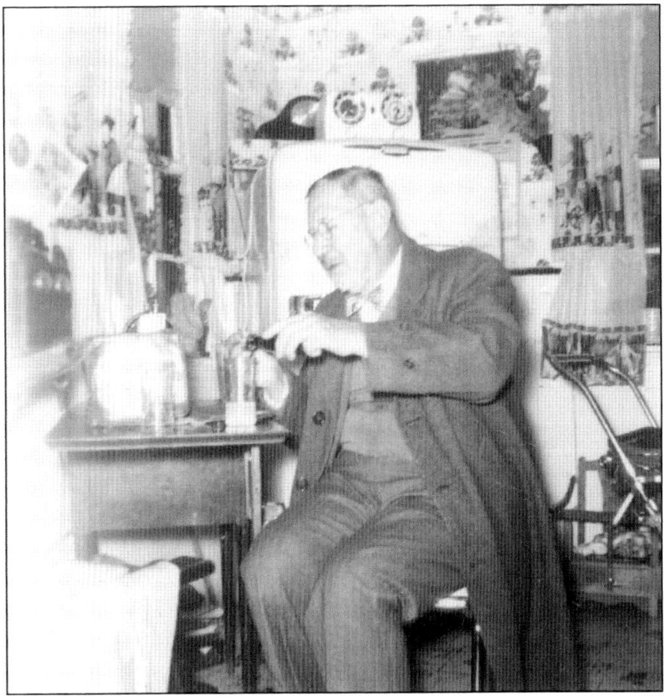

Dr. Franklin Diffenbach Zimmerman I (1878–1958) often prepared medicine for patients in his kitchen. "Doc" Zimmerman and his son Dr. Frank D. Zimmerman II (not pictured) were well loved by area residents and, between the two, practiced medicine in the community for close to 100 years. (Courtesy of Betsy Nolt.)

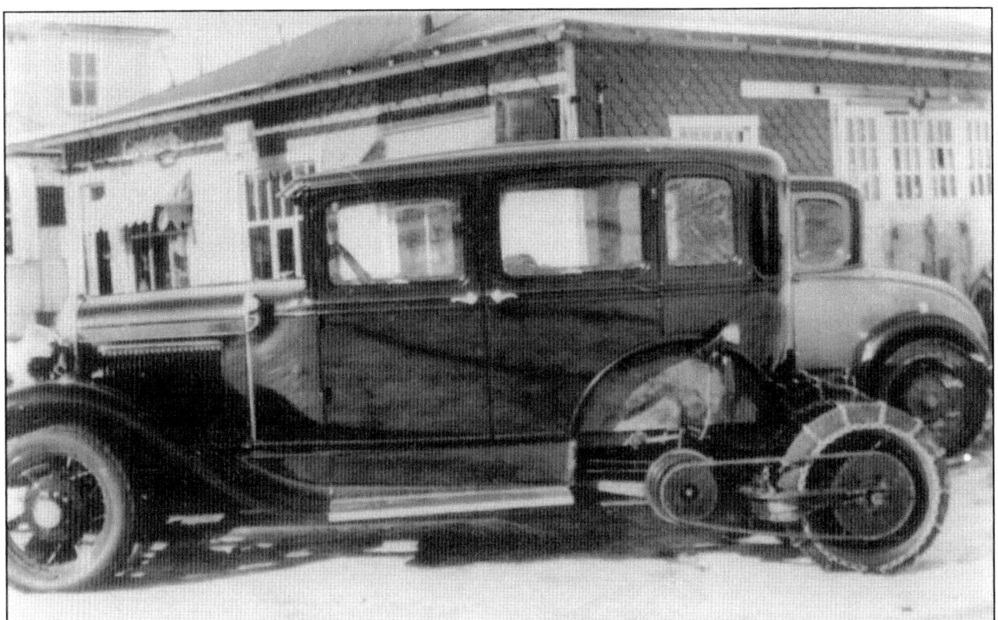

Dr. Zimmerman I was interested in all mechanical things. In the mid-1920s, he invented several vehicles designed as transportation to patients' homes during snowstorms. Dr. Zimmerman's "snow planes" had a propeller and skis. This photograph, taken in front of the Keller Brothers Ford in Buffalo Springs, shows his version of a "snow cat"—a modified Model A with four chain-driven rear wheels. (Courtesy of Betsy Nolt.)

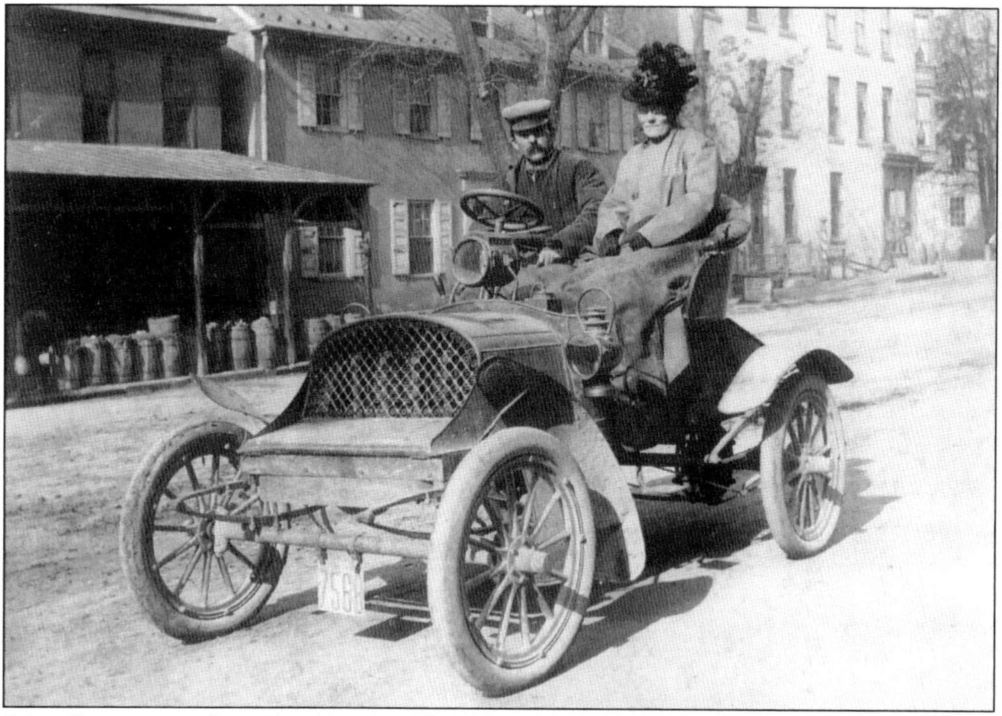

Schaefferstown residents Franklin B. and Jenny Beckley Horst drive on a street in Lebanon. Horst's automobile was reputed to be the first in Schaefferstown. It was delivered to the railway station in Lebanon, from which he had to drive it home. Horst was a prominent farmer and businessman in Heidelberg Township and a member of Schaefferstown United Brethren Church. (Courtesy of Ray Horst.)

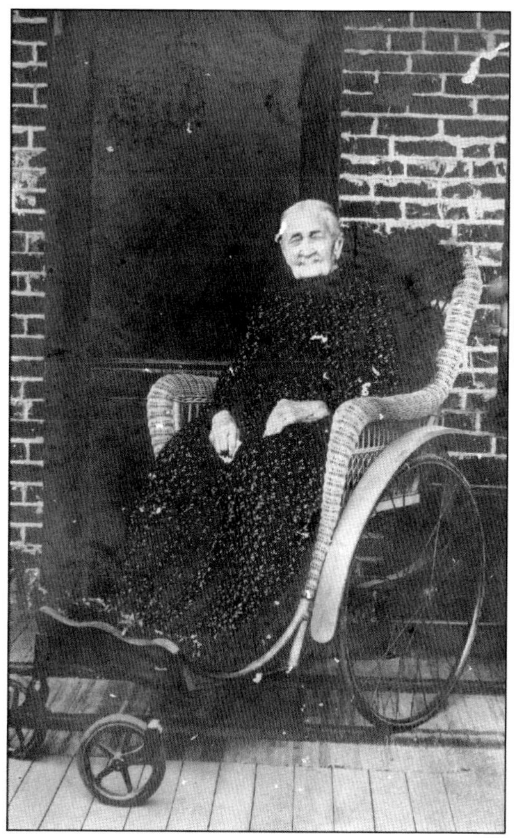

Mollie Seibert (1814–1910) addressed this photographic postcard to Alice Bomberger (1861–1944), writing that on November 1, 1908, she would be 94 years old. Seibert is seated in a wicker wheelchair padded with a fleece. Mollie, also known as Magdalena, was currently living with her daughter Mary and son-in-law Abraham S. "A.S." Brendle, author of *A Brief History of Schaefferstown*. Both Brendle and Alice Bomberger were descendants of Alexander Schaeffer.

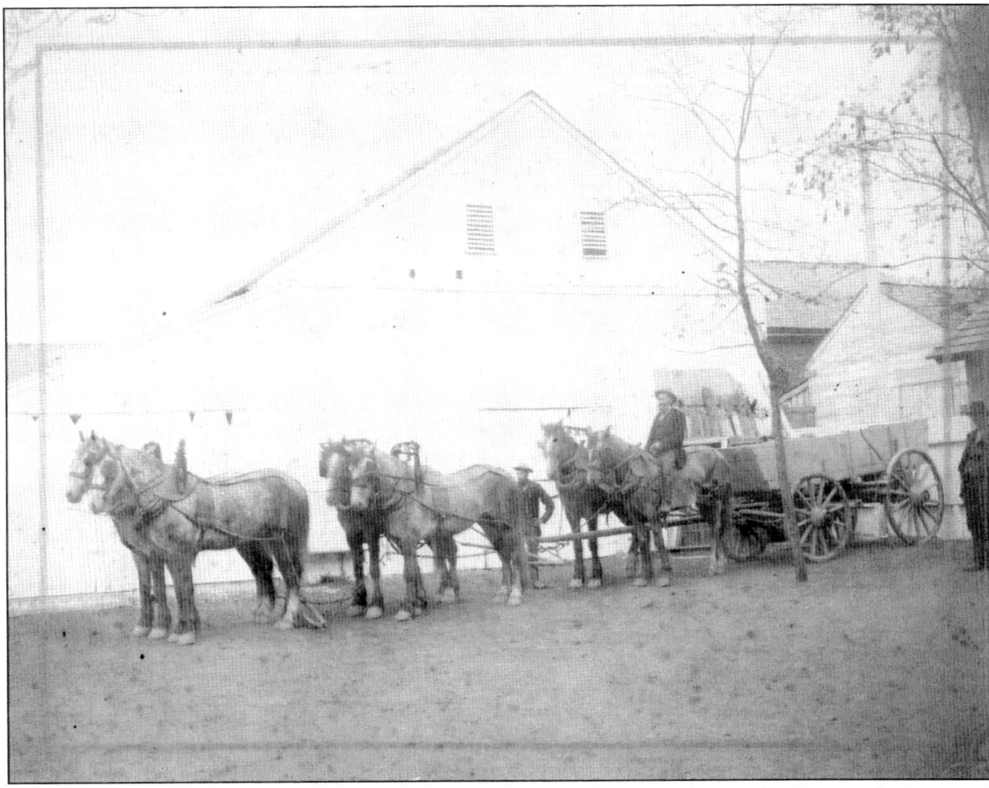

Jacob Binkley's teams are ready for hauling, complete with unusual sets of bells attached to each horse collar. Binkley owned considerable acreage in the southeast corner of the township. On the 1875 atlas map, it appears that he may have intended to sell lots to create the small community that is labeled "Binckley." Today, this land is part of Middle Creek Wildlife Management Area. (Courtesy of Diana Wike Castor.)

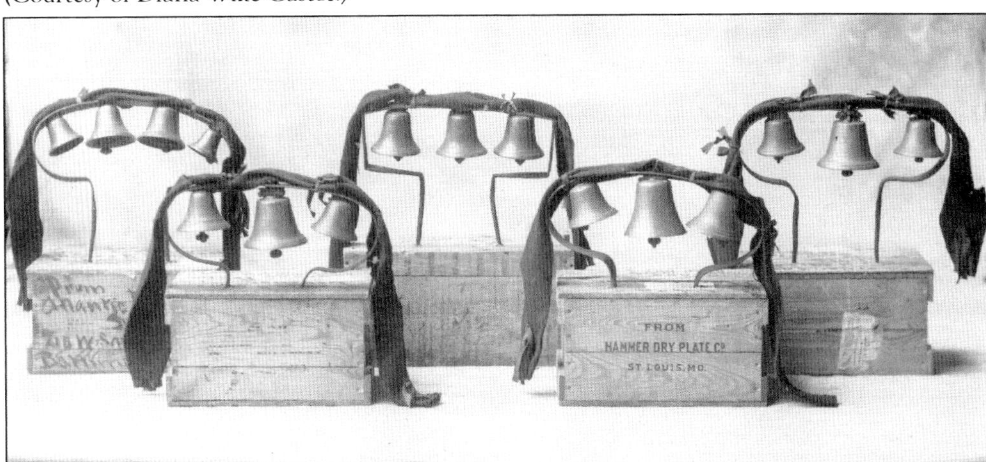

These bells, the same as those shown in the previous photograph, are a precious part of Binkley family history. They were passed from generation to generation, perhaps originating in Germany, from whence the Binkleys emigrated in the mid-1700s. Today, the whereabouts of the bells are unknown; only the photograph remains to tell this family's story. (Courtesy of Diana Wike Castor.)

Three

The Waterworks

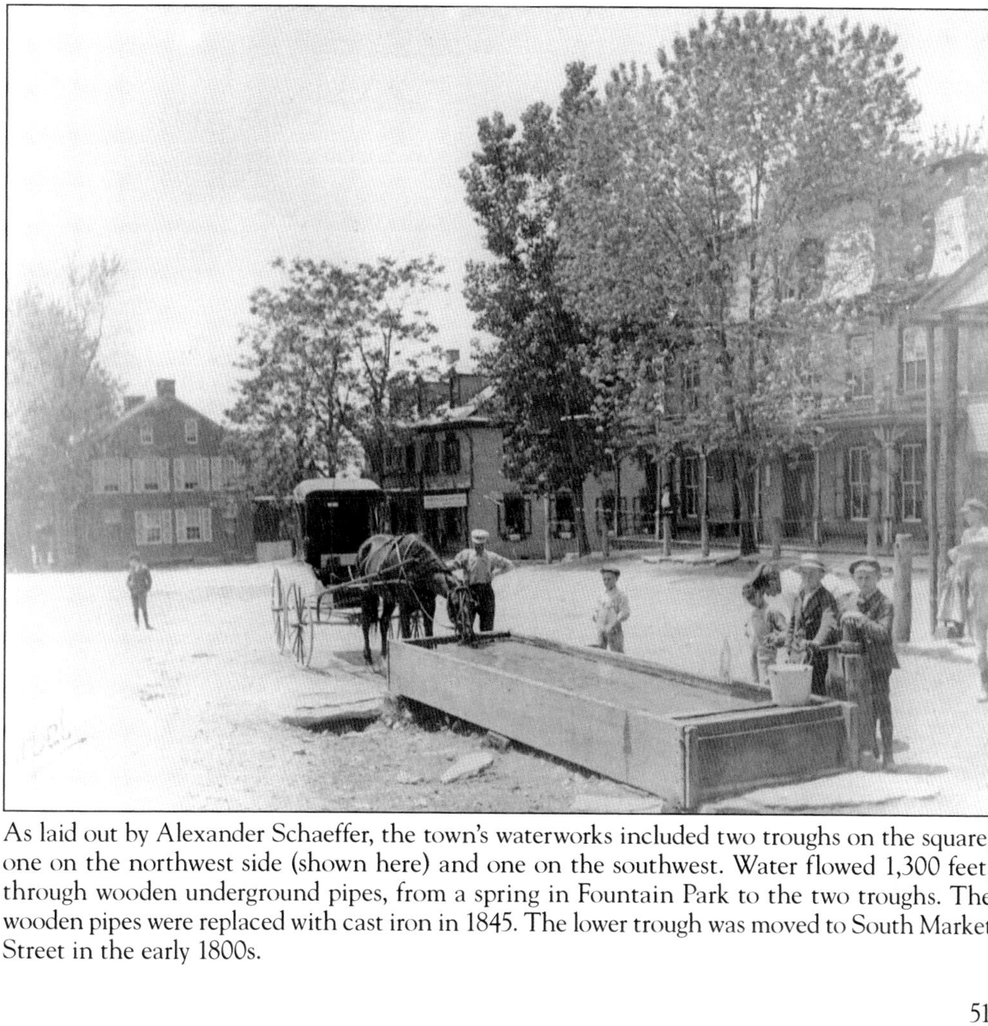

As laid out by Alexander Schaeffer, the town's waterworks included two troughs on the square, one on the northwest side (shown here) and one on the southwest. Water flowed 1,300 feet, through wooden underground pipes, from a spring in Fountain Park to the two troughs. The wooden pipes were replaced with cast iron in 1845. The lower trough was moved to South Market Street in the early 1800s.

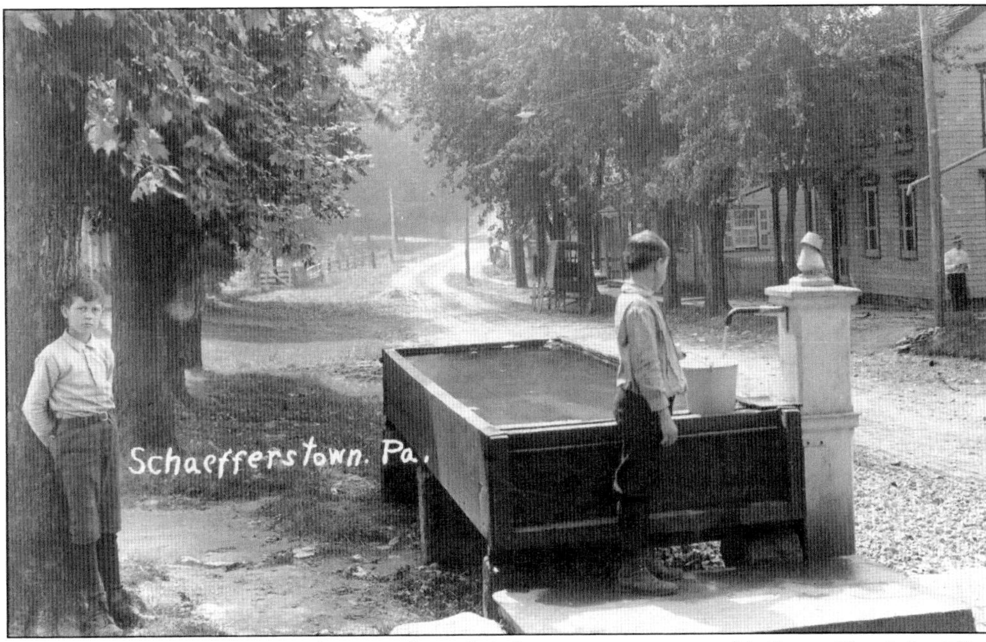

Charles Mock (left) eyes the photographer while his companion, possibly James Keath Jr., fills a bucket at the lower trough, or "fountain," as they were somewhat grandly known, on South Market Street. In 1936, this wooden trough was replaced with a granite basin. A tin cup was attached to both fountains, and it was used by thirsty kids and adults well into the 20th century.

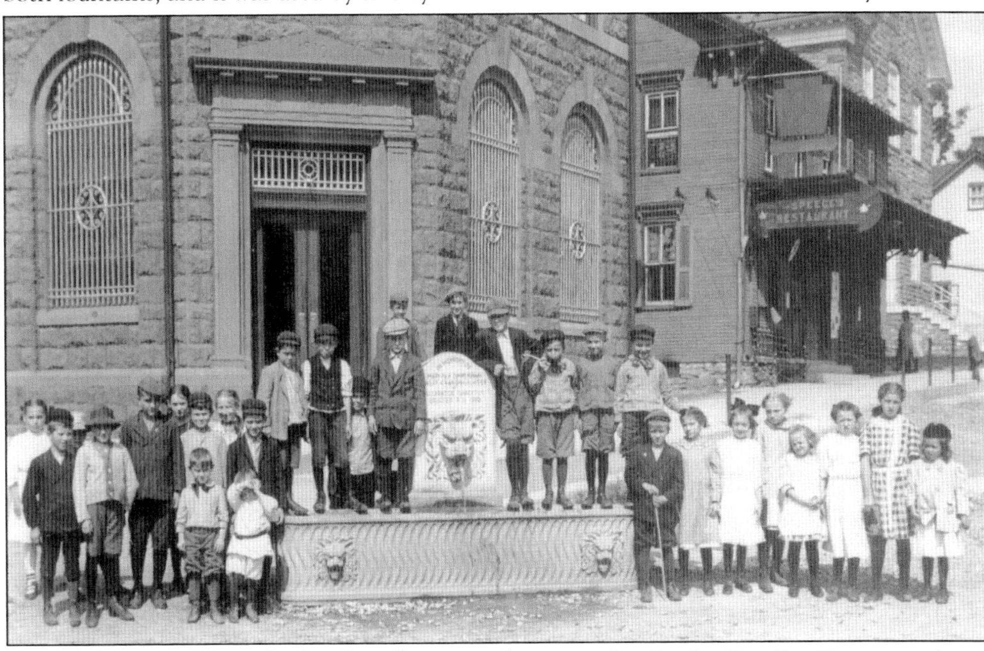

A. Matilda Zimmerman, who lived in what is now known as the Gemberling-Rex House, purchased this elaborate fountain in 1909 to replace the wooden trough and to honor her family's heritage. The fountain was a perennially popular place to pose for a group photograph, but its position, jutting out into the street, became a traffic hazard, and it was moved away from the street to its present location in 1944.

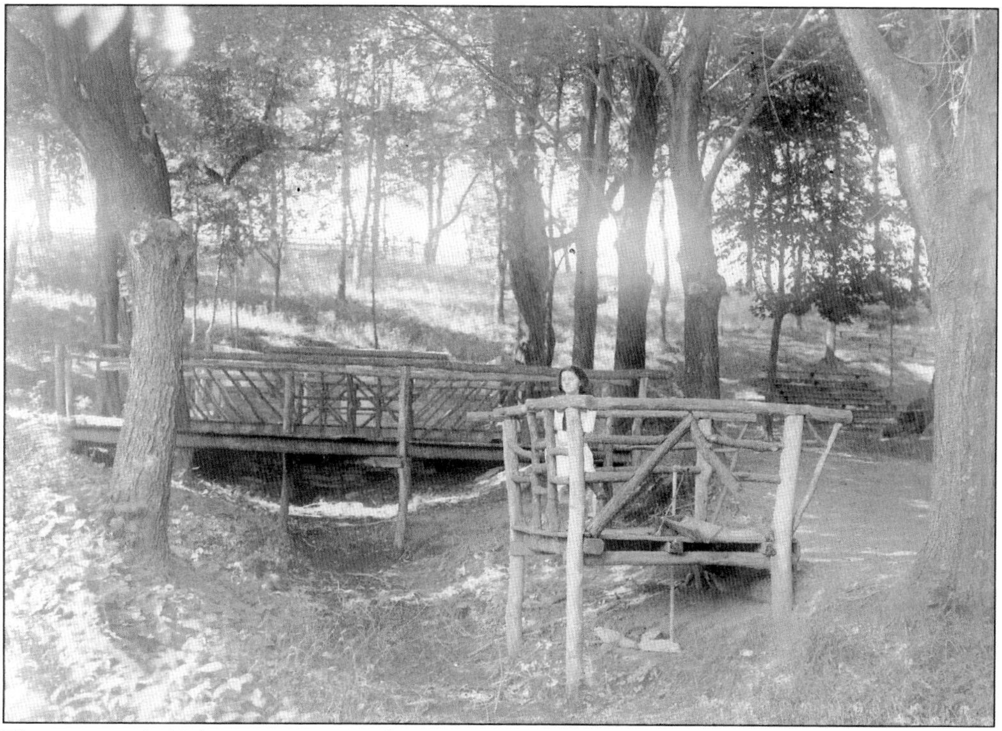

These are early-20th-century views of Fountain Park, the tract of land containing the spring and reservoir that Alexander Schaeffer deeded to the residents of Market Street in 1763. All people living on this street are still members of the water company and responsible for maintaining the water system and park. Originally calling themselves the Fountain Company, they obtained a charter from the Commonwealth of Pennsylvania in 1845 as Schaefferstown Water Company. Fountain Park was—and still is—a pleasant place for an outing with friends. (Above, courtesy of Diana Wike Castor; below, courtesy of Dona Nye.)

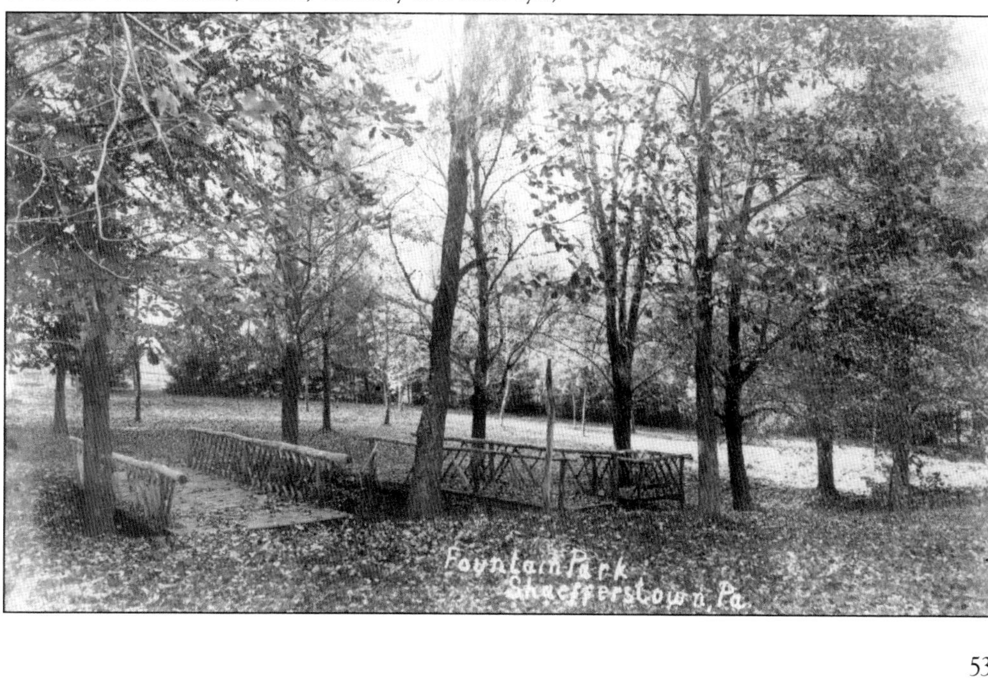

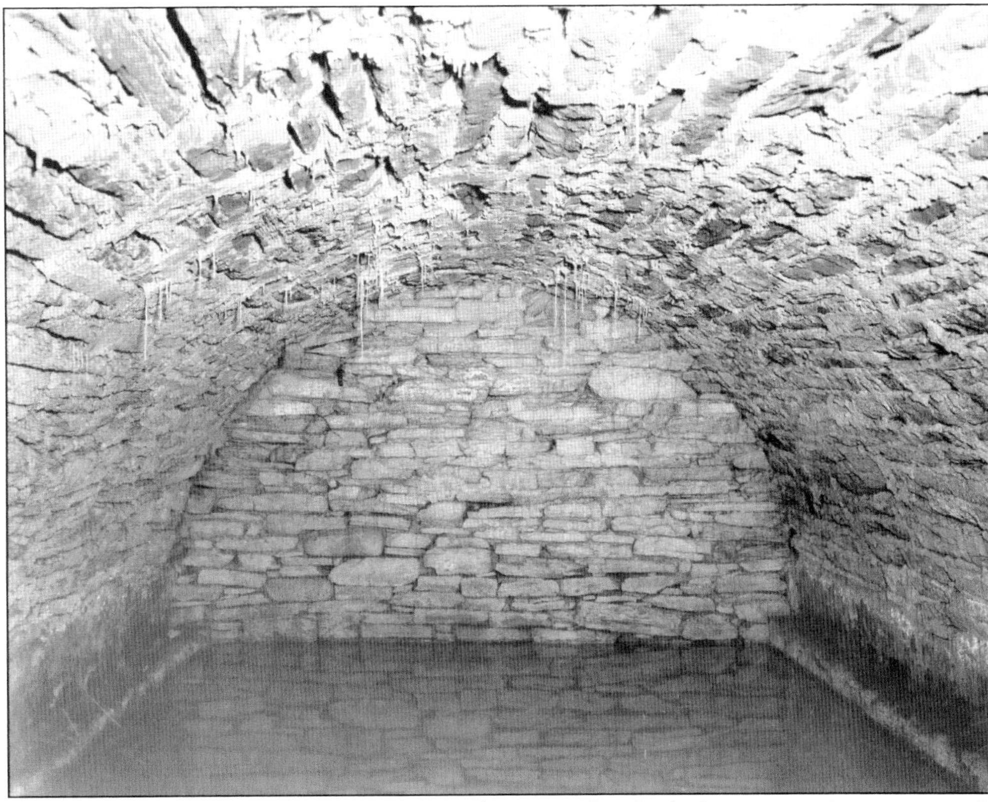

The spring that feeds the waterworks is contained in this vaulted springhouse, dating from the 18th century. Originally, the front of the structure was open with a dam containing the water, but in the 1840s, Fountain Company overseers walled in the front to enclose the entire structure. The reservoir has an estimated capacity of 13,000 gallons. (Courtesy of the Institute of American Deltiology.)

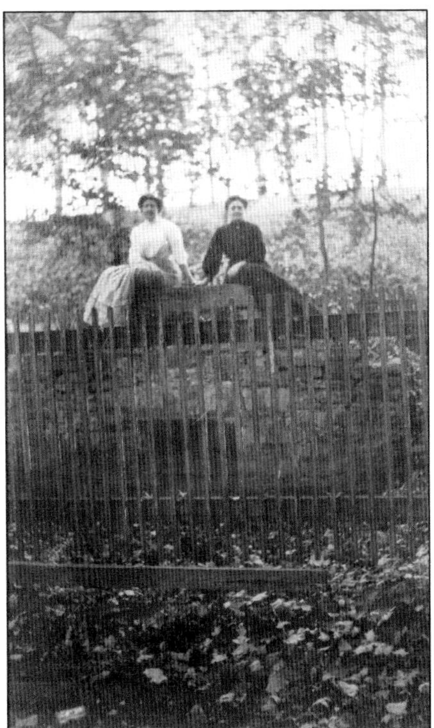

This photograph of the reservoir with two visitors perched on top predates 1909, when the water company rebuilt the front wall of the structure. During that project, workers found a stone engraved with the date 1736. This was two years before Schaeffer arrived in the country, suggesting the spring was already walled in when Schaeffer laid out the town. (Courtesy of the Institute of American Deltiology.)

Four

BUSINESS AND INDUSTRY

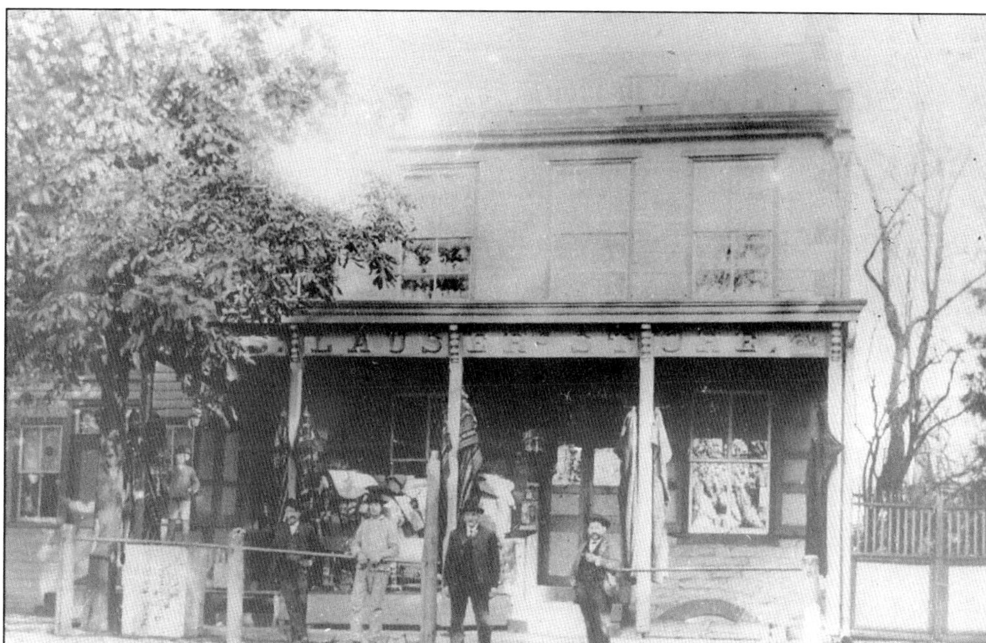

In 1850, Joseph Lauser purchased this property from George F. Miller, who had built the limestone store building just a few years earlier. Lauser and, later on, his son ran the store until 1928, when John Reinhold and Taylor Zerbe took over. Reinhold and Zerbe sold general merchandise and groceries, competing directly for customers with Umberger's, just across the street. The Reinhold-Zerbe store closed in the mid-20th century.

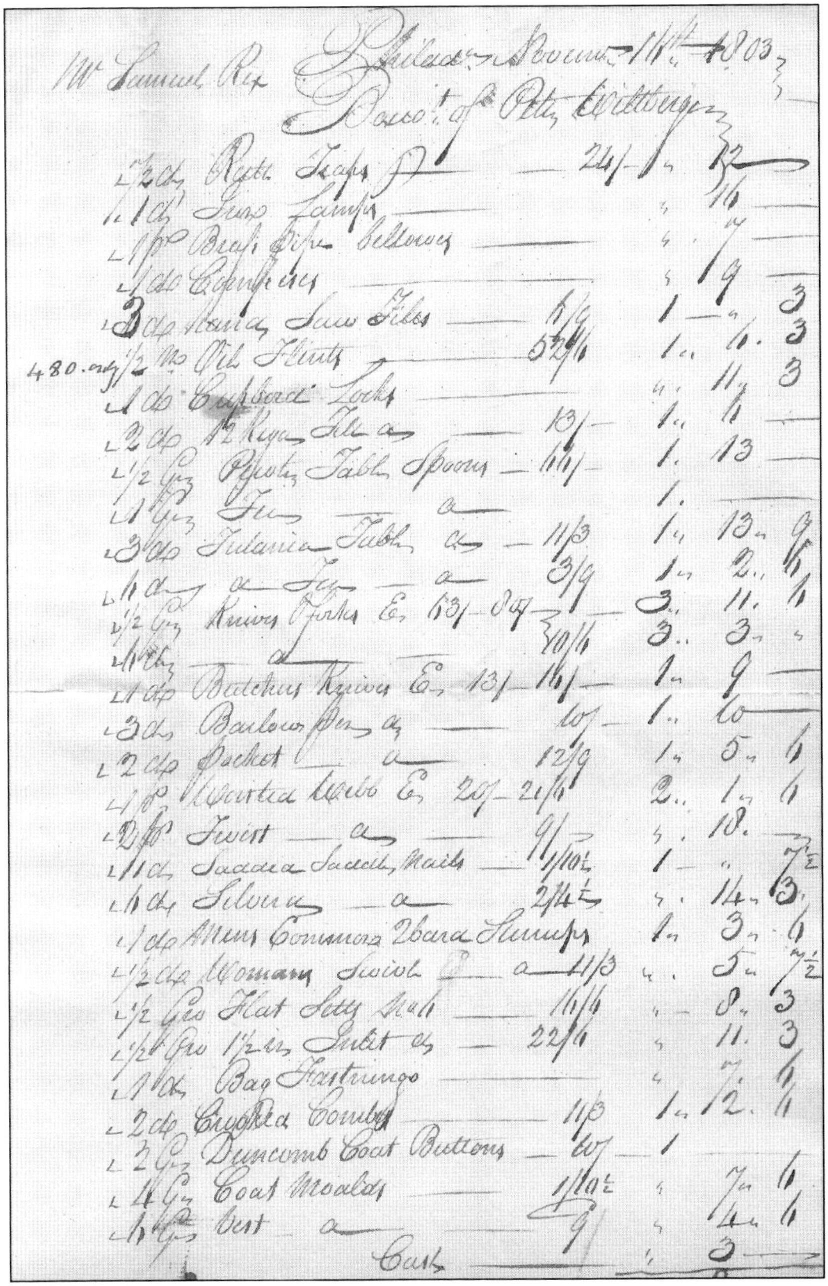
Mr Samuel Rex Philada Novem 11th 1803
Bo't of Peter Wiltberger

Samuel Rex ran his general store in what is now the Franklin House, Schaefferstown, from 1790 to 1807. Along with his brother-in-law, Michael Valentine, Rex rented the building from Henry Schaeffer. Valentine operated a tavern on one side of the building, and Rex had his store on the other. Although living in a small rural village, Schaefferstown's people could buy almost any utility and luxury goods they needed at the Rex store. Rex bought some of his merchandise and produce locally from farmers and craftsmen, and he went to Philadelphia twice a year for other items. This receipt, one of many documents surviving from Rex's business, lists hardware and notions he bought in the city from merchant Peter Wiltberger. The first item on the list is rat traps. Prices are listed in pounds, shillings, and pence.

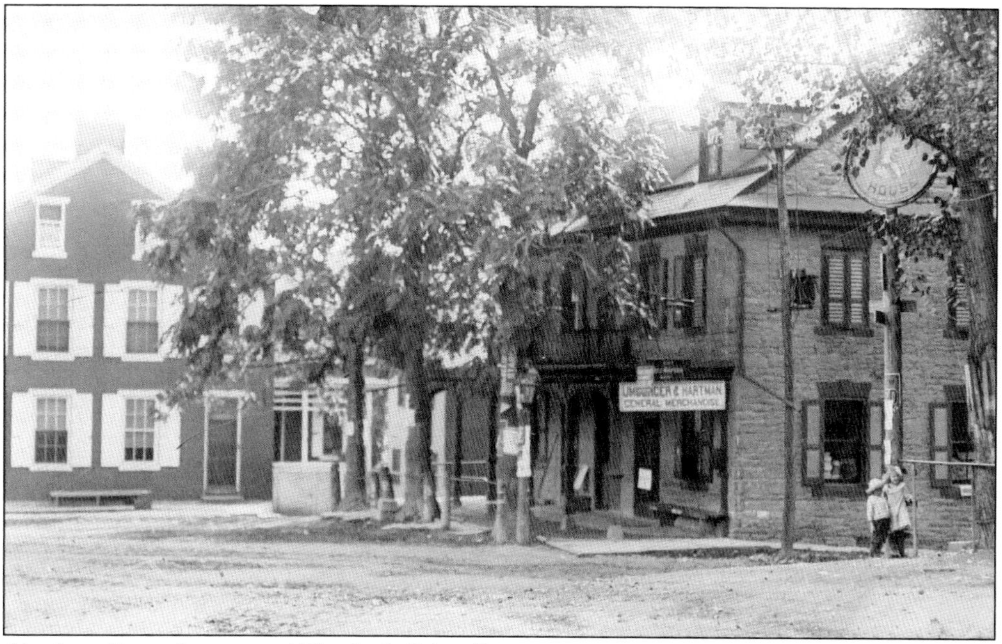

Abraham Rex, who married Elizabeth Schaeffer (Alexander Schaeffer's daughter), took over his brother Samuel's business in 1807. He built this store and residence across Main Street from the Franklin House around 1815. In 1834, Abraham Rex retired, and his sons took over the store. They sold the business five years later to their brother-in-law, William M. Weigley, who built a large mansion behind the store. (Courtesy Diana Wike Castor.)

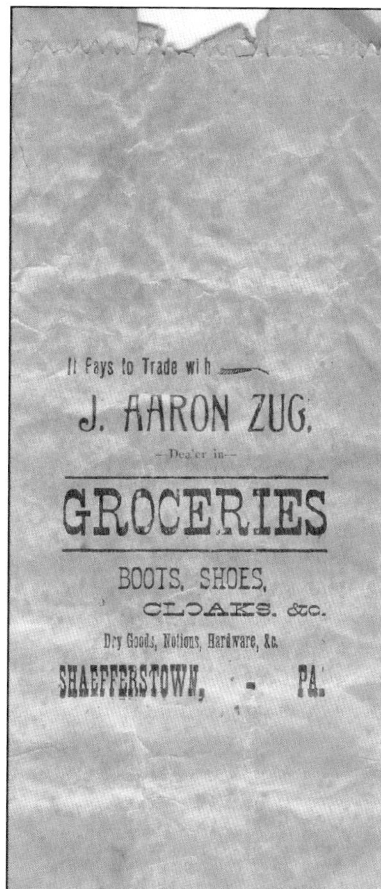

J. Aaron Zug, whose paper bags boasted of his wide range of goods, operated the former Weigley store in the 1890s, though the building was still owned by a member of the Weigley family. In 1903, Milton Hartman, who ran the post office in Zug's store, took over, in partnership with Michael Umberger. From 1940 to 1988, the business operated as Umberger's Grocery.

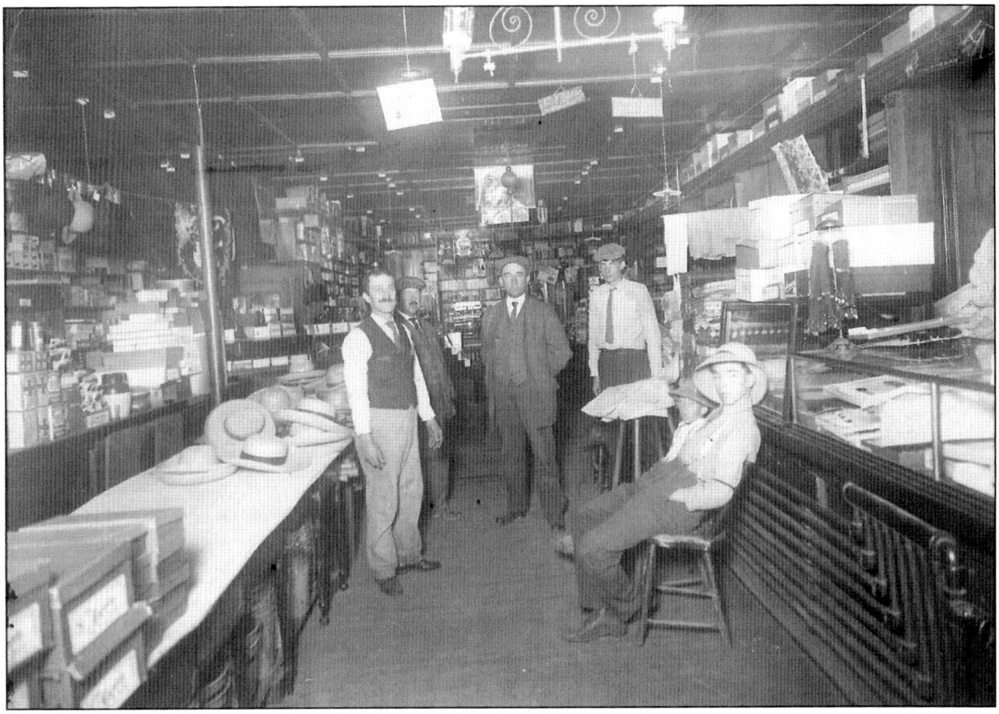

This photograph of the interior of one of Schaefferstown's stores was donated to Historic Schaefferstown by Kathryn Umberger, who ran Umberger's Grocery for many years. It shows the large selection of goods available, although one wonders how the storekeeper remembered what was in all those boxes. General stores were also places where locals gathered, as the boy on the right may have done, to visit and hear the latest news.

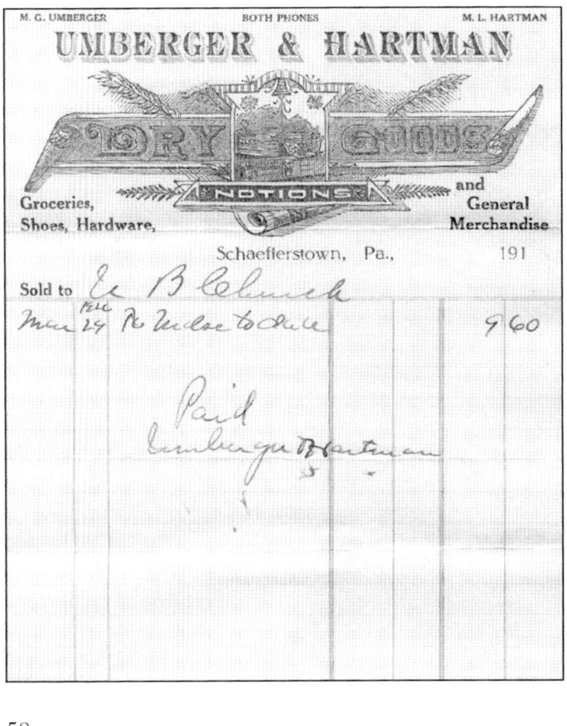

M. G. UMBERGER BOTH PHONES M. L. HARTMAN

UMBERGER & HARTMAN

DRY GOODS

NOTIONS

Groceries, Shoes, Hardware, and General Merchandise

Schaefferstown, Pa., 191

Sold to E B Church

Mar 24 To Mdse to date 9 60

Paid Umberger & Hartman

Well into the 20th century, Schaefferstown store owners allowed individuals as well as businesses to run a tab for their purchases. The elaborate illustration on this invoice emphasizes the dry goods department of Umberger & Hartman's store, but the partners sold a variety of goods, including groceries. This bill, dated March 1926, is for unspecified merchandise purchased by the United Brethren Church.

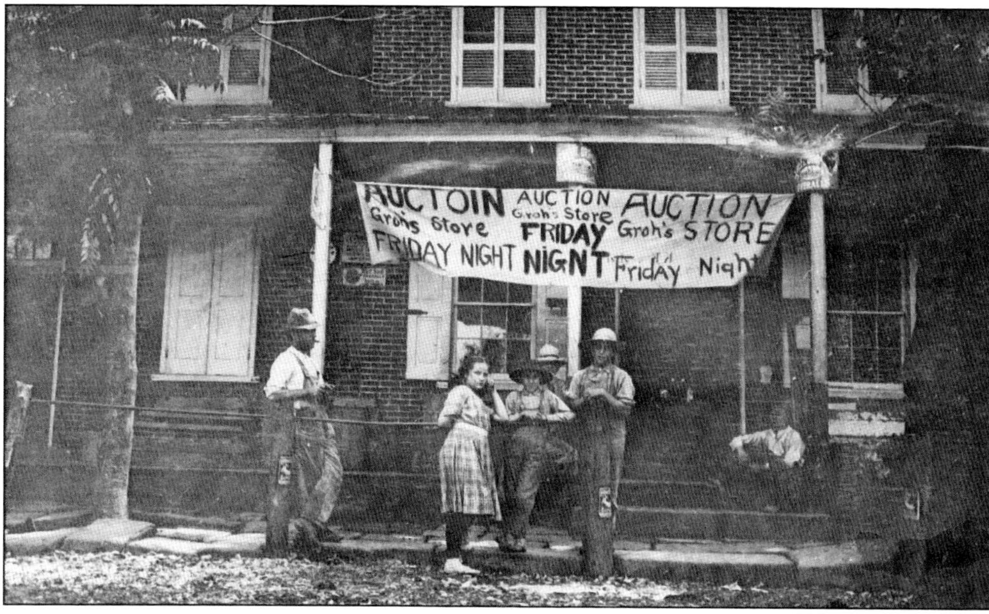

Abraham S. Groh owned a general store in Buffalo Springs on the corner of Distillery Road and Route 419 (Schaeffer Road). In 1875, he advertised the sale of queensware (dishes), drugs, boots, and shoes in addition to groceries and hardware. In this early-1900s photograph, the store is doing a little advertising.

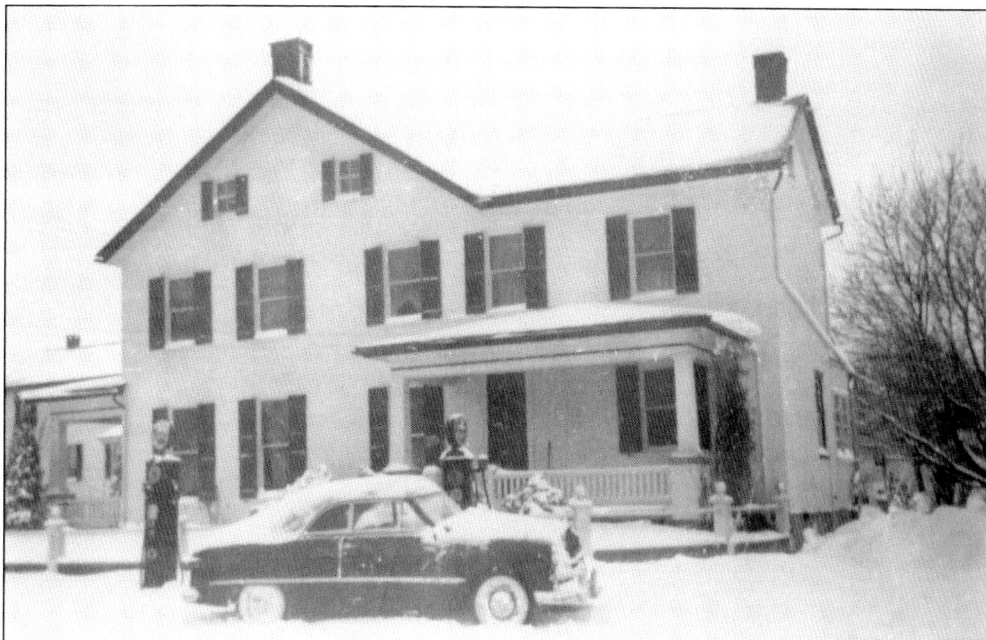

This large building, its brick facade still concealed by a coat of white paint, stands at the crossroads in Reistville. In the late 19th century, it was the Farmers and Drovers Hotel, operated by livestock dealer Isaac Phillippy and his wife. In the 1920s, Ira M. Schlosser converted the stable behind the hotel into a garage; it currently houses a farm-implement business. (Courtesy of Institute of American Deltiology.)

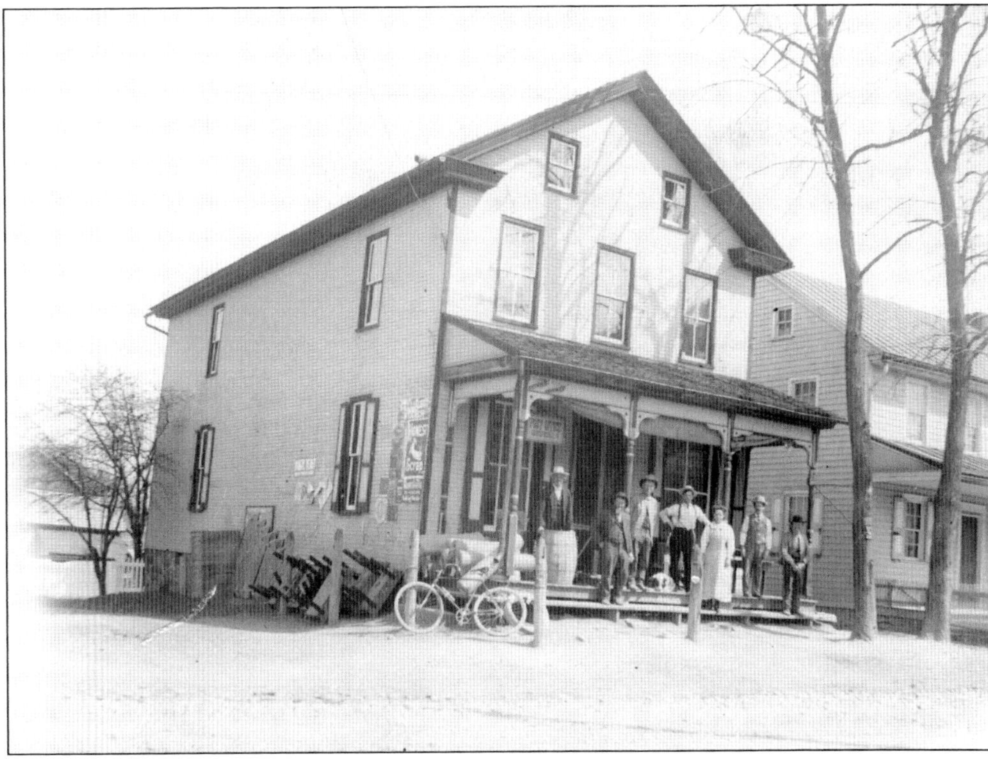

Weik's Store, seen here in 1911, served the community of Kleinfeltersville as an all-purpose grocery store, hardware store, and post office. Weik's was located on Millbach Road, across from Trinity Evangelical United Brethren Church. Later, Weik's became Doster's Market, and a gasoline pump was installed. (Courtesy of Institute of American Deltiology.)

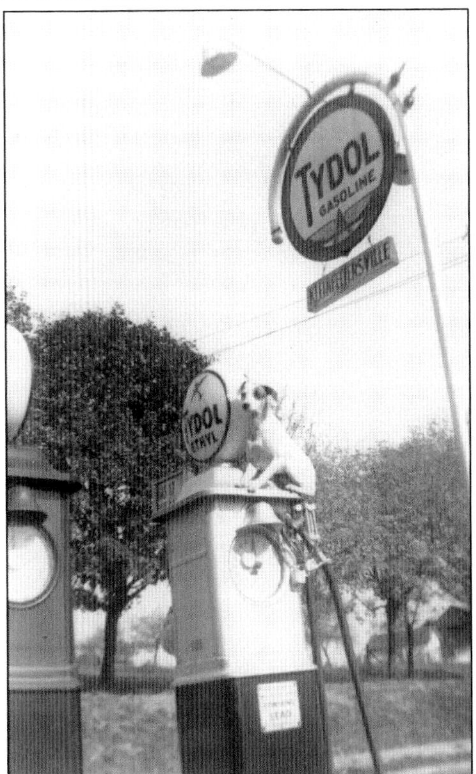

The gas pumps at Doster's Market in Kleinfeltersville seem an odd place to find a dog. The local market was often a place to visit with friends, catch up on news from near and far, purchase gas, buy a soda, or even have a little fun posing a puppy! (Courtesy of Rita Mock.)

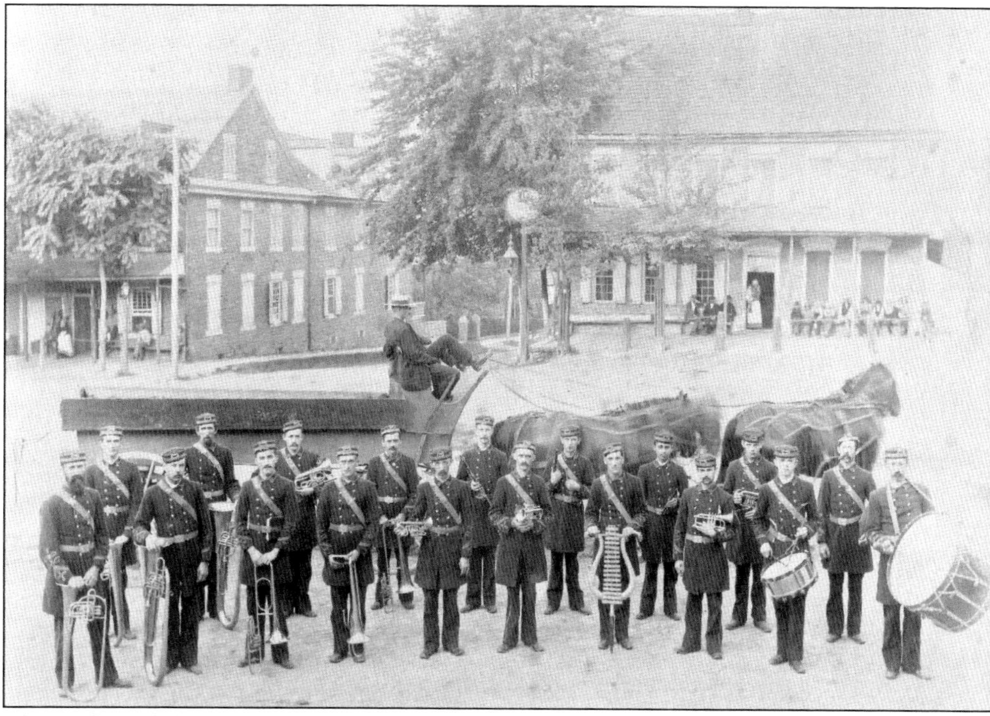

This is the only known image of the Franklin House hotel, built by Alexander Schaeffer, as it looked before John L. Graybill enlarged and remodeled it in 1883. Note the gable roof and single-front doorway. Ironically, it was not the building that the photographer was interested in, but the town band, proudly posing on the Schaefferstown square with the hotel as backdrop.

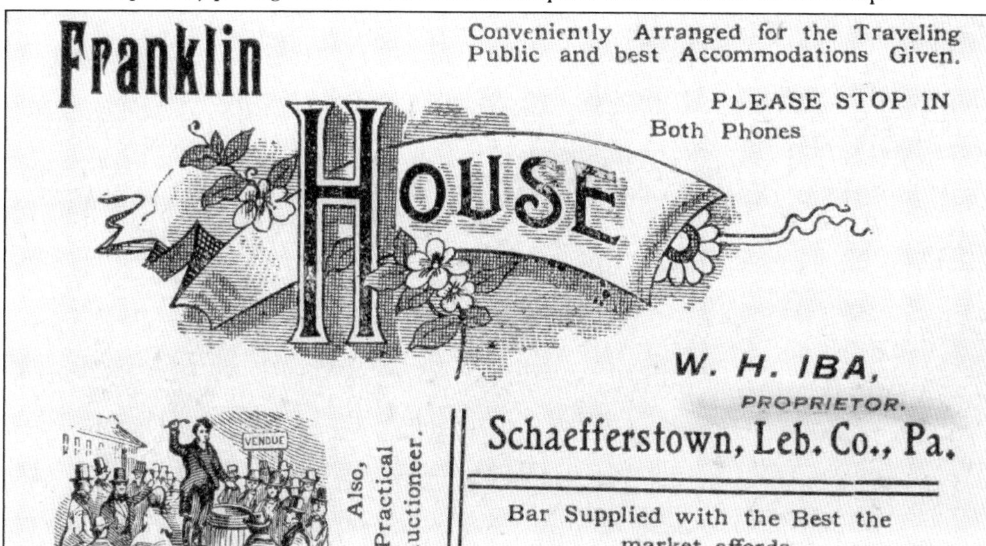

William H. Iba, son of Civil War veteran William B. Iba, used this business card during the time he was proprietor of the Franklin House. Iba also was somewhat of an entrepreneur. In addition to keeping the Franklin House, he was a trolley conductor from at least 1914 to 1921 and, as indicated by this card, a "Practical Auctioneer."

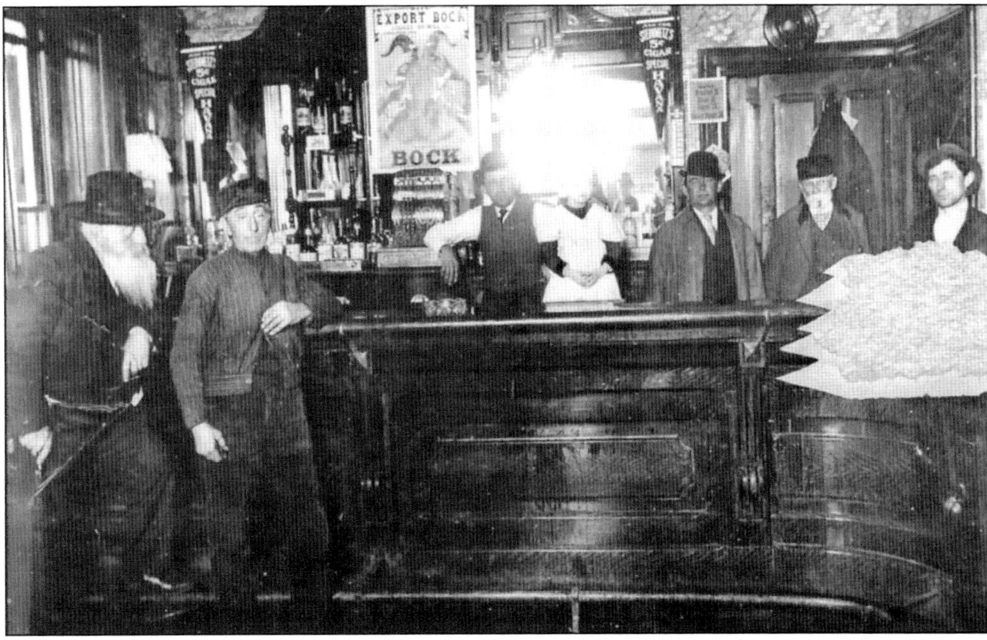

The tavern in the Franklin House was—and still is—a popular place for locals to relax and enjoy food and drink. A sign behind the bar advertises breakfast, lunch, and dinner, with prices ranging from 25¢ to 50¢. Built by local carpenter Benjamin Hartman, the bar is still in use, although barstools have replaced the foot rail.

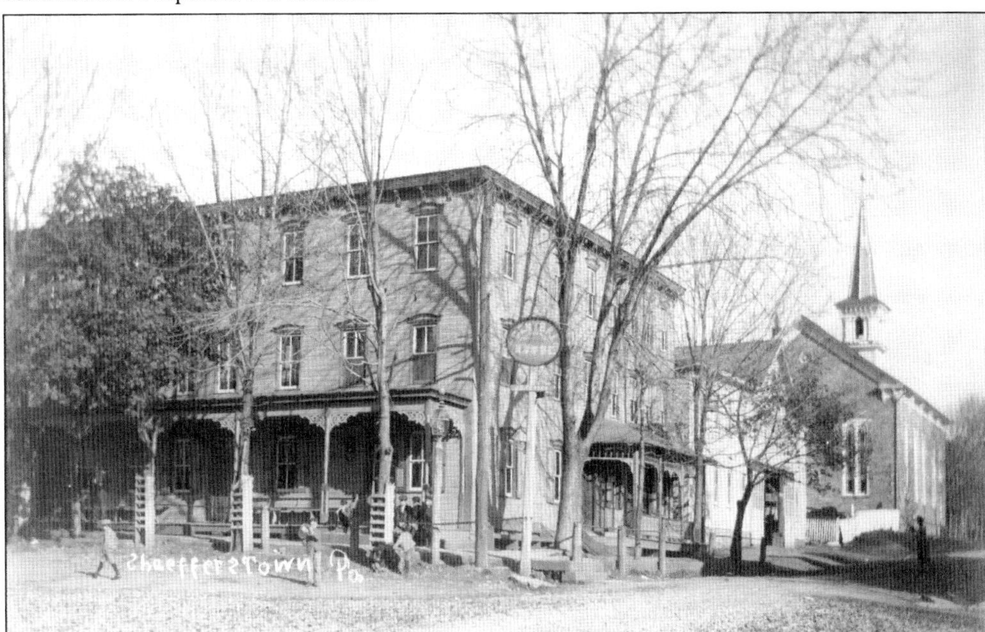

The Central House stood on the northeast side of Schaefferstown's square. Described by A.S. Brendle as one of Schaefferstown's "first-class hotels," it was run by the Fetter family, who enlarged it in 1882. The Central House was demolished in 1976 to provide parking for St. Luke Church. During demolition, an early log building with carved corner post and arched cellar was found under the larger frame structure. (Courtesy of Dona Nye.)

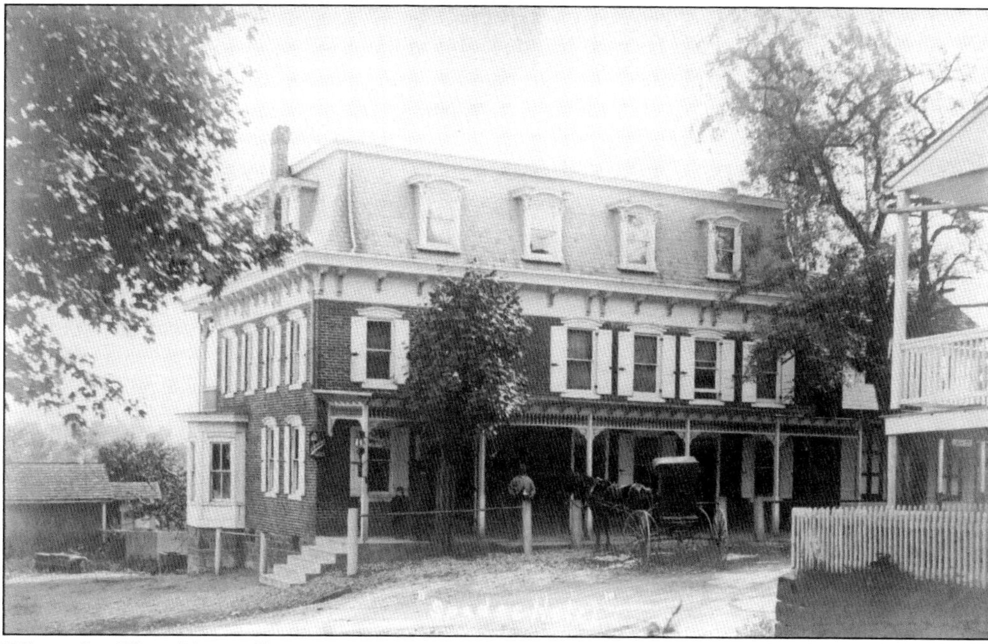

When the Kleinfeltersville Hotel was built prior to 1860, it was a two-story structure. Like its counterparts in Schaefferstown, it was enlarged in the late 19th century to accommodate increasing trade. Proprietor Henry Noll put on an addition to the east in 1884, and Adam Spayd added a third story with mansard roof in 1889. It remains a popular restaurant and bar with local residents.

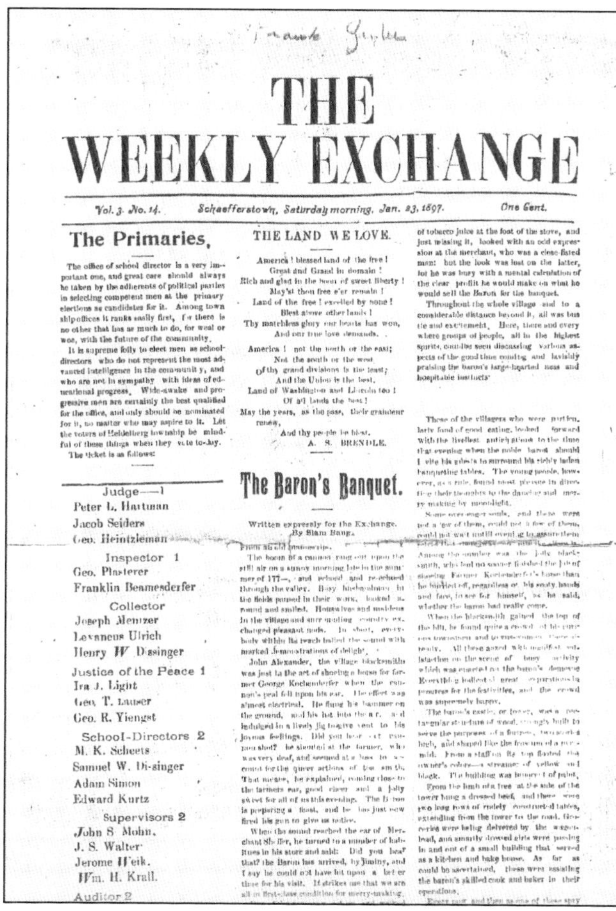

THE WEEKLY EXCHANGE

Vol. 3. No. 14. Schaefferstown, Saturday morning, Jan. 23, 1897. One Cent.

The Primaries,

The office of school director is a very important one, and great care should always be taken by the adherents of political parties in selecting competent men at the primary elections as candidates for it. Among township offices it ranks easily first, for there is no other that has as much to do, for weal or woe, with the future of the community.

It is supreme folly to elect men as school-directors who do not represent the most advanced intelligence in the community, and who are not in sympathy with ideas of educational progress. Wide-awake and progressive men are certainly the best qualified for the office, and only should be nominated for it, no matter who may aspire to it. Let the voters of Heidelberg township be mindful of these things when they vote to-day.

The ticket is as follows:

Judge—1
Peter L. Hartman
Jacob Seiders
Geo. Heintzleman

Inspector 1
Geo. Plasterer
Franklin Beamesderfer

Collector
Joseph Menzer
Levaneus Ulrich
Henry W Dissinger

Justice of the Peace 1
Ira J. Light
Geo. T. Lauser
Geo. R. Yiengst

School-Directors 2
M. K. Scheets
Samuel W. Dissinger
Adam Simon
Edward Kurtz

Supervisors 2
John S Mohn.
J. S. Walter
Jerome Weik.
Wm. H. Krall.

Auditor 2

THE LAND WE LOVE.

America! blessed land of the free!
Great and Grand in domain!
Rich and glad in the boon of sweet liberty!
May'st thou free e'er remain!
Land of the free! excelled by none!
Blest above other lands!
Thy matchless glory our hearts has won,
And our true love demands.

America! not the north or the east;
Not the south or the west
Of thy grand divisions is the least;
And the Union is the best.
Land of Washington and Lincoln too!
Of all lands the best!
May the years, as the pass, their grandeur renew,
And thy people be blest.

A. S. BRENDLE.

The Baron's Banquet.

Written expressly for the Exchange.
By Slam Bang.

of tobacco juice at the foot of the stove, and just missing it, looked with an odd expression at the merchant, who was a close-fisted man: but the look was lost on the latter, for he was busy with a mental calculation of the clear profit he would make on what he would sell the Baron for the banquet.

Throughout the whole village and to a considerable distance beyond it, all was bustle and excitement. Here, there and every where groups of people, all in the highest spirits, could be seen discussing various aspects of the good time coming and lavishly praising the baron's large-heartedness and hospitable instincts.

Those of the villagers who were particularly fond of good eating, looked forward with the liveliest anticipations to the time

From 1896 to about 1901, Schaefferstown had its own newspaper, the *Weekly Exchange*. The *Exchange* was published each Saturday morning by Rex R. Griswold, who had his printing company in the Central House hotel. Local lawyer and historian A.S. Brendle served as editor-in-chief. The paper was four pages long and sold for 1¢ per copy or 50¢ a year.

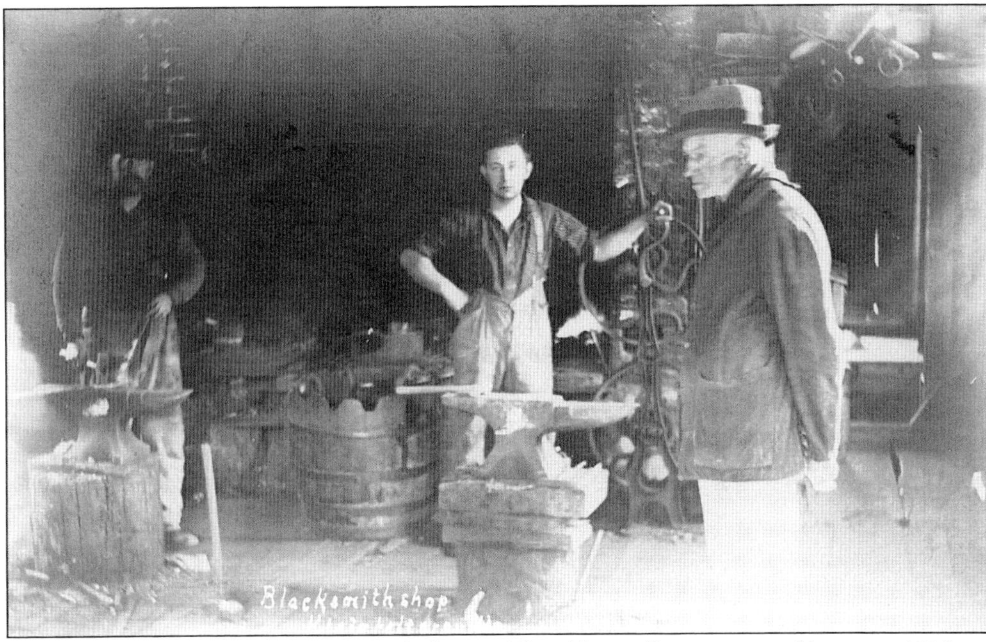

This may be Irvin Eiceman's blacksmith shop in Kleinfeltersville, operational between 1905 and 1910. An unusual crank-and-gear system worked the bellows for this forge. Blacksmithing was often done by farmers on the side, but skilled smiths were necessary to do large or intricate jobs. Many blacksmith shops are marked on the 1875 Lebanon County atlas map for the township. (Courtesy of Susan Horst Kerschner.)

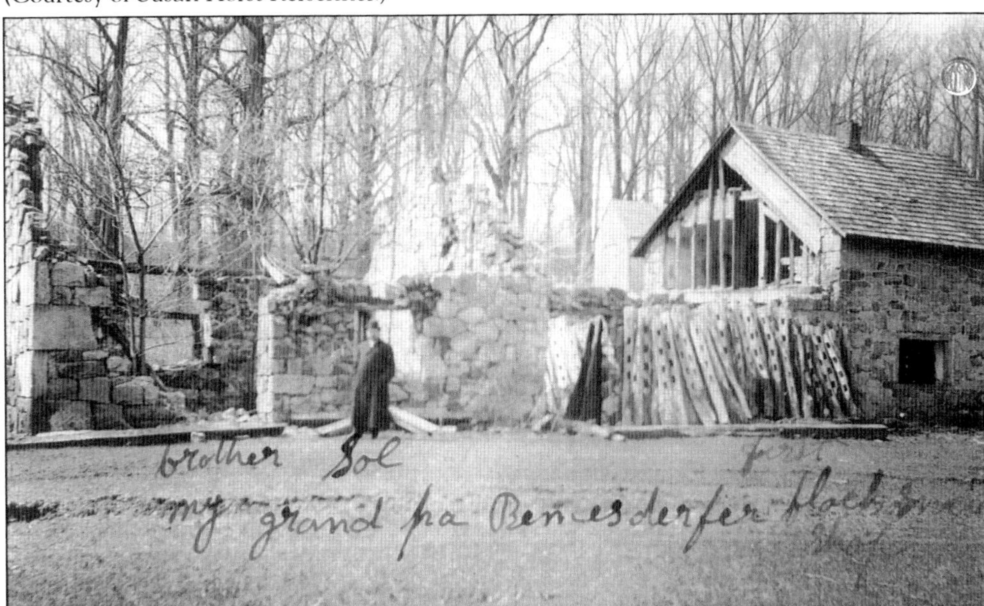

Cyrus Beamesderfer's blacksmith shop, visible on the 1875 atlas map, was located on the north side of Old Mill Road, south of Schaefferstown. This undated photograph includes the youngest of his nine children, tinsmith Solomon Beamesderfer. Several of his other children joined the 1860s westward movement and settled in Sterling, Illinois. (Courtesy of Frank Summers.)

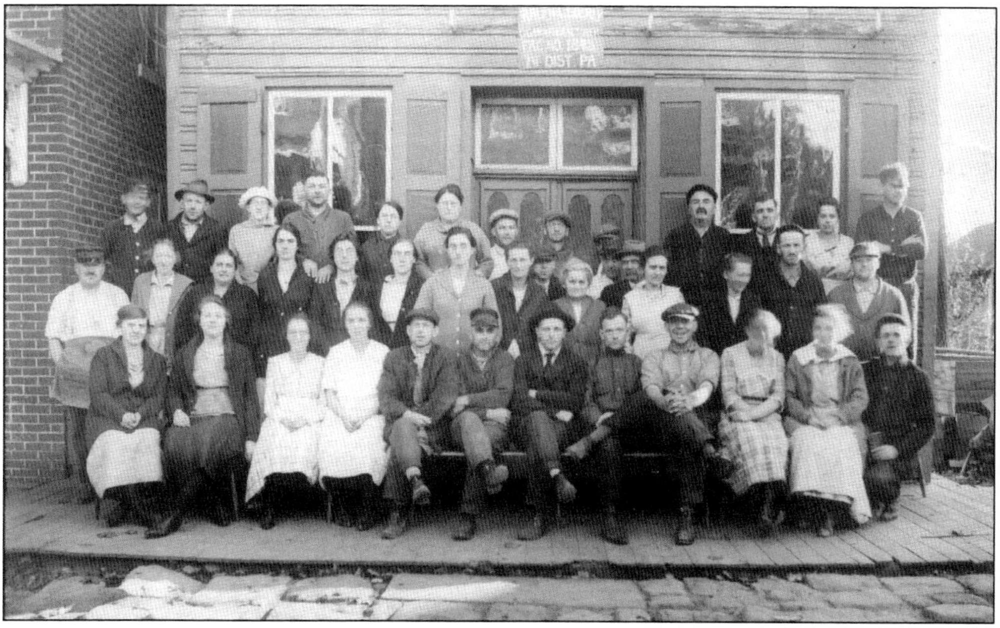

From the late 1800s through the first decades of the 20th century, Kleinfeltersville and Schaefferstown, like many towns in the region, were home to a number of small factories that employed local men and women in processing tobacco and rolling cigars. In 1921, the employees of Ralph Eberly's cigar factory in Kleinfeltersville posed for this group photograph. (Courtesy of Rita Mock.)

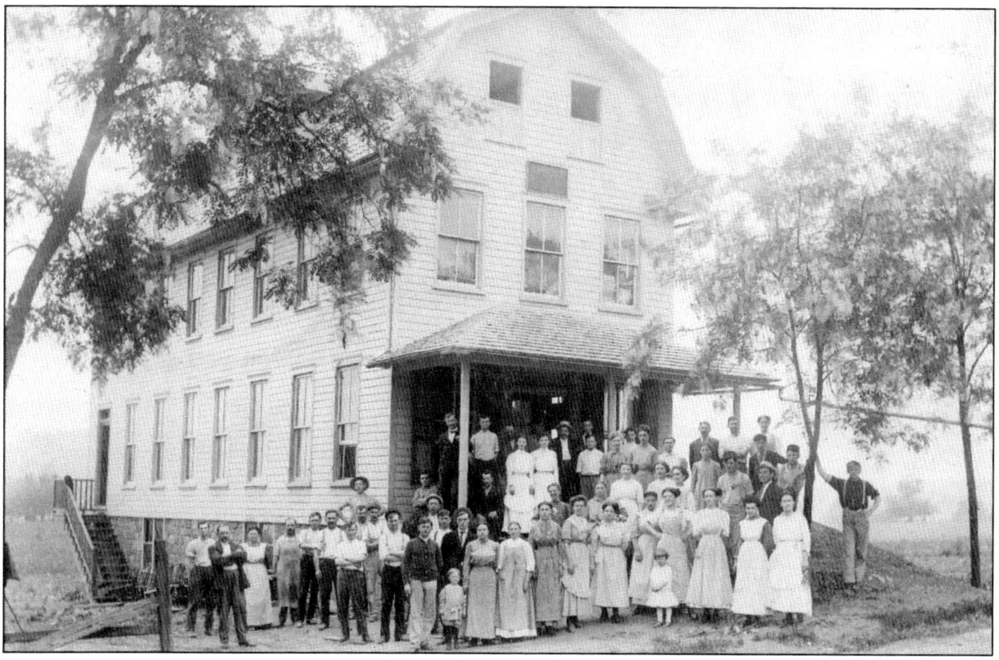

This photograph, taken around 1912, shows workers and two children in front of Witter's Cigar Factory, Kleinfeltersville. The building was the former Carpenter's Hall, which, in 1909, had been moved from Schaefferstown, where it had also been one of Witter's factories. Cigars were enormously popular in the United States in the Victorian era; consumption peaked in 1920, when over eight billion cigars were sold. (Courtesy of Rita Mock.)

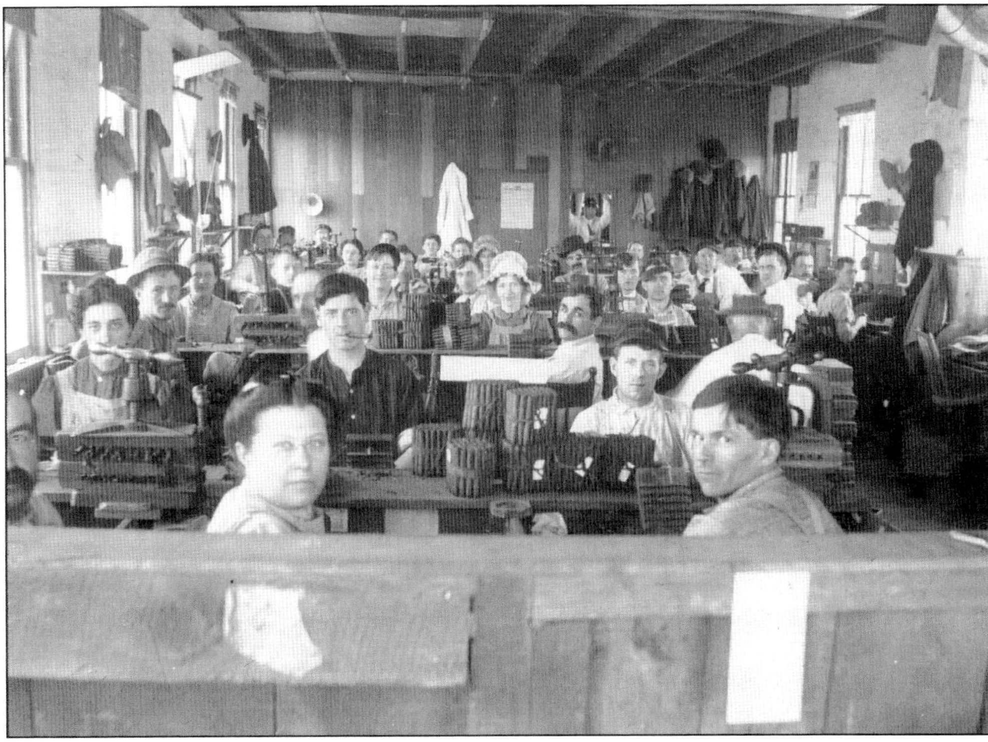

Inside Witter's cigar factory in Kleinfeltersville, men and women sit at wooden tables with tools of their trade. Note the tobacco leaves, cigar molds and presses, and the bundles of finished cigars. After the tobacco was dried and allowed to ferment, workers sorted the leaves and removed the large center rib. At first, cigar making was done entirely by hand by skilled craftsmen. After the introduction of the wooden mold in the early 20th century, there was a division of labor. "Bunch makers" rolled strips of filler tobacco inside a larger binder leaf; these were put into the molds, and the molds put into the presses. After the pressing was complete, a worker known as a "roller" removed the cigars from the mold and applied the outer wrapper leaf. (Both, courtesy of Rita Mock.)

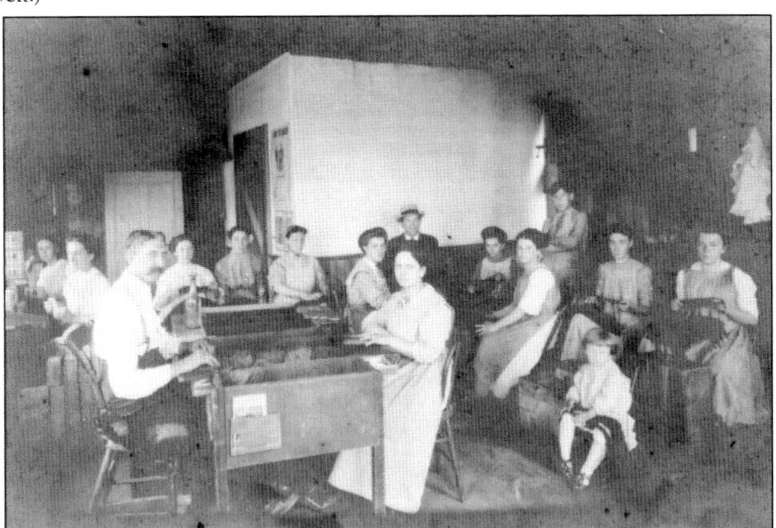

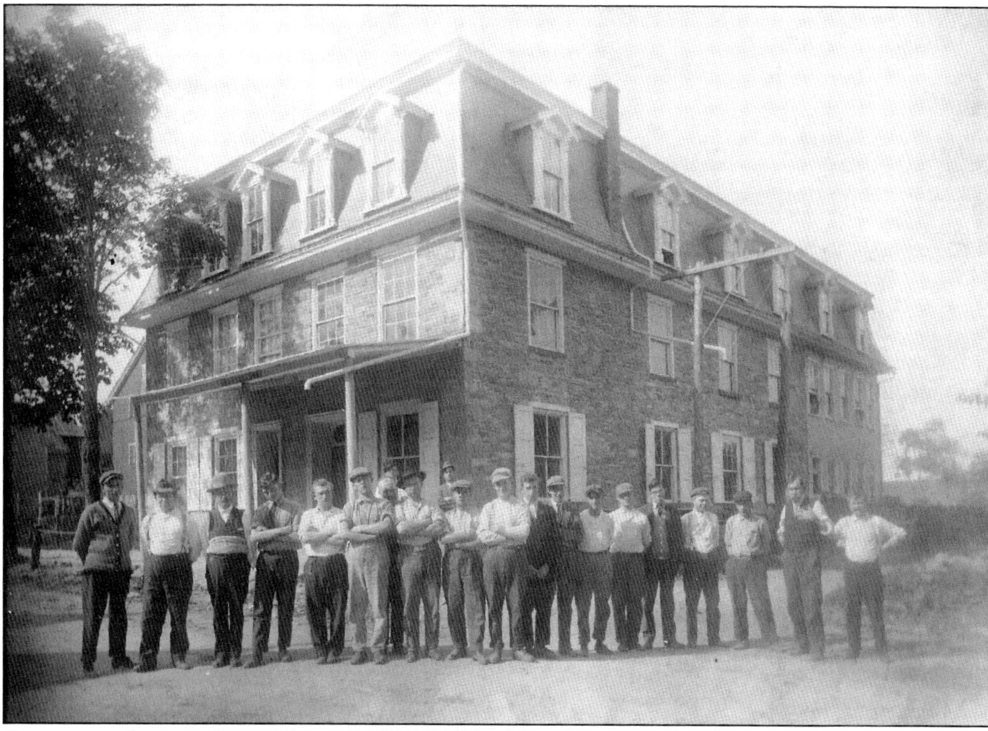

Cigar manufacturer Irwin Horst (1869–1956) had his factory in the former Krall family store on the northwest corner of Lancaster Avenue and Main Street, Schaefferstown. Horst opened his factory around 1900, and he went on to be a justice of the peace and local tax collector. Later on, this building became the township office. It is now divided into apartments.

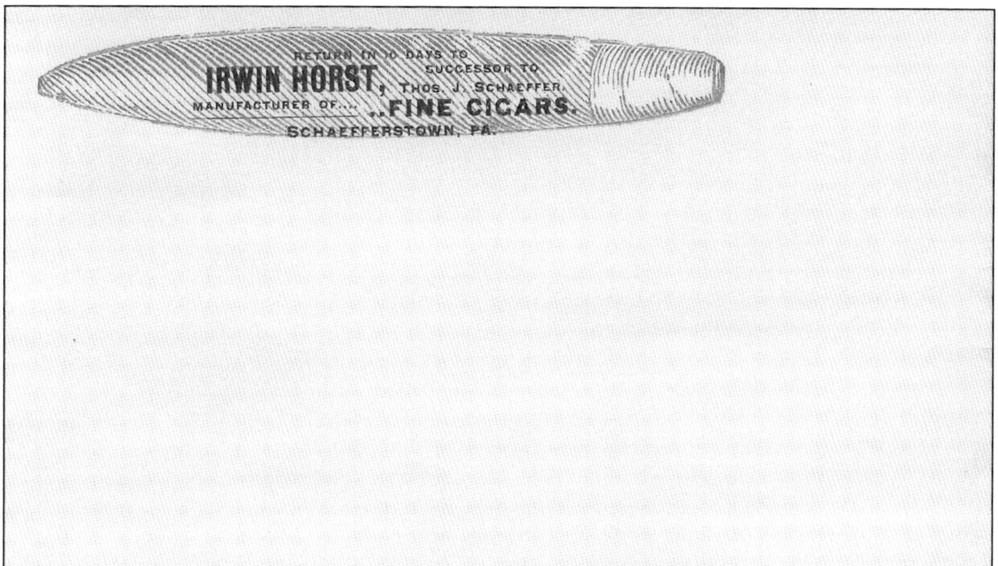

Irwin Horst's business envelope rather proudly announces that he was successor to cigar manufacturer Thomas J. Schaeffer, who was a descendant of the town founder. Following Schaeffer's death in 1899, Horst took over his factory next to the United Brethren Church on West Main Street. According to a directory published in 1902, Horst was one of five cigar manufacturers in Schaefferstown.

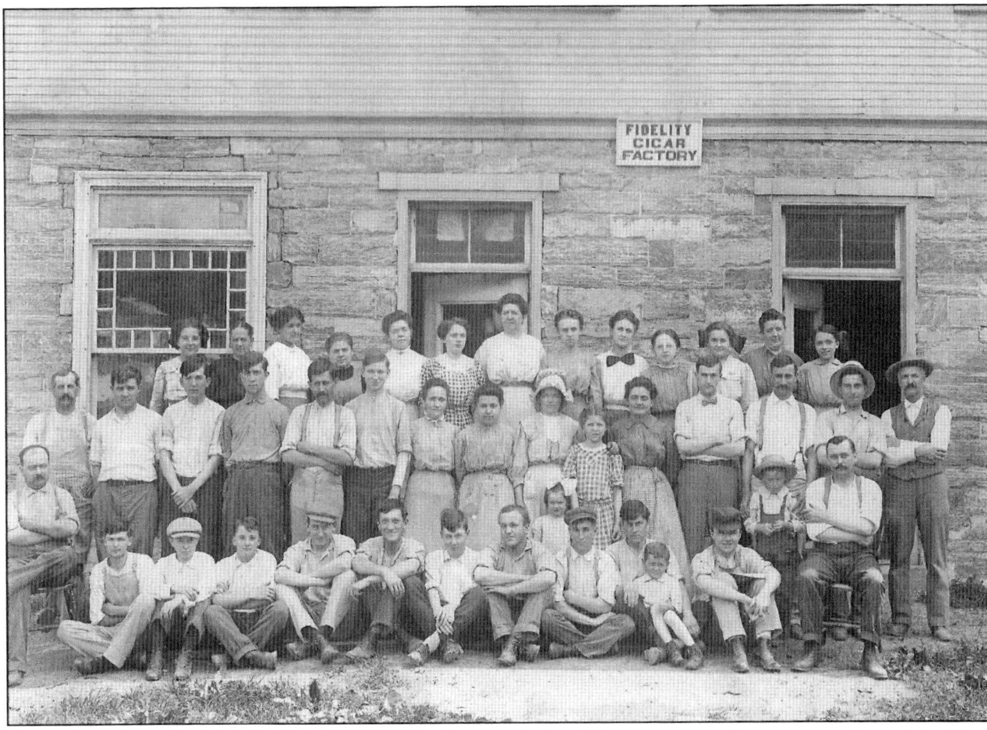

Fidelity Cigar Factory stood on West Main Street, Schaefferstown, on the current site of the Zion United Methodist Church parking lot. In 1883, Thomas J. Schaeffer bought this building, which had been a schoolhouse, and converted it to cigar manufacturing. Schaeffer enlarged it several times as his business grew. He employed over 60 people at the time of his death.

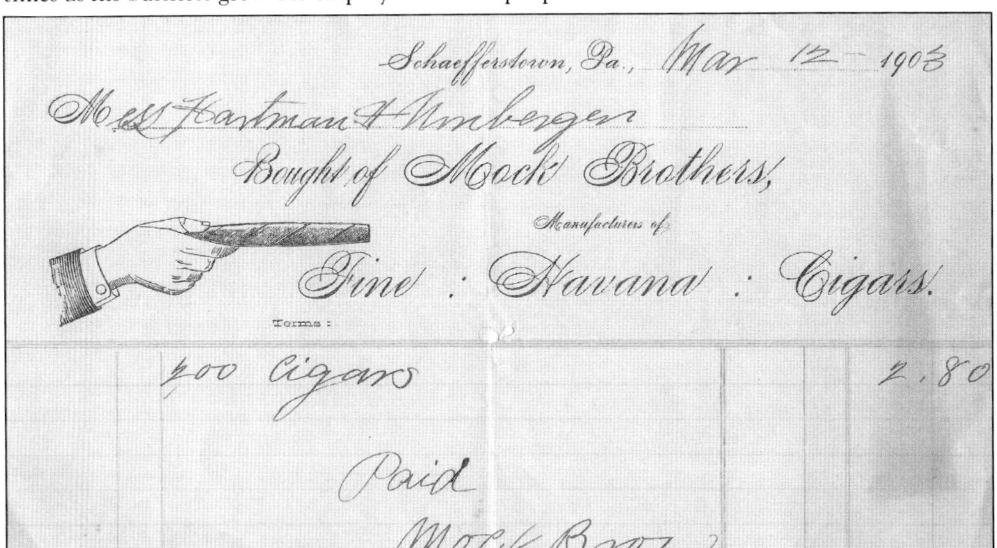

Schaefferstown, Pa., Mar 12 1903

Mess Hartman & Umberger

Bought of Mock Brothers,

Manufacturers of

Fine : Havana : Cigars.

Terms :

200 Cigars	2.80

Paid

Mock Broz

When Mock Brothers of Schaefferstown sold 200 cigars wholesale to Umberger & Hartman's Store in 1903, they cost a mere $2.80. Mock Brothers had their factory in a building on West Main Street that was later converted into a double home. By 1906, according to A.S. Brendle, there were 300 people employed in cigar factories in Schaefferstown.

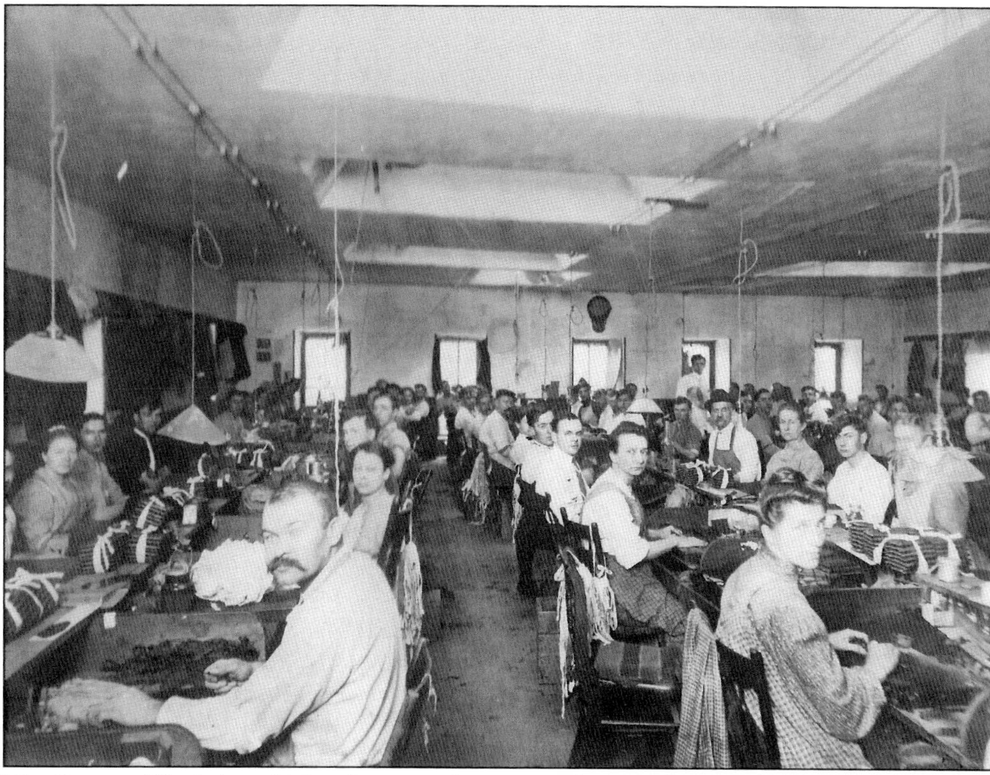

The Grim and Rush (cigar) Manufacturing Company, whose workers are shown here, was located on South Church Street, Schaefferstown. In 1900, Grim and Rush took over from Thomas and B. Frank Zerbe, who had converted this former brewery to a cigar factory in 1883. In 1938, Grim and Rush closed, victims of competition from machine-produced cigars. The building was subsequently used as a feed storage house and garment factory.

Charles Beamesderfer, his wife, Mary (Peiffer), daughter, Clare, sons, Norman and Harry, and a mill worker stand outside their sawmill along the Hammer Creek, south of Schaefferstown. Photographed around 1890, this mill, built of local sandstone, produced long wooden roofing shingles. Family tradition puts its location at the intersection of Obie and Michter's Roads. (Courtesy of Frank Summers.)

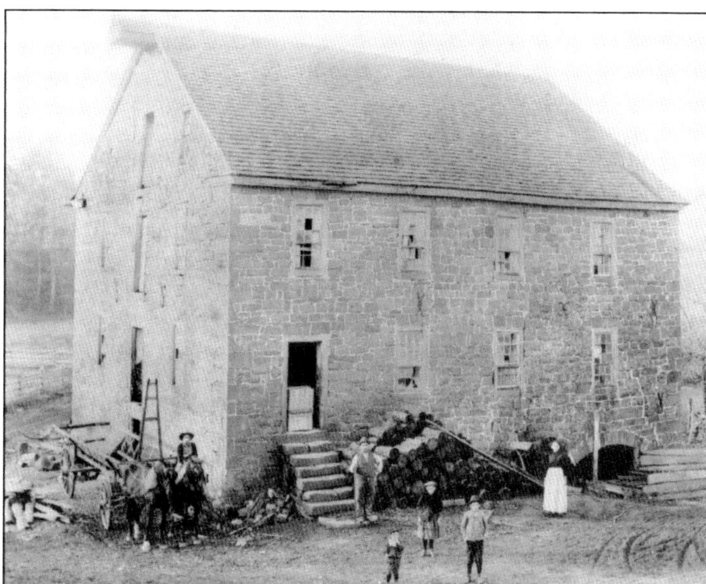

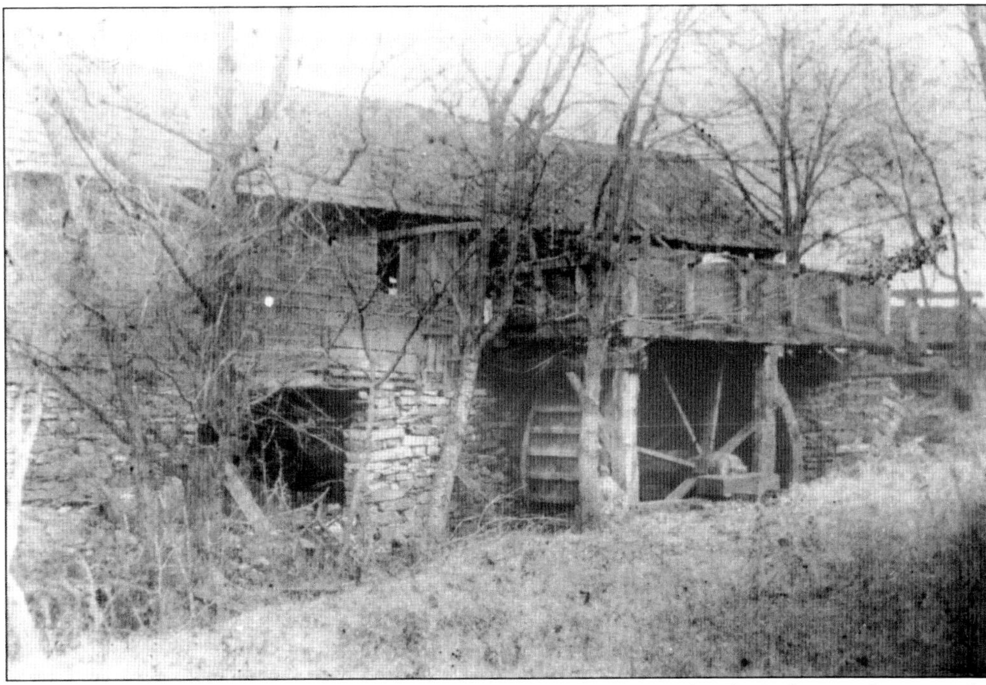

This old mill may also have been located along the Hammer Creek. The Lebanon County atlas maps for 1860 and 1875 show at least five mills along this creek's two major branches: the main branch flowing south from Buffalo Springs, and its eastern branch originating east of Schaefferstown. This mill's limestone foundation indicates a location where limestone was easily obtained, rather than where red sandstone was more prevalent.

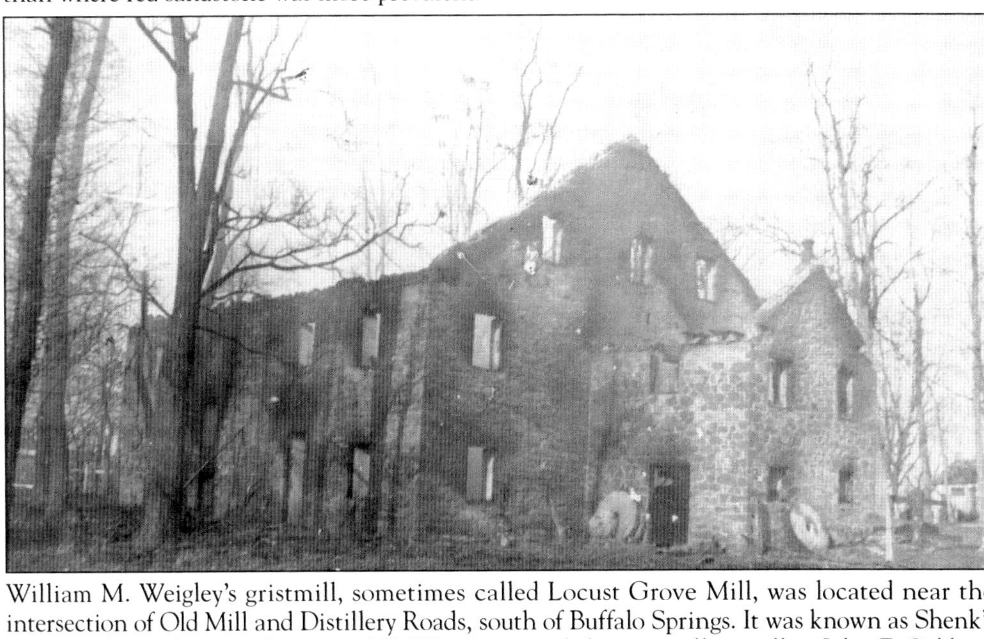

William M. Weigley's gristmill, sometimes called Locust Grove Mill, was located near the intersection of Old Mill and Distillery Roads, south of Buffalo Springs. It was known as Shenk's Mills until Weigley's purchase in 1855. Weigley rented the gristmill to millers John F. Gable of Waldeck and Henry M. Huber. This photograph was taken after January 1, 1917, when Weigley's Mill was destroyed by fire. (Courtesy of Glenn Wolgemuth.)

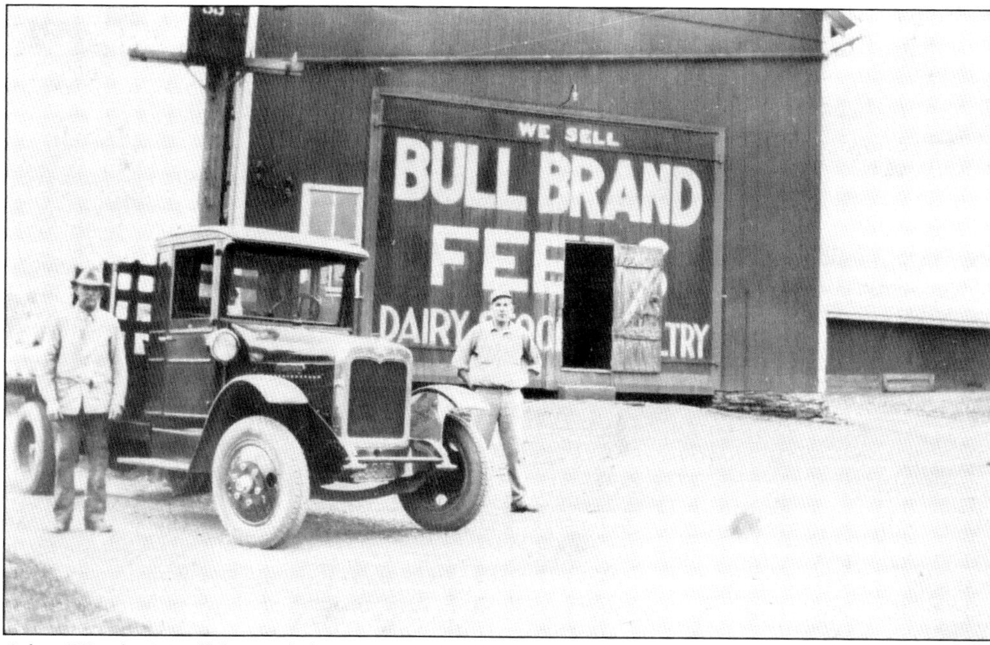

After Weigley's Mill burned down, miller Henry M. Huber bought this property on West Main Street in Schaefferstown, which included a small brick house and a large tobacco shed that he converted into a mill. He added a belt-driven grinder powered by a gasoline engine. This may be Henry and his son Irwin Huber with their work truck outside the newly painted structure that became Huber Mills. (Courtesy of Glenn Wolgemuth.)

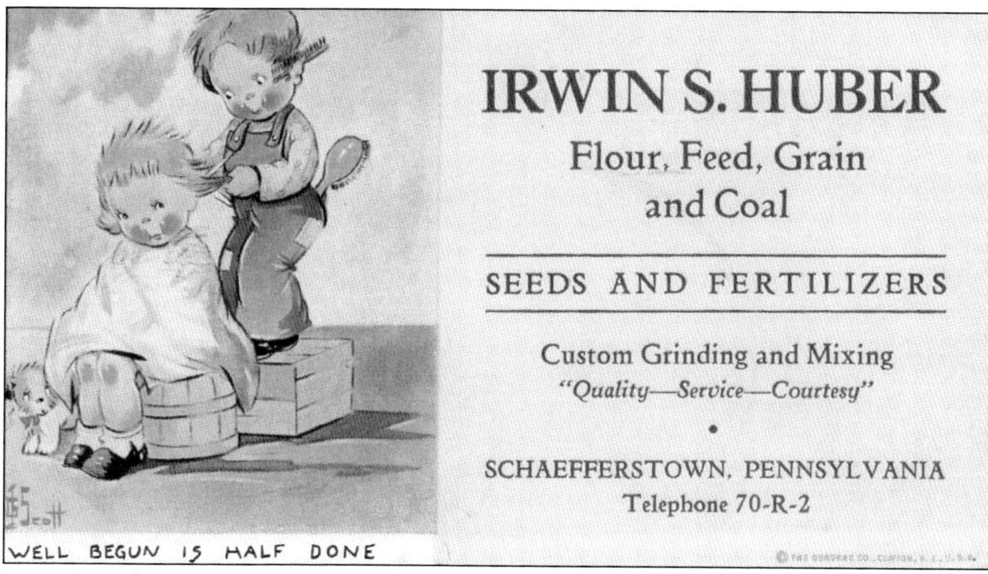

Irwin S. Huber (1904–1989) used this colorful card to advertise his services at Huber Mills. After Henry Huber died in 1937, Irwin carried on the milling business. He was eventually joined by brothers Charles and John, and they formed Huber Brothers Feed & Grain. They ran the business successfully until 1966, when the mill was sold to Charles Alspaugh, who operated it as Schaefferstown Milling Company.

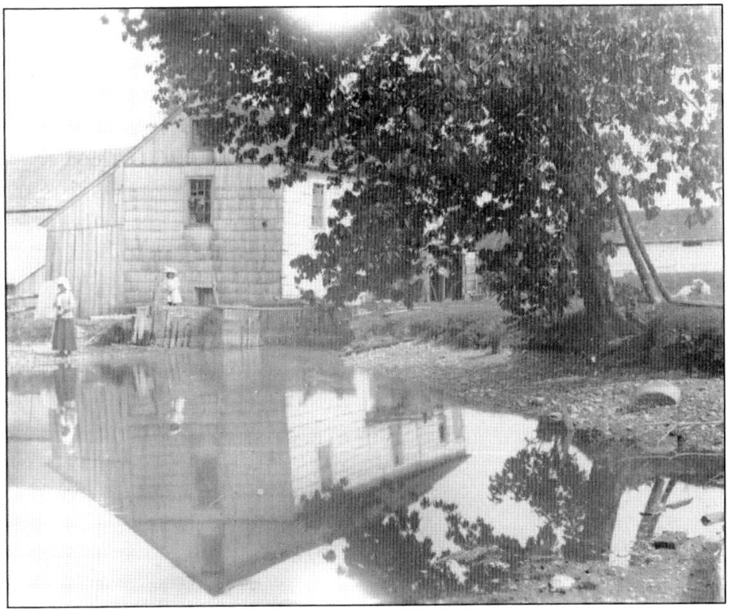

Labeled "Eberly's Mill & Dam, 5/19/14," this photograph may be of a mill located in what is now Middle Creek Wildlife Management Area. Both the 1860 and 1875 Lebanon County atlas maps for Heidelberg Township show a sawmill as well as a carding mill on Middle Creek. Sawmills were located with the same frequency as gristmills on the major streams in the township. (Courtesy of Glenn Wolgemuth.)

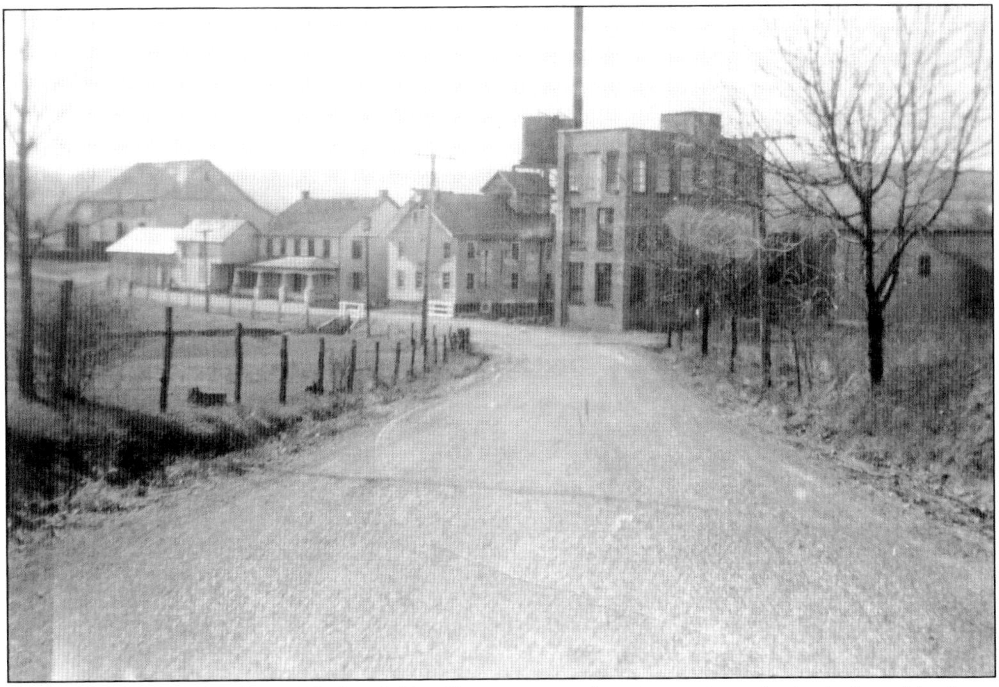

This 1937 photograph shows Michter's Distillery very much as it may have looked when Abraham S. Bomberger and his sons owned and operated it before Prohibition. Reputed to be the oldest distillery in America, Bomberger's/Michter's expanded a common farm-based distilling operation, started in 1753, into a large-scale industry. The distillery achieved national landmark status in 1980. Today, however, it is abandoned and deteriorating. (Courtesy of Raynor Seltzer Leed.)

Five

TRANSPORTATION

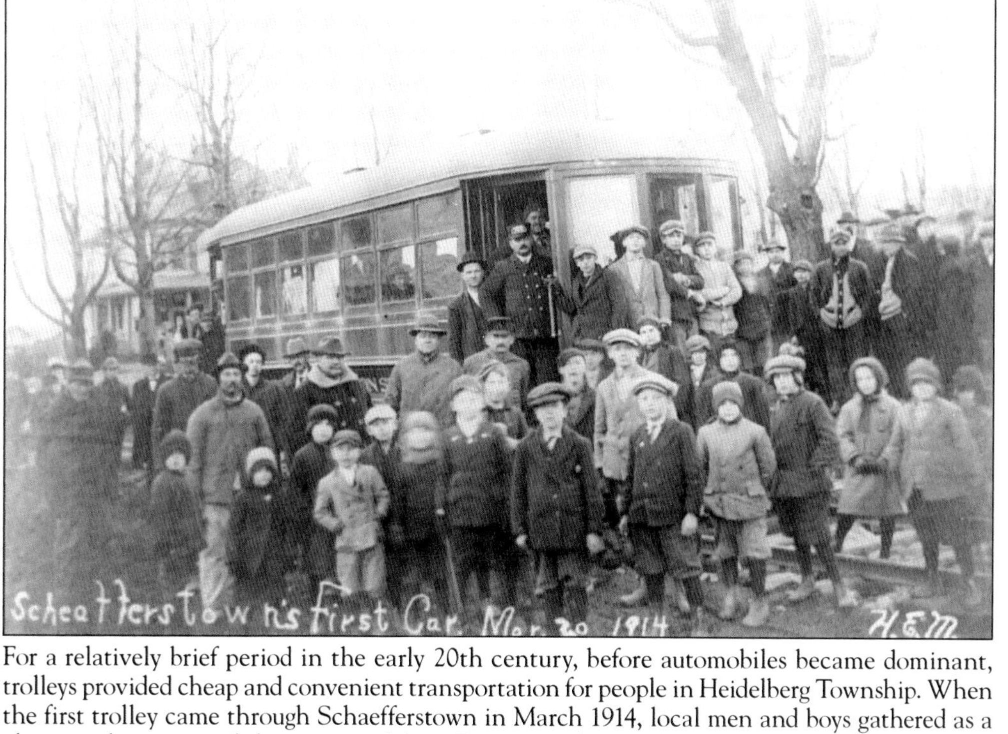

For a relatively brief period in the early 20th century, before automobiles became dominant, trolleys provided cheap and convenient transportation for people in Heidelberg Township. When the first trolley came through Schaefferstown in March 1914, local men and boys gathered as a photographer captured the moment. Moses Fetter was the conductor.

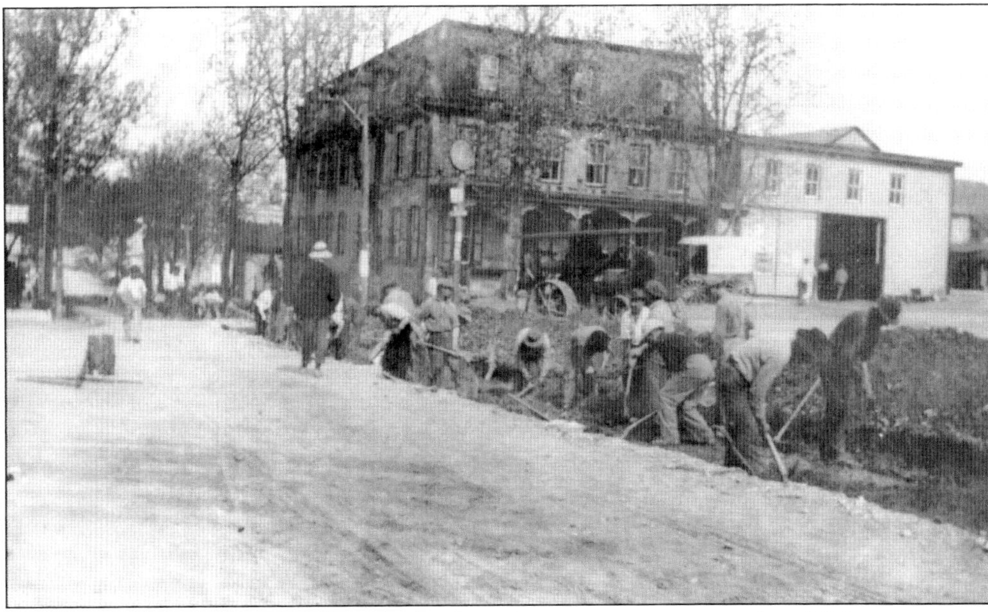

The Ephrata & Lebanon (E&L) Street Railway Company was organized in 1909; construction of the lines began in 1911. It took a lot of men, working by hand, to dig up Schaefferstown's Main Street in preparation for laying tracks. As the company name suggests, the trolley ran from Lebanon to Ephrata by way of Iona, Reistville, Schaefferstown, Kleinfeltersville, South Mountain, Hopeland, Clay, Weidmansville, and Lincoln. (Courtesy of Dona Nye.)

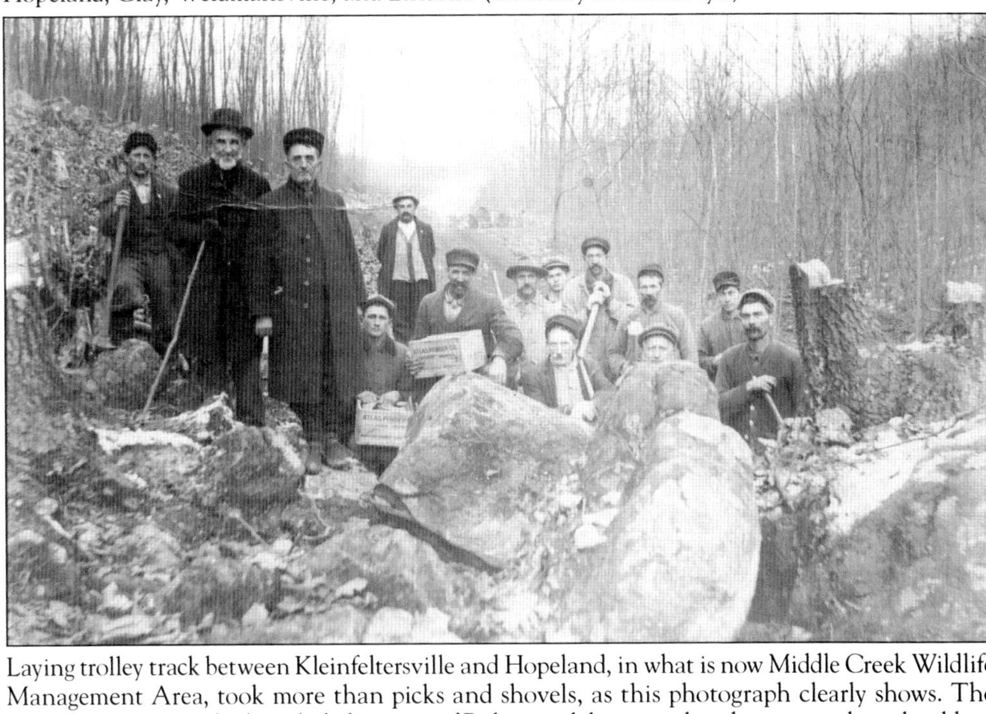

Laying trolley track between Kleinfeltersville and Hopeland, in what is now Middle Creek Wildlife Management Area, took more than picks and shovels, as this photograph clearly shows. The construction crew, which included a group of Bulgarian laborers, is lined up among large boulders, displaying the blasting powder needed to get through the mountainous terrain. The well-dressed gentlemen may be officials inspecting the project. (Courtesy of Rita Mock.)

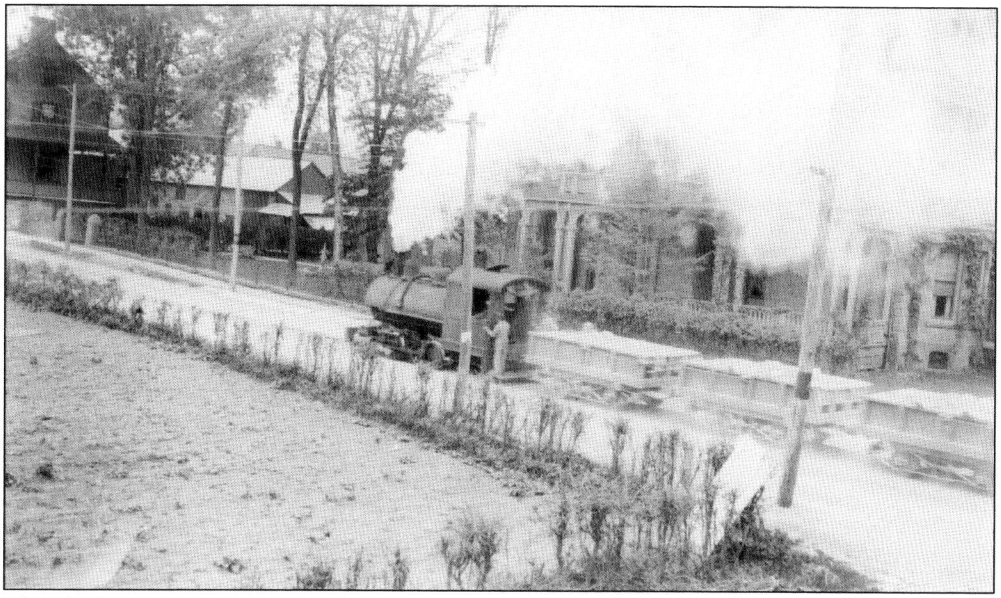

This dinky steam locomotive with dump cars was used to haul materials while the trolley lines were being built; it later carried coal and other heavy freight along the line. Here, it heads east, going past the Weigley mansion on Main Street, Schaefferstown. Note the vacant lot in the foreground; the large Victorian house that now occupies that site had not yet been built. (Courtesy of Ray Horst.)

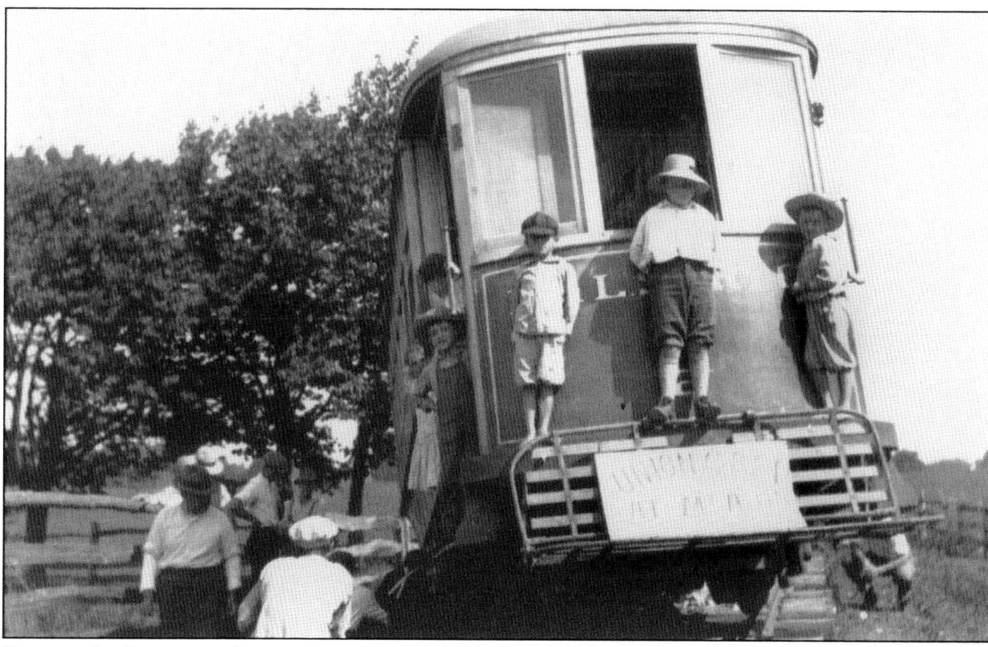

During the first year of operation, cars on the Ephrata & Lebanon line ran on batteries that were recharged after every trip. If the battery car broke down, the dinky locomotive was used to pull the car and passengers from Schaefferstown to Lebanon. In this photograph, battery car No. 2 has derailed. While adults inspect the damage, youngsters seize the opportunity to climb on the car. (Courtesy of Dona Nye.)

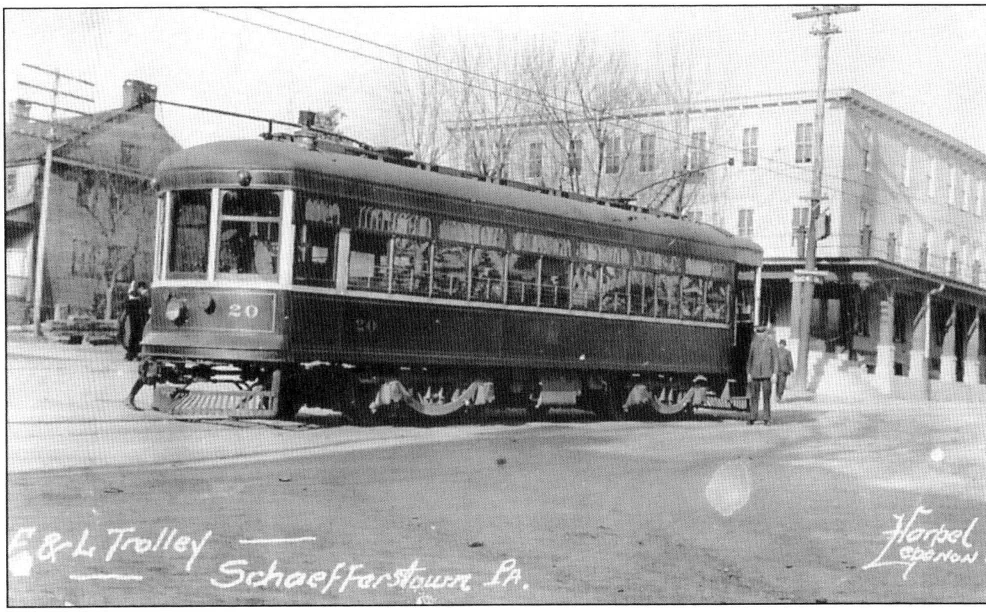

By 1915, Ephrata & Lebanon Traction Company was chartered to equip the E&L Street Railway Company for electric cars with overhead lines. Car No. 20 is shown here, waiting to load passengers in front of the Central House in Schaefferstown. Numbers 20 and 21 were all-steel, double-truck cars manufactured by Cincinnati Car Company. They were quite handsome, with dark green exterior trimmed in white with gold lettering. (Courtesy of Lyle and Loretta Krall.)

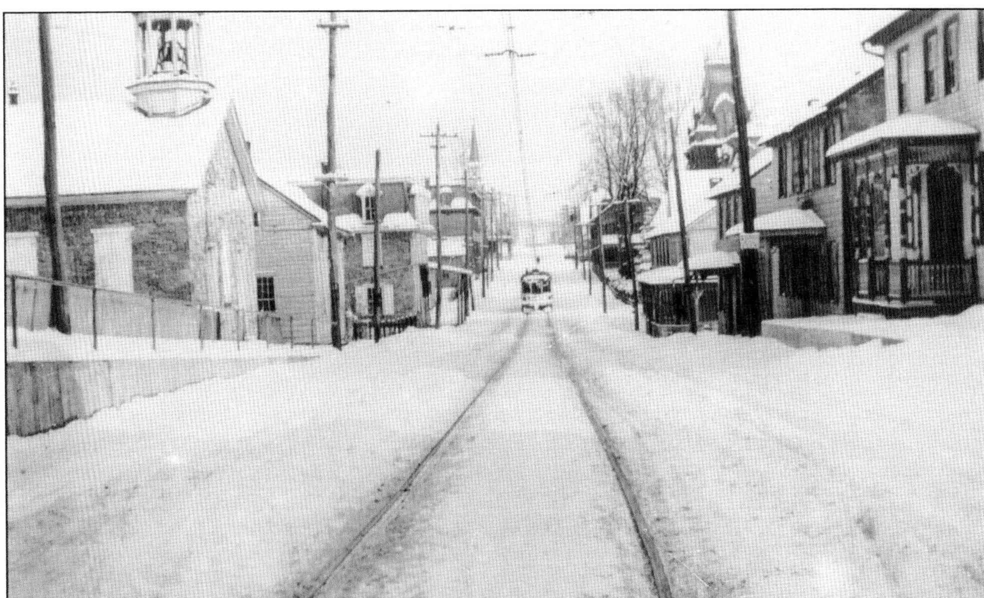

Bad weather did not stop the trolley as it made its run on snow-covered West Main Street, Schaefferstown. For passenger comfort and convenience, each car was equipped with a hot-air stove fueled by coal, as well as a telephone. The electric cars made the run from Eighth and Walnut Streets in Lebanon to Main and State Streets in Ephrata in one and one-quarter hours. (Courtesy of the Institute of American Deltiology.)

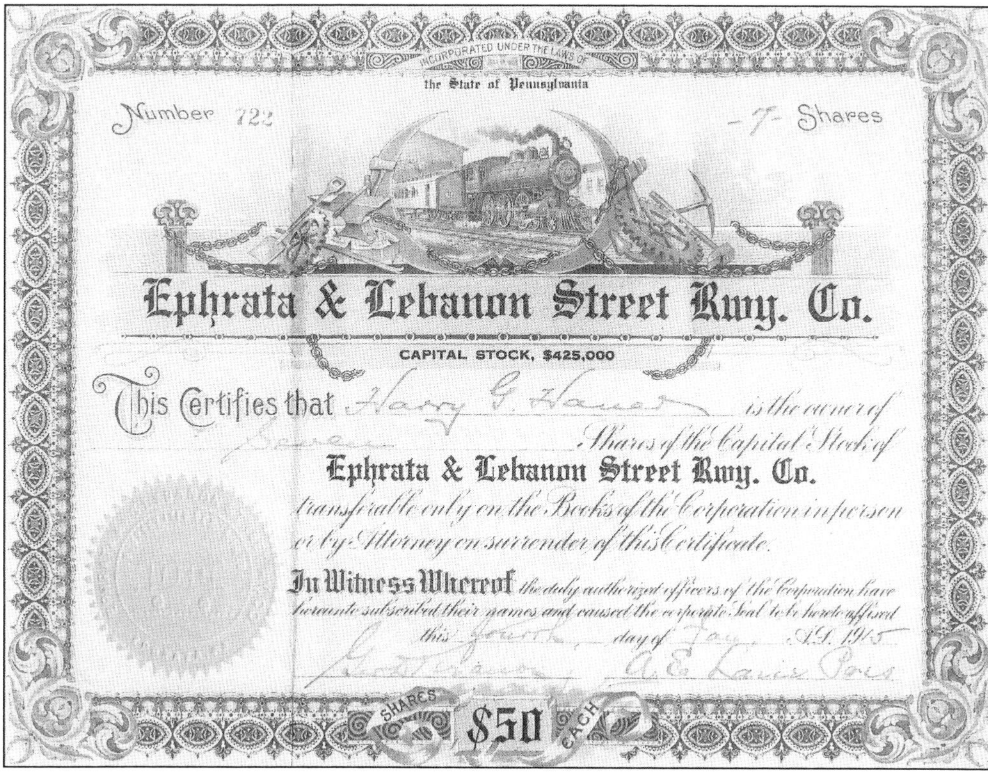

Incorporated under the laws of the State of Pennsylvania

Number 722 — -7- Shares

Ephrata & Lebanon Street Rwy. Co.

CAPITAL STOCK, $425,000

This Certifies that Harry G. Hauer is the owner of Seven Shares of the Capital Stock of **Ephrata & Lebanon Street Rwy. Co.** transferable only on the Books of the Corporation in person or by Attorney on surrender of this Certificate.

In Witness Whereof the duly authorized officers of the Corporation have hereunto subscribed their names and caused the corporate Seal to be hereto affixed this fourth day of Jan. A.D. 1915

Shares $50 Each

Financing of the Ephrata & Lebanon Street Railway Company was done through sales of stock at $50 each; total capitalization was $425,000. Cars hauled both passengers and freight; an important source of revenue was carrying milk from family farms for the Hershey Chocolate Company. It was a serious blow to the trolley company when Hershey purchased its own trucks to haul milk in 1929.

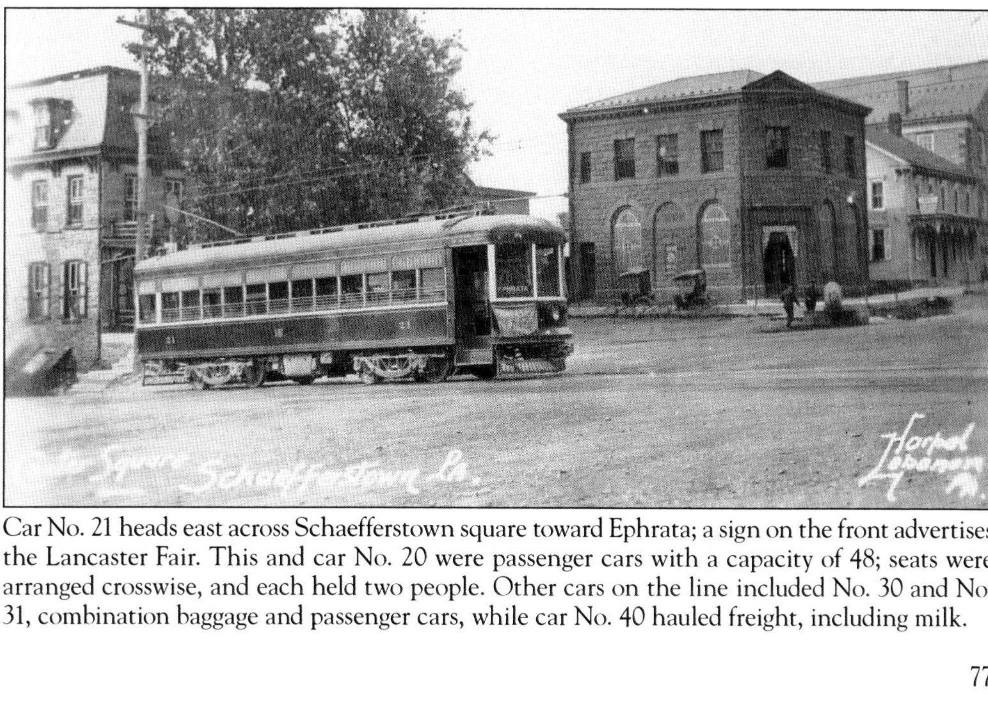

Car No. 21 heads east across Schaefferstown square toward Ephrata; a sign on the front advertises the Lancaster Fair. This and car No. 20 were passenger cars with a capacity of 48; seats were arranged crosswise, and each held two people. Other cars on the line included No. 30 and No. 31, combination baggage and passenger cars, while car No. 40 hauled freight, including milk.

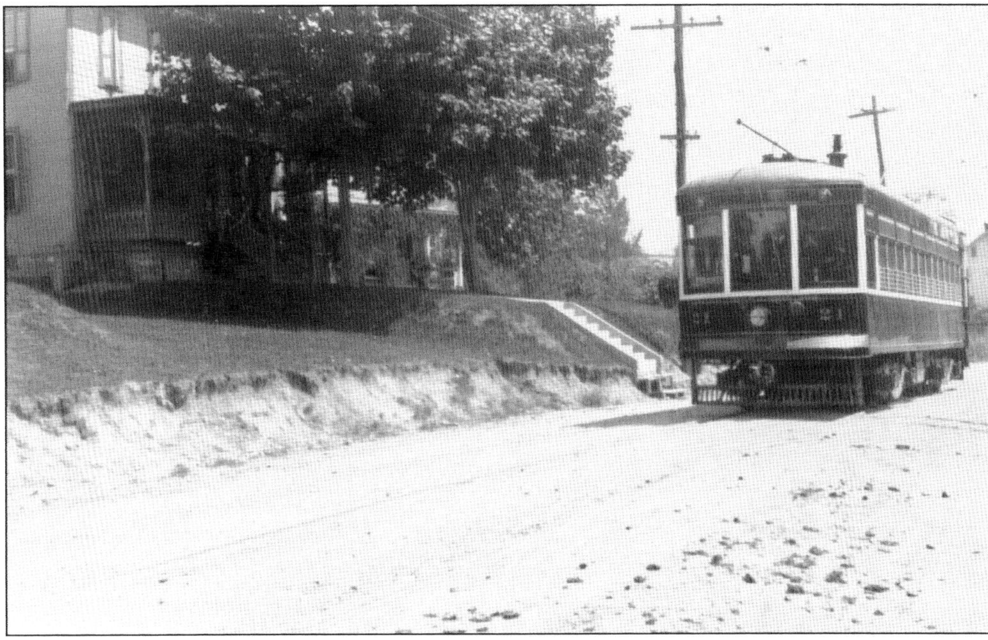

Car No. 21 heads out of town at the far end of East Main Street, Schaefferstown, on its way to Kleinfeltersville. In Schaefferstown, the tracks were in the center of the street, as they were in Ephrata, Lincoln, Clay, and Lebanon. Outside of towns, however, the lines ran alongside roads and across private fields. (Courtesy of Dona Nye.)

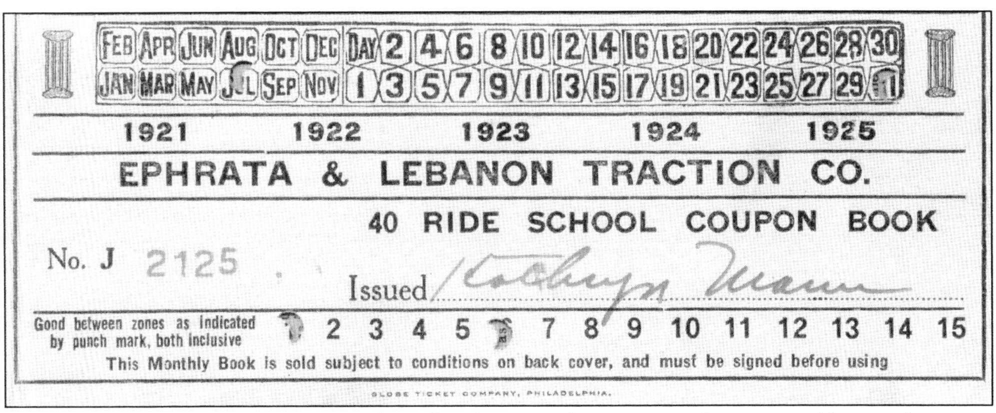

When storage battery cars were used, trolley fare was 5¢ per zone; there were 10 zones between Lebanon and Ephrata. When the line switched to electric cars, the fare went up to 6¢ a zone. Buying coupons or a weekly pass was advertised as a cheaper way to ride. Kathryn Mann Krall used this "Ride School Coupon Book" in the 1920s. (Courtesy of Loretta and Lyle Krall.)

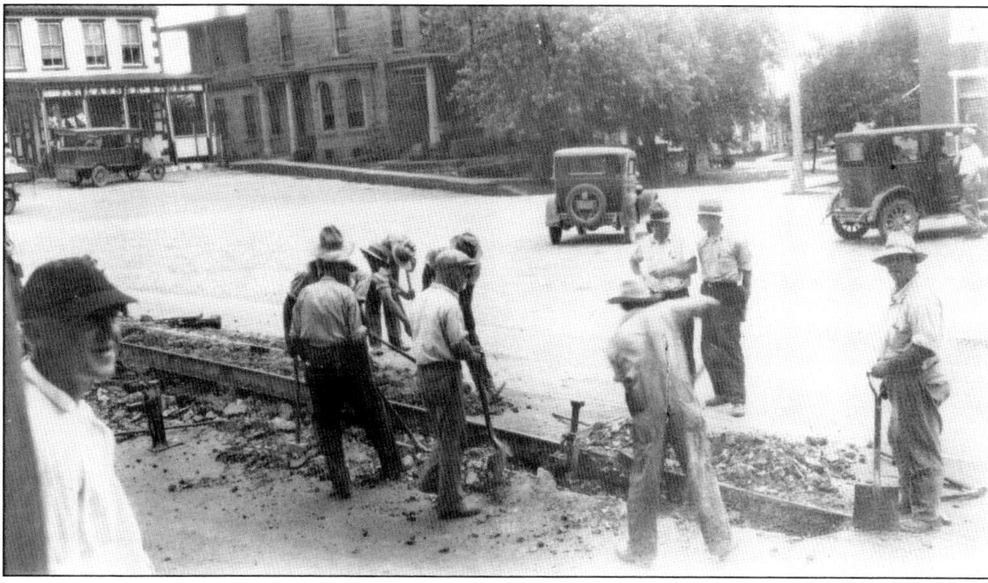

The loss of Hershey Chocolate's contract in 1929 severely cut into E&L's profits; at the same time, passenger traffic fell, as more and more people purchased automobiles. By 1931, the company went out of business. In this photograph, workers remove tracks from the Schaefferstown square so they can be sold for scrap. (Courtesy of Glenn Wolgemuth.)

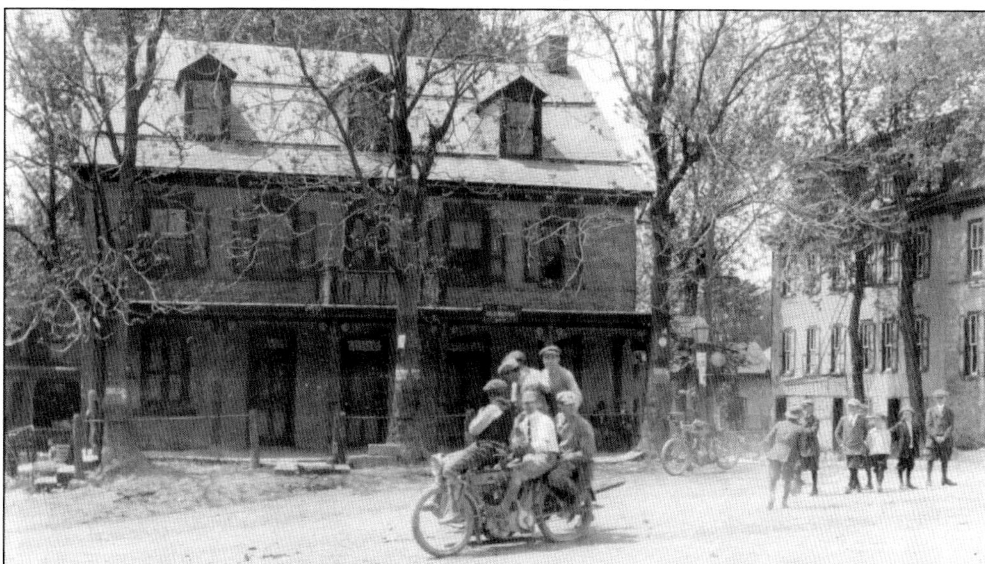

Although the trolley was disappearing, Schaefferstown residents found other means of transportation—and recreation. In the town square, in front of Umberger & Hartman's Store, three young men pile on a motorcycle; a second motorcycle is parked behind them. The older men sitting on the porch of the store and the young boys on the street are watching the antics.

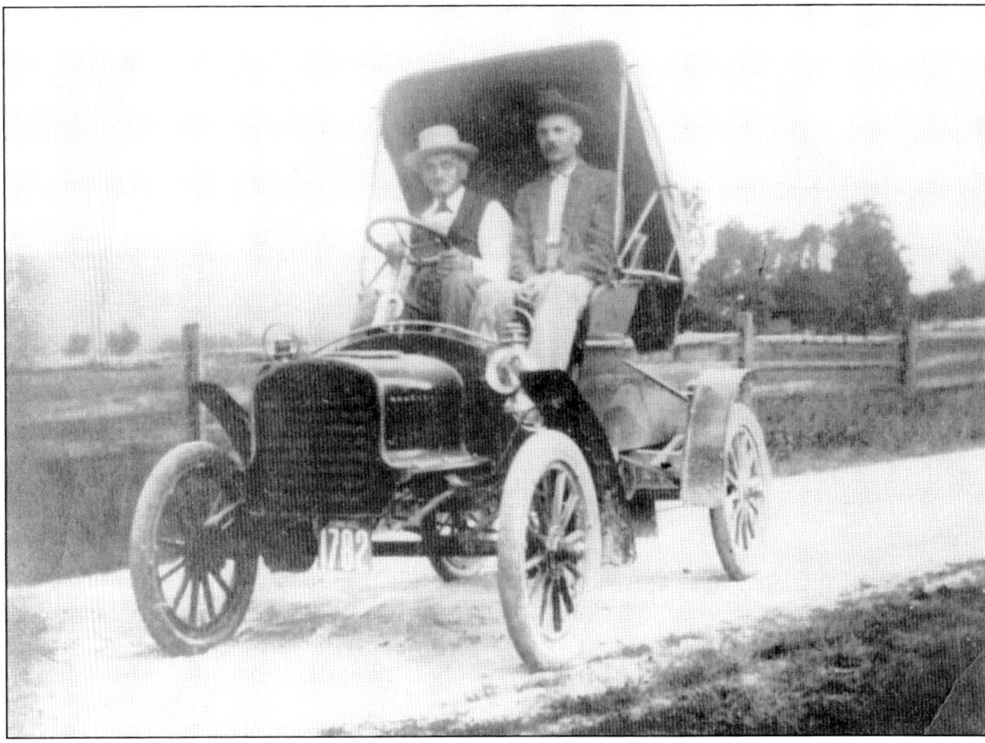

In the above photograph, business partners George H. Lesher (1844–1913) (left) and John K. Dierwechter (1868–1938) of Kleinfeltersville are shown out for a drive, perhaps to one of their customers, in an early automobile. Formerly known as Dierwechter & Good, the firm of Dierwechter & Lesher sold and repaired all sorts of carriages and wagons, as evidenced by their business stationery (below). Dierwechter married Lesher's daughter Mary. His primary profession was farming, but he also had training at the Lebanon Business College. He used this business training initially as a clerk in Lebanon, then as director of Schaefferstown's rural telephone company. Going into business with his father-in-law, however short-lived, was a natural extension of his experience. (Both, courtesy of Glenn Wolgemuth.)

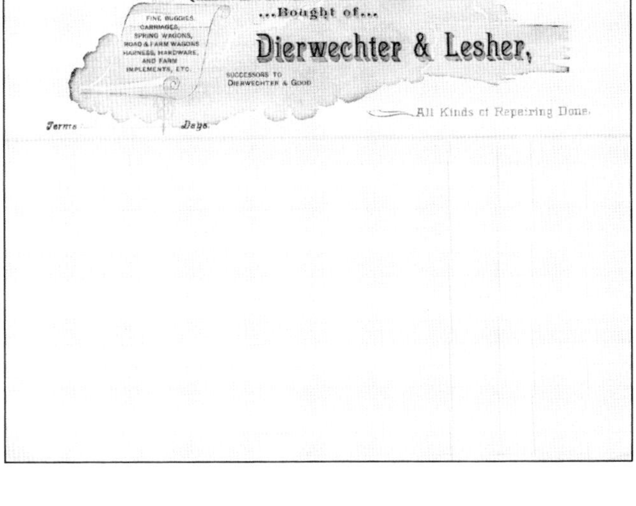

J. K. DIERWECHTER
GEO. H. LESHER

Kleinfeltersville, Pa., 190

M

FINE BUGGIES
CARRIAGES,
SPRING WAGONS,
ROAD & FARM WAGONS
HARNESS, HARDWARE,
AND FARM
IMPLEMENTS, ETC.

...Bought of...

Dierwechter & Lesher,

SUCCESSORS TO
DIERWECHTER & GOOD

All Kinds of Repairing Done.

Terms Days.

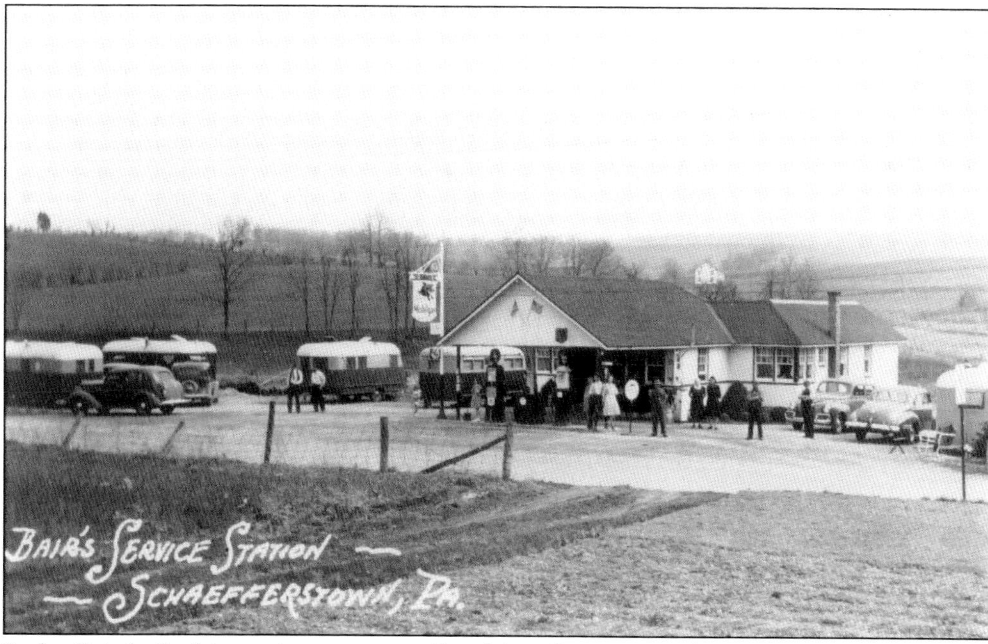

Staley Bair built this service station on East Main Street around 1949. The vista behind the station shows Sheep Hill and other hills to the south in pastureland, rather than the tree-lined hills of today. Bair and his wife, Annie, operated the gas station until 1955, when it passed to a new owner. This property housed a gas station until the early 1980s. (Courtesy of Rita Mock.)

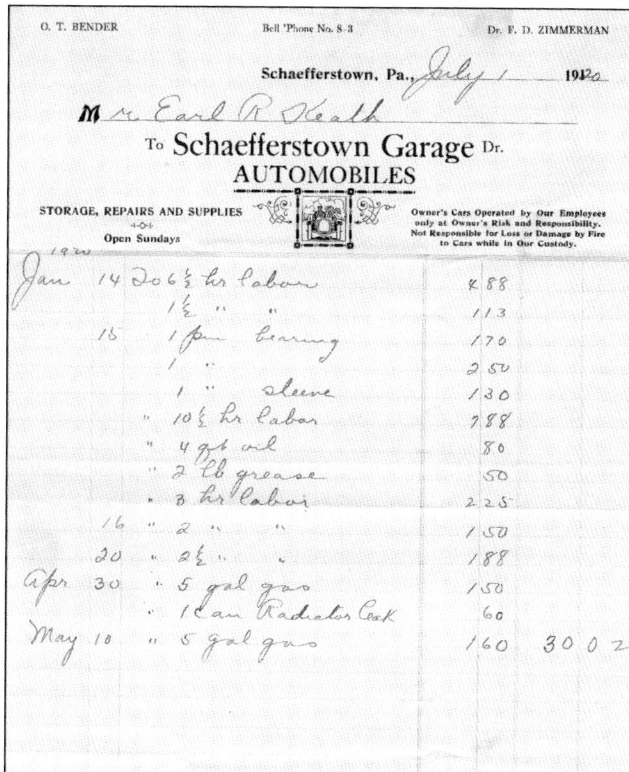

O. T. BENDER Bell 'Phone No. 8-3 Dr. F. D. ZIMMERMAN

Schaefferstown, Pa., July 1 1920

Mr. Earl R Keath

To Schaefferstown Garage Dr.

AUTOMOBILES

STORAGE, REPAIRS AND SUPPLIES

Open Sundays

Owner's Cars Operated by Our Employees only at Owner's Risk and Responsibility. Not Responsible for Loss or Damage by Fire to Cars while in Our Custody.

1920				
Jan	14	206½ hr labor	4 88	
		1½ " "	1 13	
	15	1 pin bearing	1 70	
		1 "	2 50	
		1 " sleeve	1 30	
		" 10½ hr labor	7 88	
		" 4 qt oil	80	
		" 2 lb grease	50	
		" 3 hr labor	2 25	
	16	" 2 " "	1 50	
	20	" 2½ " "	1 88	
Apr	30	" 5 gal gas	1 50	
		" 1 can Radiator Cock	60	
May	10	" 5 gal gas	1 60	30 02

Dr. Frank Zimmerman I started this garage in an old barn behind his house on West Main Street, Schaefferstown. Recognizing a need for automotive repair facilities, he partnered with mechanics Oliver T. Bender and Ira Schlosser. In 1917, they built the enlarged Schaefferstown Garage (now Zimmey's Automotive). Contrast this bill with today's prices for gas and labor! The garage was even open on Sundays. (Courtesy of Carol Fetter.)

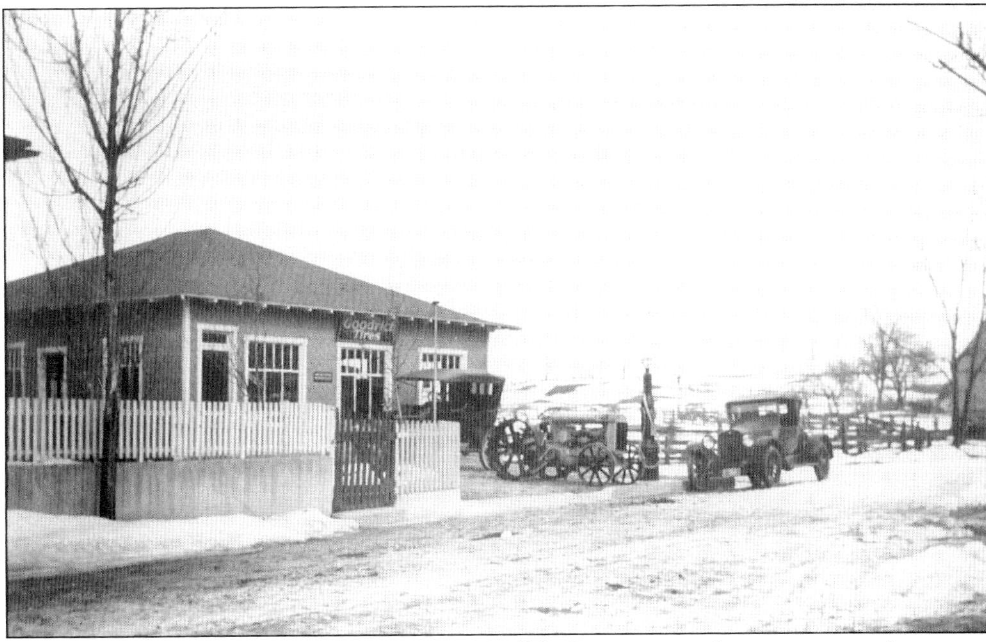

This photograph of Keller Brothers Garage in Buffalo Springs was taken one wintry day around 1921. Mark B. Keller (1899–1948) built the garage in the yard of his parents' home and, joined by his brothers, sold and serviced automobiles here from 1921 until 1931, when a new, larger Keller Brothers Ford Sales and Service was built just east of here. (Courtesy of the Institute of American Deltiology.)

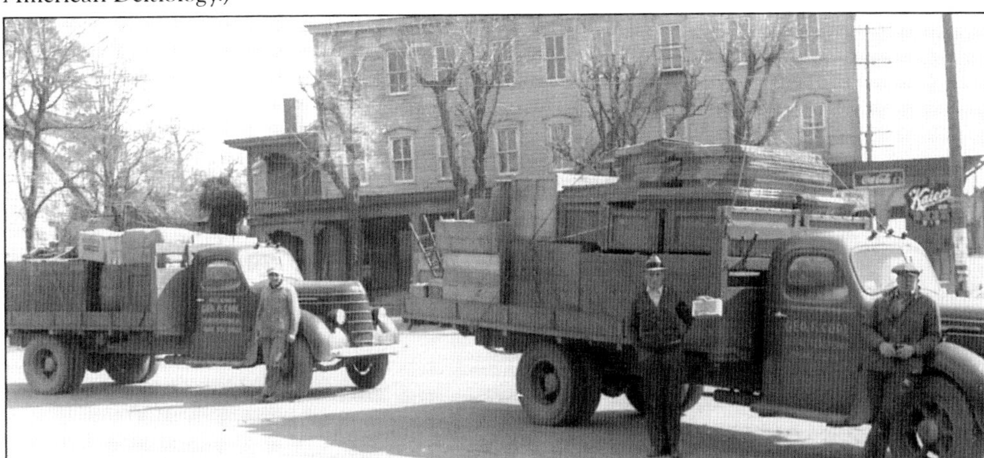

George F. Corl's trucks park in the square, with the Central House as a backdrop. George Corl ran a versatile business in Schaefferstown. In the mornings, he operated a milk run, collecting cans of milk and delivering them to Hershey Creamery in Cleona. Then he trucked coal and anything else that was needed. Corl probably took this photograph of Earl Royer (left), Ben Miller (center), and George Achey. (Courtesy of Dona Nye.)

Six

SCHOOLS AND CHURCHES

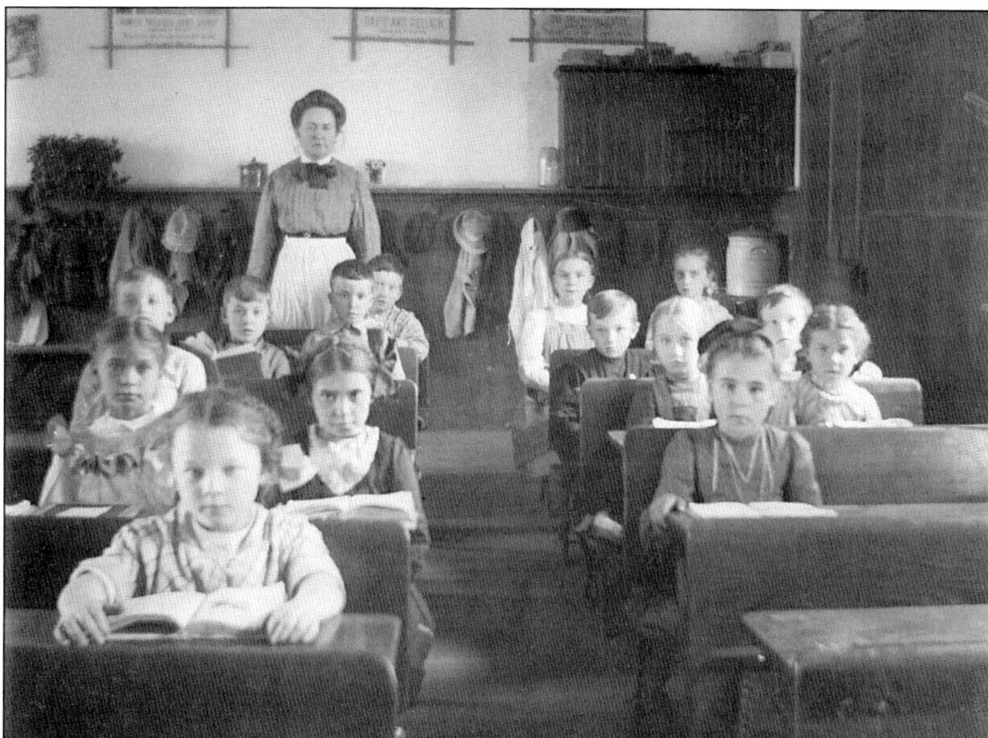

Some very serious-looking primary school pupils and their teacher take a break from their lessons in this photograph of a Heidelberg Township class taken around 1911. Note the water cooler and one lunch box in the back of the room as well as the religious-themed pictures on the rear wall. (Courtesy of Rita Mock.)

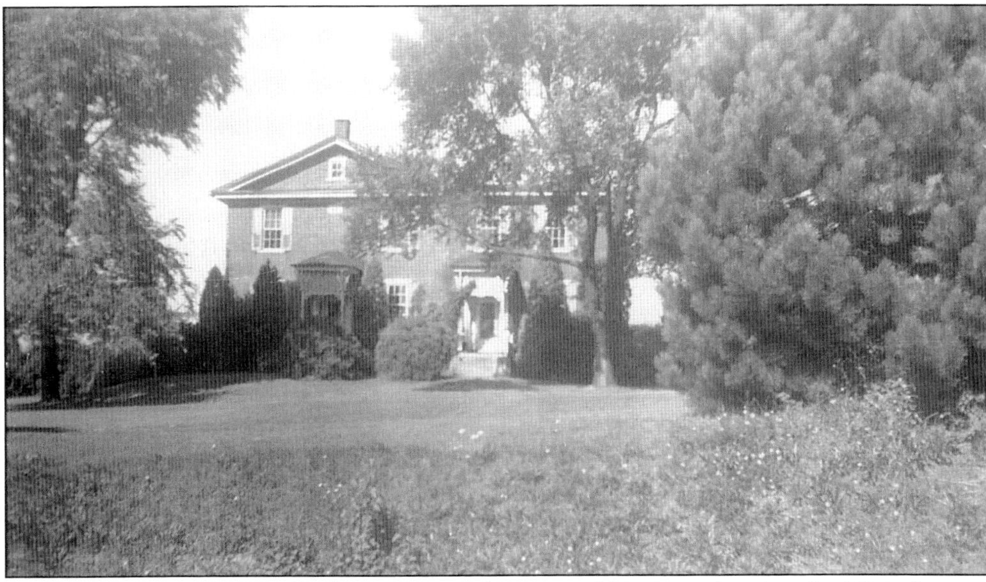

Early on, Schaefferstown schools were privately operated by town churches. In 1834, the state established a common school system, but not all residents were satisfied with those schools. From 1857 to 1860, this building on North Carpenter Street, Schaefferstown, housed the Schaefferstown Academy, established by local residents who desired a better education for their youngsters than that offered in public schools.

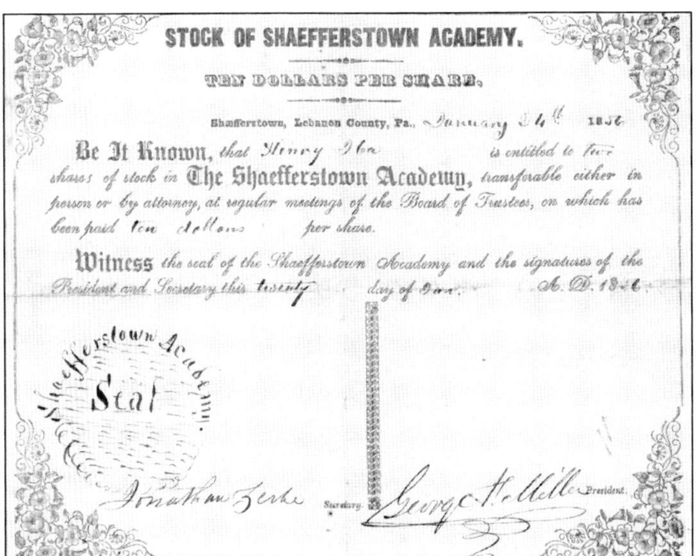

STOCK OF SHAEFFERSTOWN ACADEMY.

TEN DOLLARS PER SHARE.

Shaefferstown, Lebanon County, Pa., January [illegible] 1856

Be It Known, that Henry [illegible] is entitled to [illegible] shares of stock in The Shaefferstown Academy, transferable either in person or by attorney, at regular meetings of the Board of Trustees, on which has been paid ten dollars per share.

Witness the seal of the Shaefferstown Academy and the signatures of the President and Secretary this twenty day of Jan. A. D. 18[illegible]

Shaefferstown Academy Seal

Jonathan Zerbe Secretary. George H. Miller President.

The town's leading citizens financed the Schaefferstown Academy by purchasing stock at $10 a share. While they raised money for the new building, the academy was held on the second floor of Lauser's store. Note the alternative spelling (not unusual for the time) of Schaefferstown on the certificate. The classical education at the academy was said to be so excellent that graduates who entered college started as sophomores.

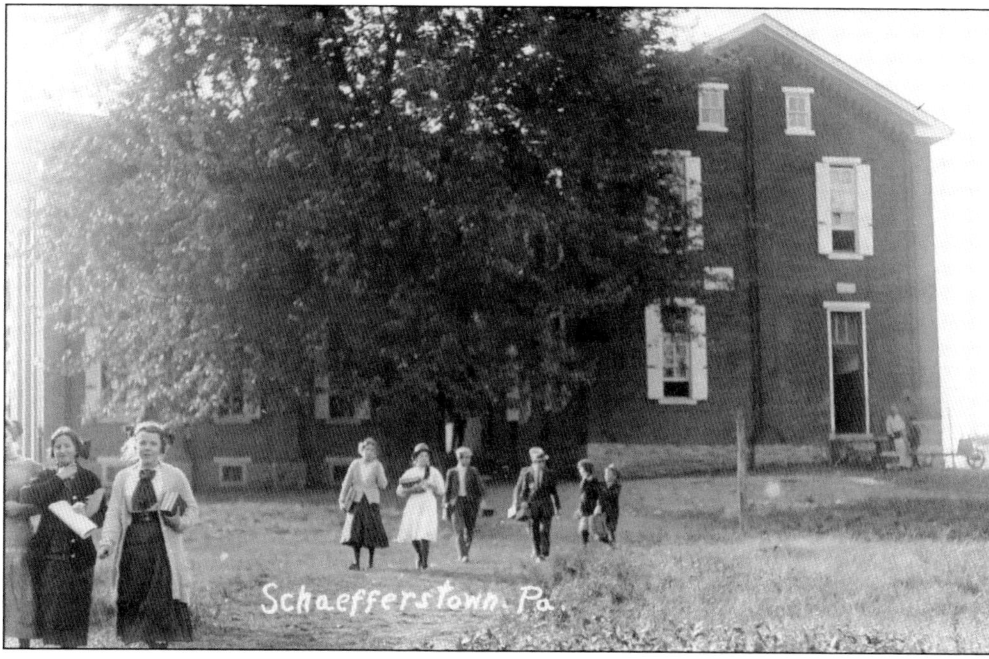

When Pennsylvania established its public school system, Schaefferstown officials built three small schools for the primary grades. In 1883, the school board upgraded facilities by erecting the large brick school shown in these photographs. In 1904, the school board added the annex to the south and expanded the curriculum to include two years of high school; a third year was added in 1911. When the new, modern limestone school was opened in 1937, the brick schoolhouse became obsolete. A few years later, in 1942, St. Paul's United Church of Christ purchased the building for use as its Sunday school and social hall, and it is still used for those purposes as well as for community functions.

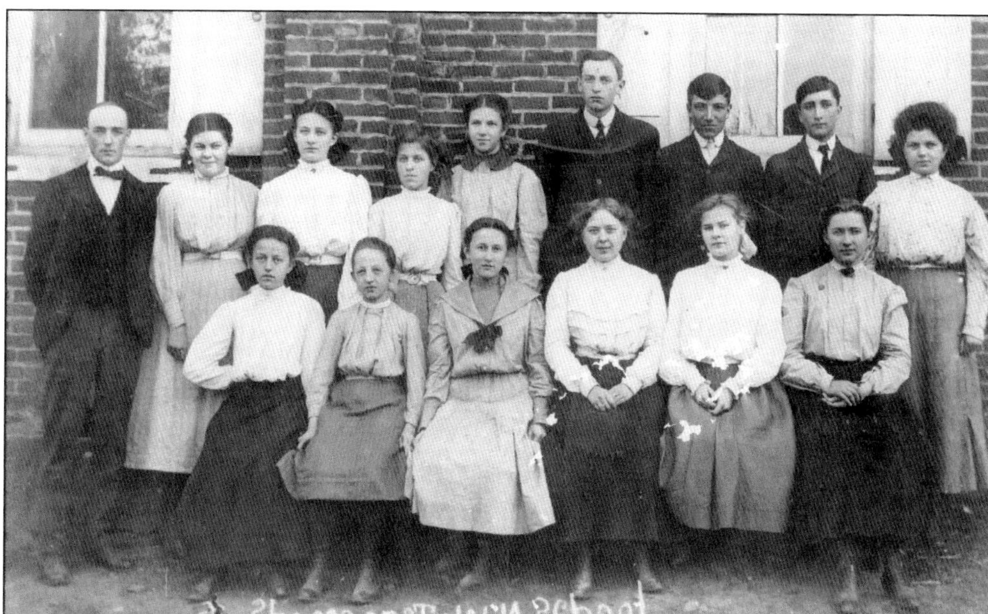

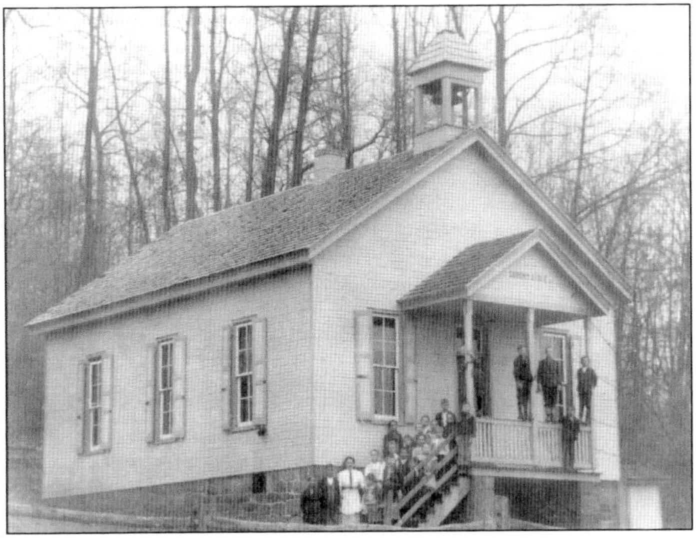

After the 1834 adoption of the common school system, many one- and two-room schools were built around the township. Sunnyside School, pictured here, was located in the southern part of the township on Sunnyside Road near its intersection with Sheep Hill Road. Between 1920 and 1926, many of these small schools were consolidated. Sunnyside School was the first to be closed. (Courtesy of Dona Nye.)

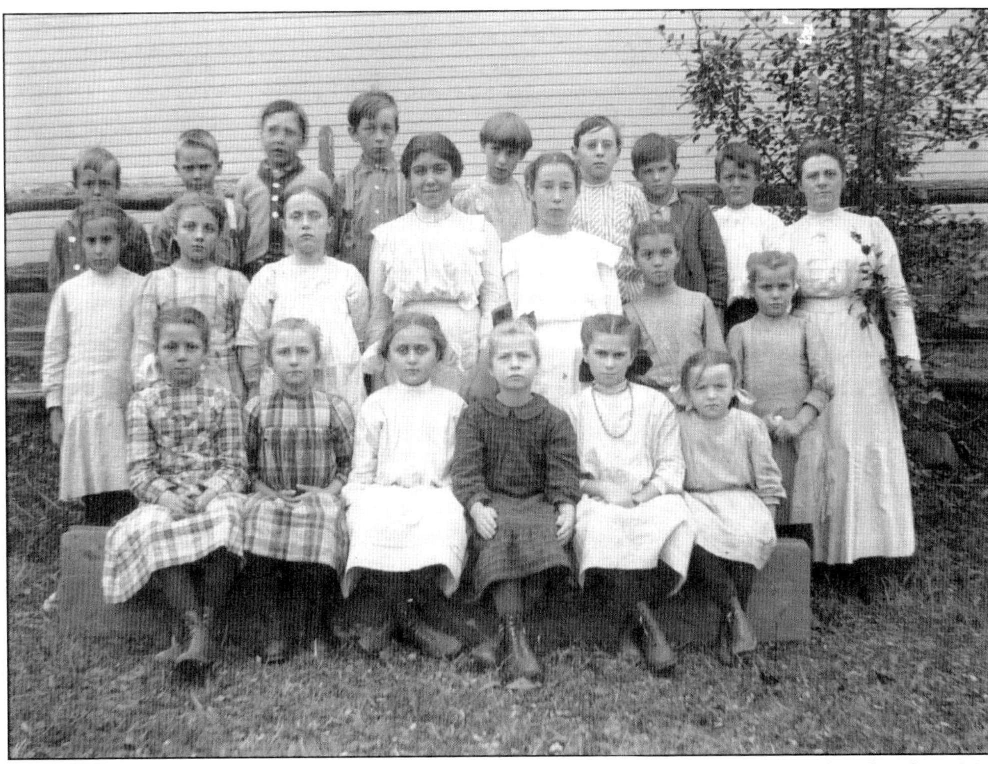

Charlotte Gable stands with her students for their 1912 class portrait at Waldeck School. Gable, daughter of John F. and Clara Gable, attended Millersville State Normal School and began teaching in Waldeck in 1902. The school is visible on the 1875 atlas map for Heidelberg Township near the southeast corner of the crossroads of Distillery Road and Route 501. (Courtesy of Rita Mock.)

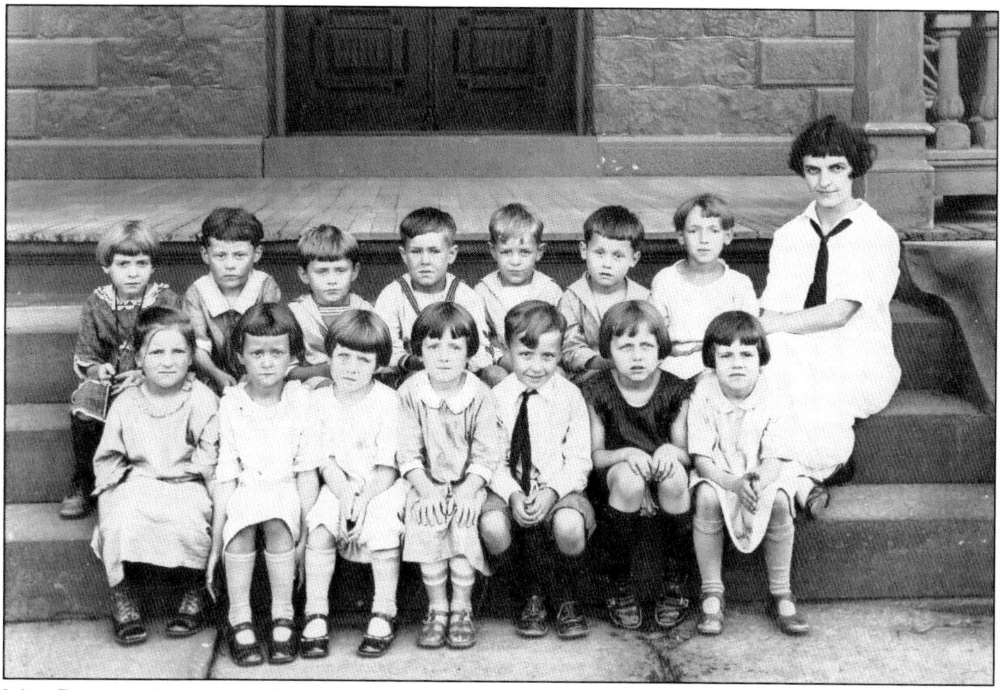

Miss Dissinger's primary class poses on the steps of the Weigley mansion for their class picture. Weigley's was a short walk from the brick Schaefferstown School. Before the 1904 annex was added, Schaefferstown's primary grades attended school in a small wooden schoolhouse slightly southwest of the brick building. All children walked to school, many from a considerable distance. (Courtesy of Ray Horst.)

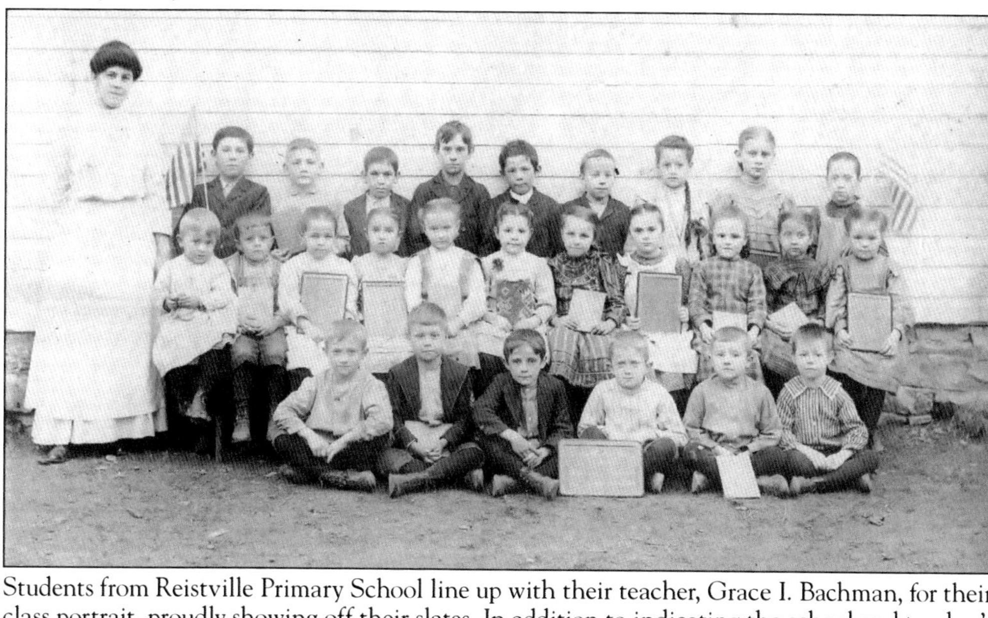

Students from Reistville Primary School line up with their teacher, Grace I. Bachman, for their class portrait, proudly showing off their slates. In addition to indicating the school and teacher's name, the large slate in front dates this photograph October 24, 1906. The young man in back holding an American flag is Raymond Horst, son of Frank Horst. Reistville School closed in 1937. (Courtesy of Ray Horst.)

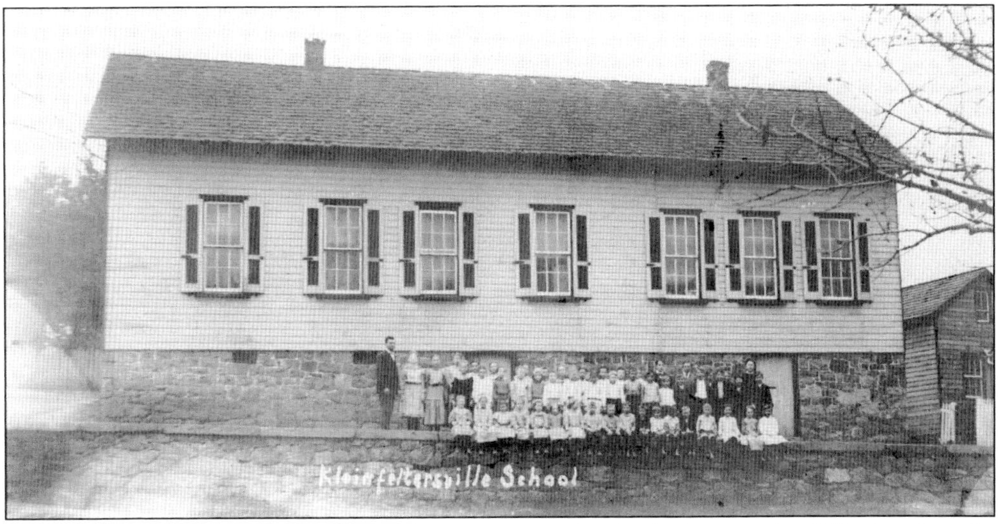

The first school in Kleinfeltersville was this two-room school, which opened in 1832. It is thought that this was converted from a barn owned by the Snavely family. It has a wooden shingle roof, clapboard siding, and nicely painted shutters and trim. Here, students of all ages gather for a photograph. The youngest seem to enjoy dangling their legs from their perch on the wall. (Courtesy of Susan Horst Kerschner.)

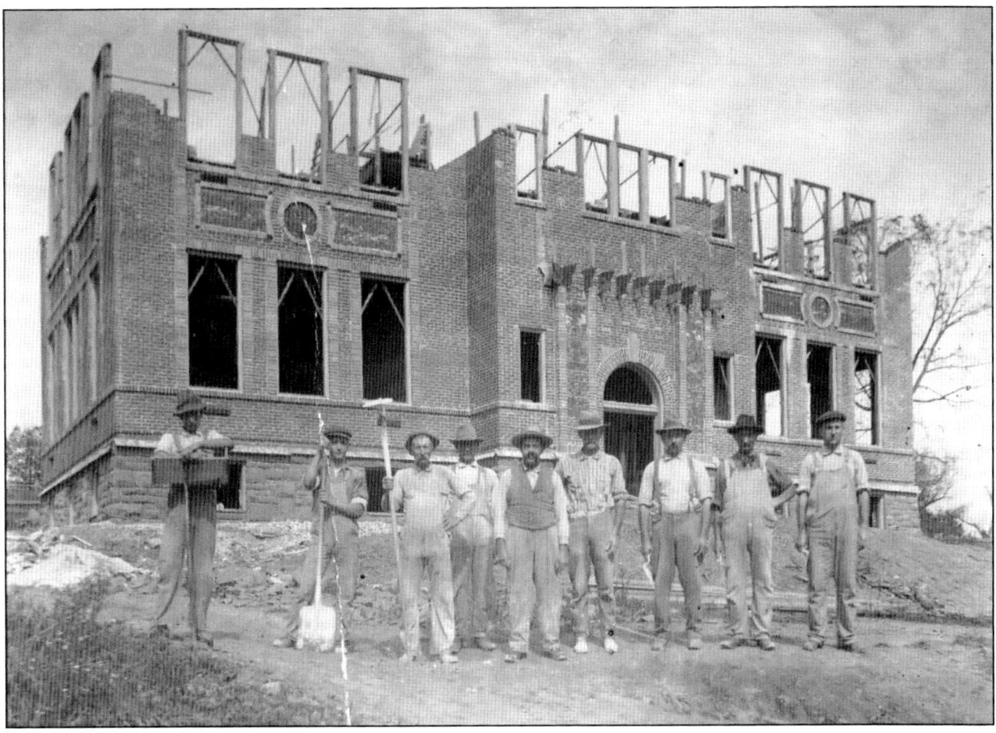

The crew building the new Kleinfeltersville School pauses for a photograph. This brick building opened in 1914 and replaced the two-room wooden schoolhouse shown above. In the 1920s, when Binkley's and other nearby one-room schools were closed, some of these children attended Kleinfeltersville School. This building was in use until the Eastern Lebanon County School jointure in 1962. (Courtesy of Rita Mock.)

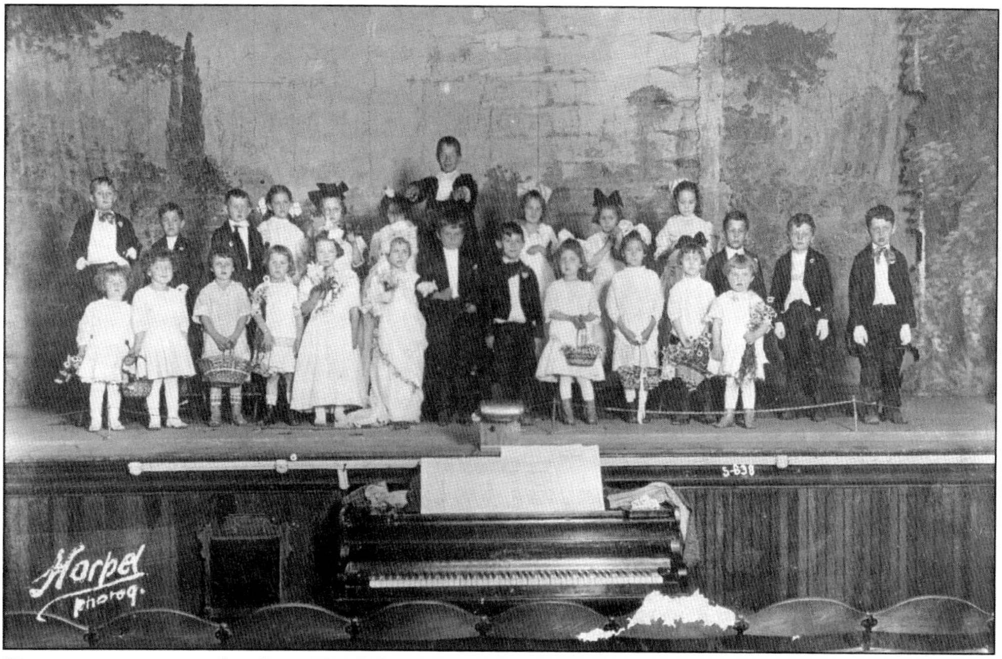

One amenity most schools in Heidelberg Township lacked was a large space for school plays and concerts. When the POS of A Hall was built, it provided a location near Schaefferstown School for these and many other functions. Above, young primary students are dressed in wedding costume on stage in a 1909 production. One student poses as a pastor to marry the bride and groom, surrounded by their wedding party. In the mid-1930s photograph of the Schaefferstown High School band in concert (below), a few students have been identified: Miles Hammer (far left), Franklin D. Zimmerman II (fifth from left), Grace Zimmerman (fourth from right, standing), and Harold Bollinger (fifth from right). (Above, courtesy of the Institute of American Deltiology.)

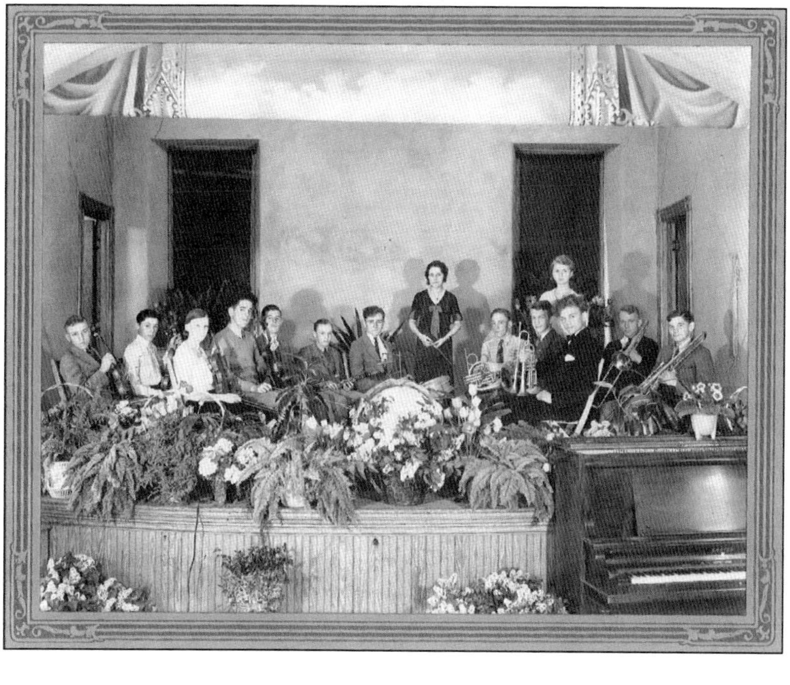

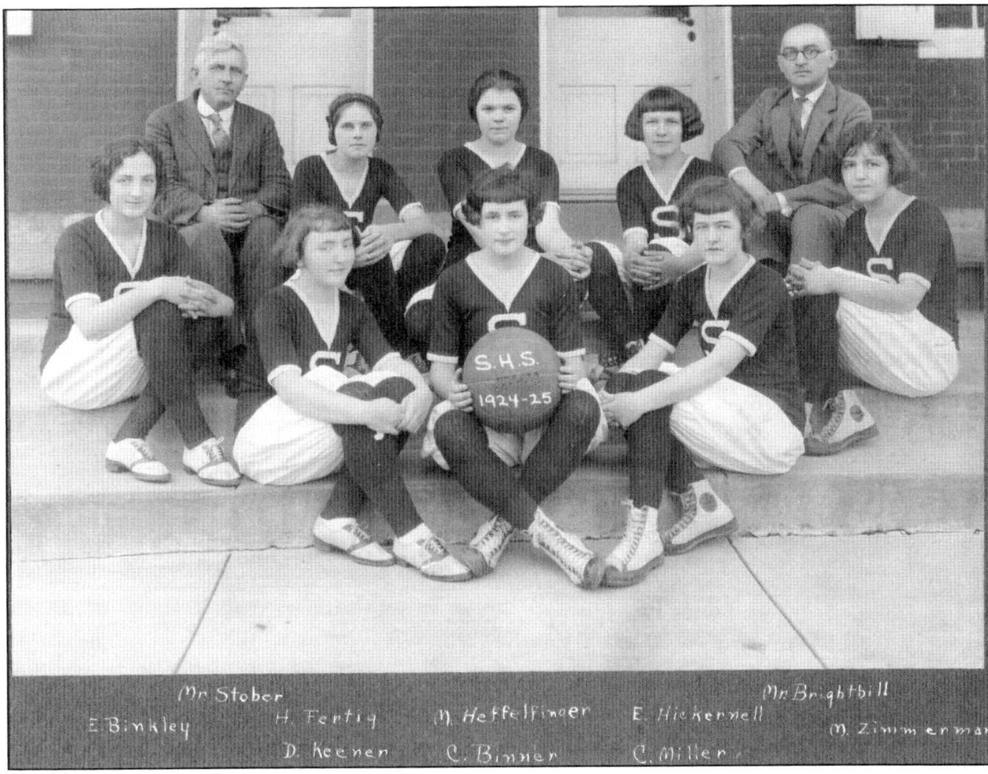

In addition to a venue for concerts and plays, the large open room of the POS of A Hall's main floor provided indoor space for physical education and some intramural sports. Pictured here are the Schaefferstown High School's boys' and girls' basketball teams for the 1924–1925 school year. The coaches, Mr. Stober and Mr. Brightbill, are the same for both teams. While the boys' uniforms seem similar to today's attire, the uniforms for the girls were designed for modesty. Bloomers and above-the-knee socks completely covered the female players' legs. High-top sneakers seem to be a favorite for both teams. These photographs, originally mounted together for framing, include the players' names below the portraits.

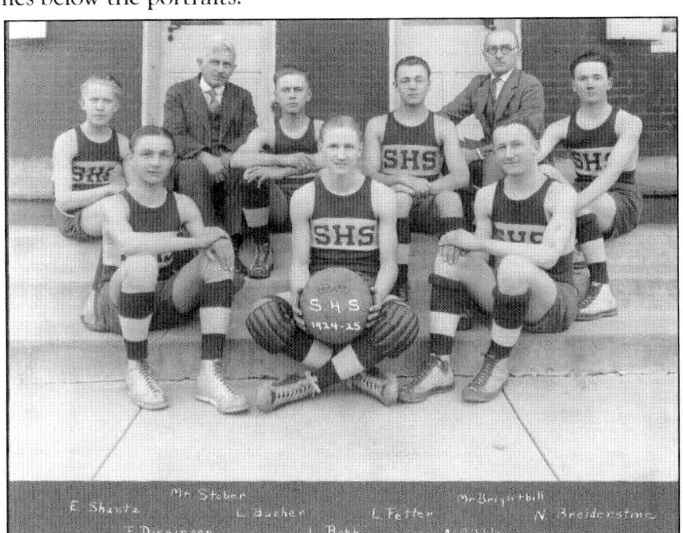

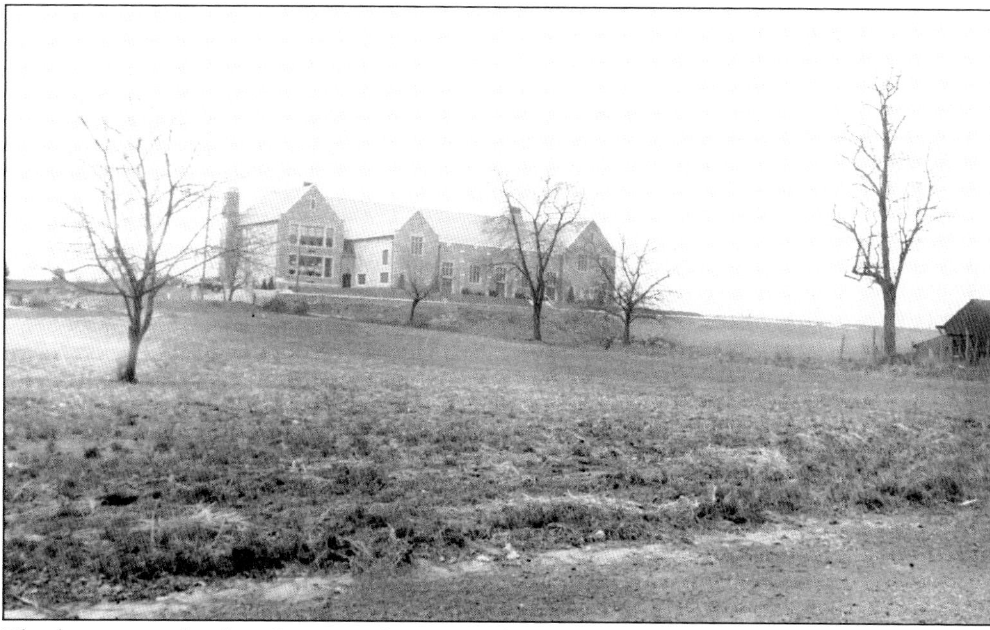

This limestone school on Carpenter Street in Schaefferstown was built in 1936. From September 1937 until June 1962, students in grades one to 12 attended classes here. In 1963, it became Schaefferstown's elementary school, housing kindergarten through grade six. It was a blow to many town residents, who appreciated the convenience of having a local school, when the Eastern Lebanon County School District consolidated classes and closed this building in 2010. (Courtesy of Dona Nye.)

The congregation of St. Paul's Reformed Church, now St. Paul's United Church of Christ, is as old as the village of Schaefferstown. This c. 1883 photograph shows the imposing brick edifice as seen from the cornfield across Main Street. To the left can be seen the Schaefferstown School, built in 1883 and enlarged in 1904. The parsonage, built about 1870, is to the right. (Courtesy of St. Paul's UCC.)

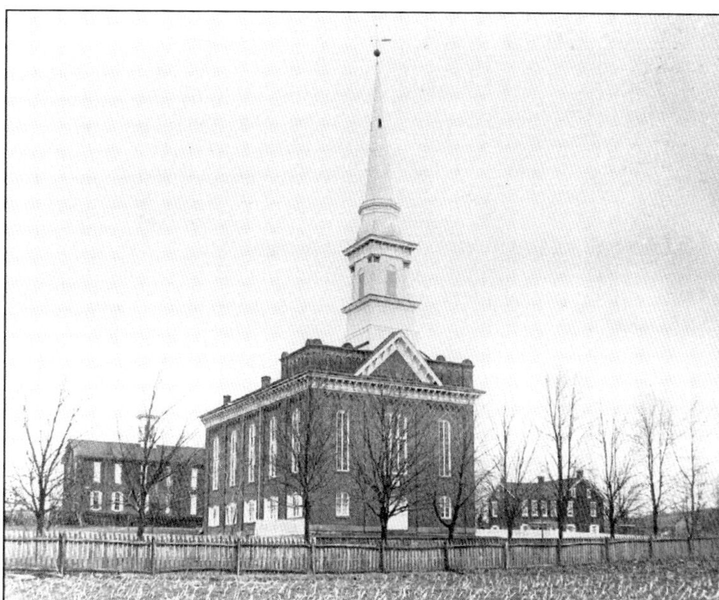

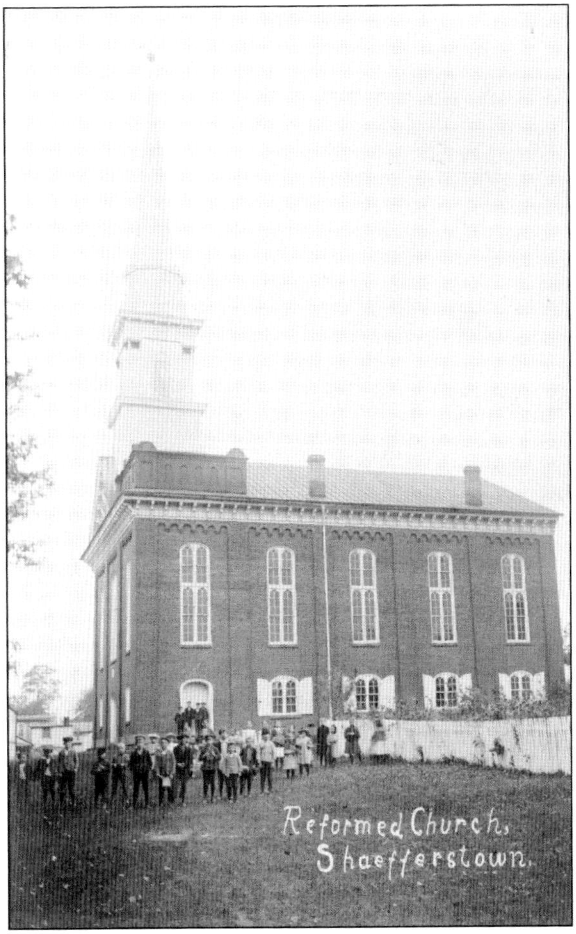

The present St. Paul's Church is actually the third structure for this congregation. A union church served both the Reformed and Lutheran congregations nearby until 1795. Then a stone church was erected on the northwest corner of Carpenter and Main Streets. In 1858, this had to be abandoned due to structural problems, and the present brick structure was built. (Courtesy of Diana Wike Castor.)

Father and son, Reverends Adam J. Bachman (left) and Adam R. Bachman, pose near the front steps of St. Paul's Reformed Church around 1937. Rev. Adam J. Bachman served St. Paul's for 52 years, from 1878 until his death in 1937. Rev. Adam R. Bachman ministered here from 1937 until 1960. Between them, the Bachmans contributed an amazing total of 82 years of ministry.

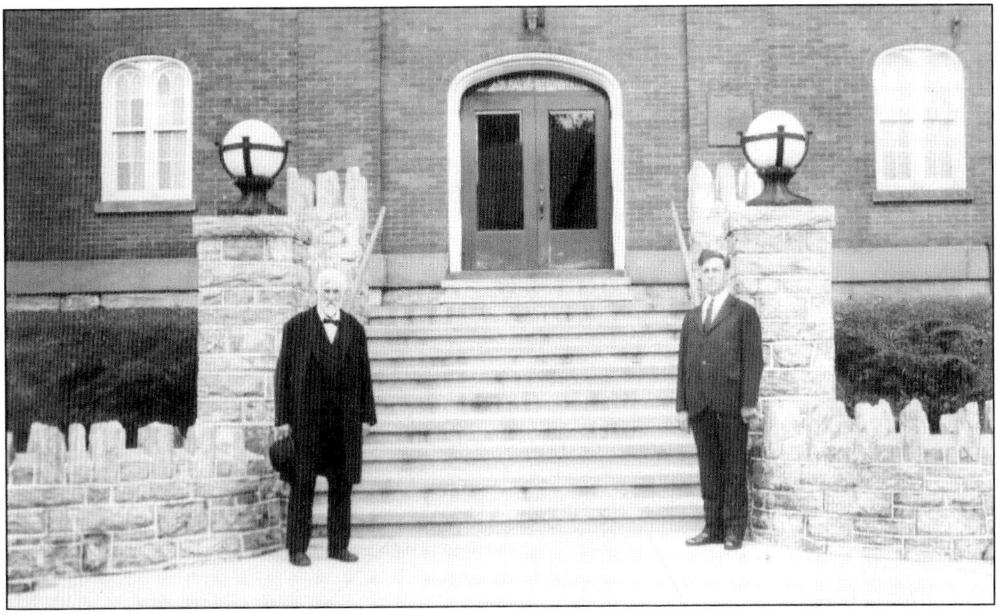

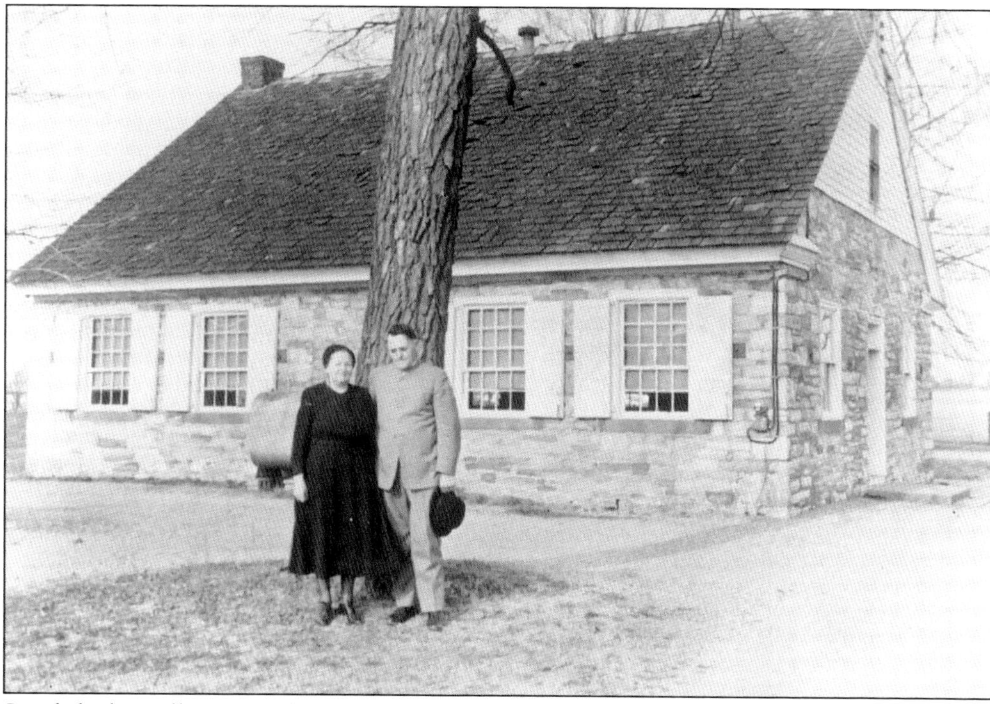

Sturdy little Krall's Meetinghouse was built on Rexmont Road in South Lebanon Township, near the border of Heidelberg Township, to serve members of the Mennonite faith in both townships. John Shenk, a prominent Mennonite landowner in Heidelberg Township, helped this congregation to purchase land for this house of worship in 1811. Krall's pastor, Martin Weaver, and his wife, Verda, are photographed at the meetinghouse. (Courtesy of Robert Martin.)

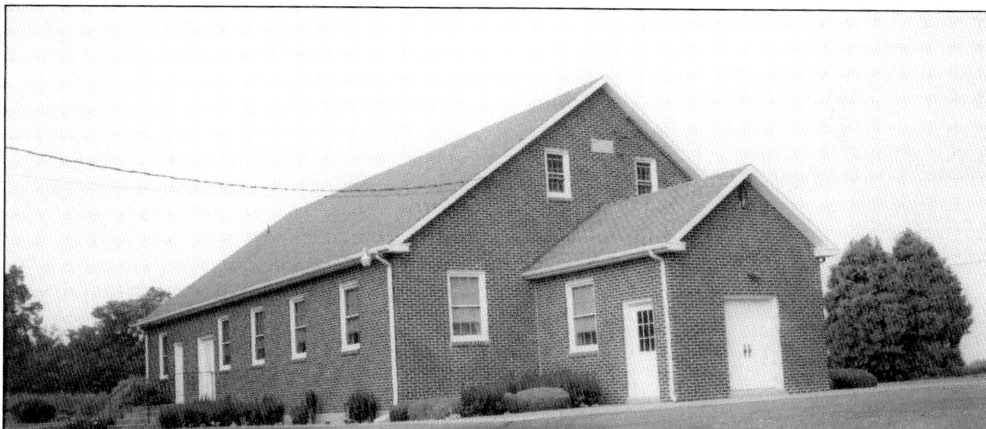

Krall's original building eventually became too small for its congregation. So, in 1956, a new, larger house of worship was erected. The present Krall's Mennonite Church is located on the northwest corner of Route 897 and Prescott Road. The original meetinghouse is now a private residence. (Courtesy of Robert Martin.)

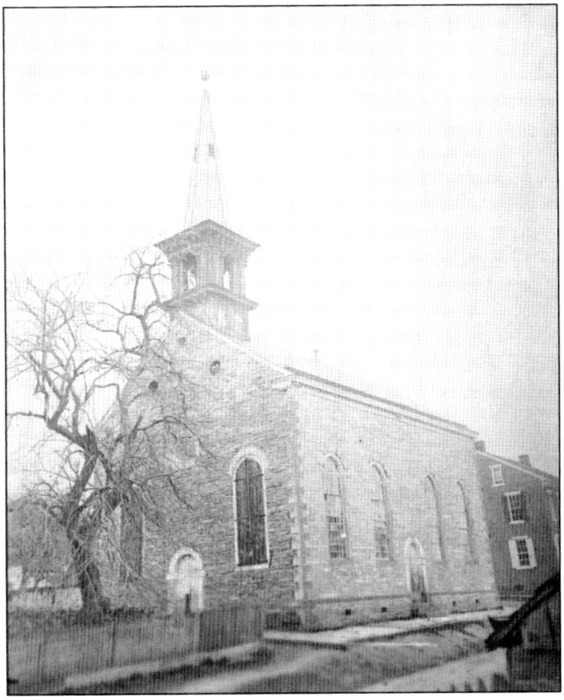

In 1765, the Lutherans sold their share of the union church to the Reformed congregation and built this impressive structure, with wineglass pulpit, on the corner of Main and Front (now Church) Streets, Schaefferstown. During the American Revolution, it served as a hospital for soldiers wounded at the Battle of Brandywine; the congregation petitioned the Continental Congress unsuccessfully for payment for damages to the building after it served as a hospital.

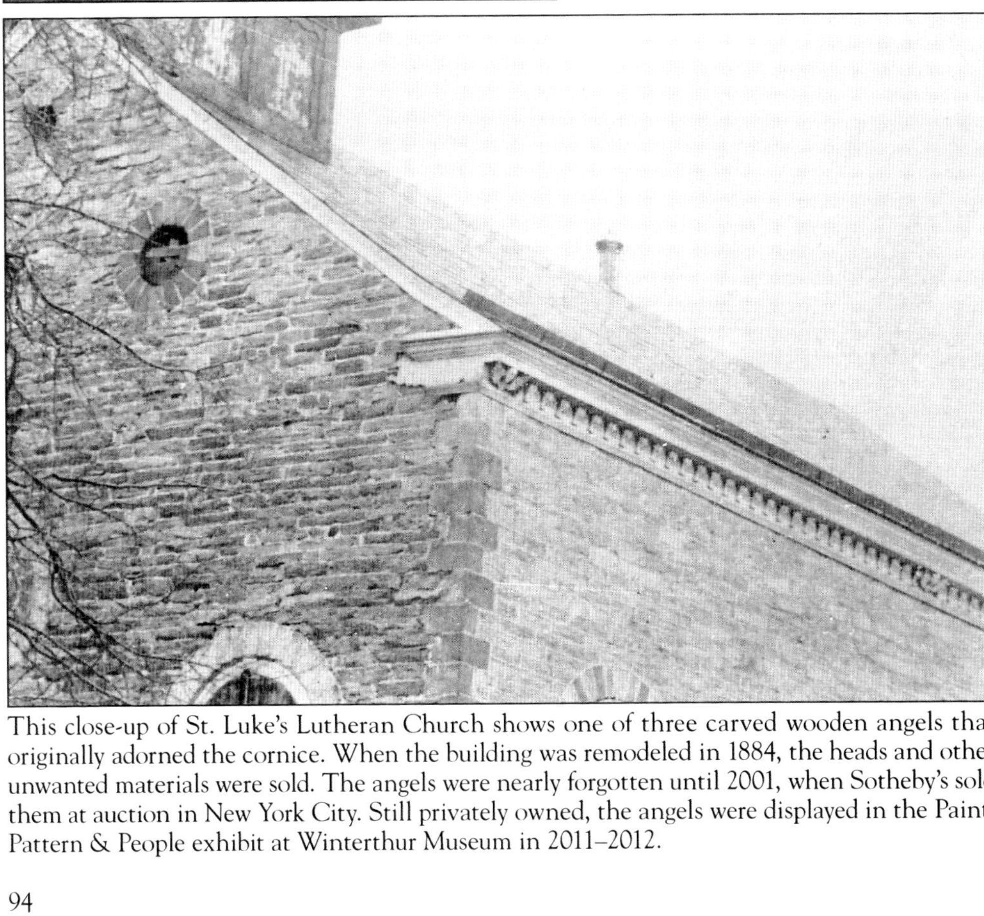

This close-up of St. Luke's Lutheran Church shows one of three carved wooden angels that originally adorned the cornice. When the building was remodeled in 1884, the heads and other unwanted materials were sold. The angels were nearly forgotten until 2001, when Sotheby's sold them at auction in New York City. Still privately owned, the angels were displayed in the Paint, Pattern & People exhibit at Winterthur Museum in 2011–2012.

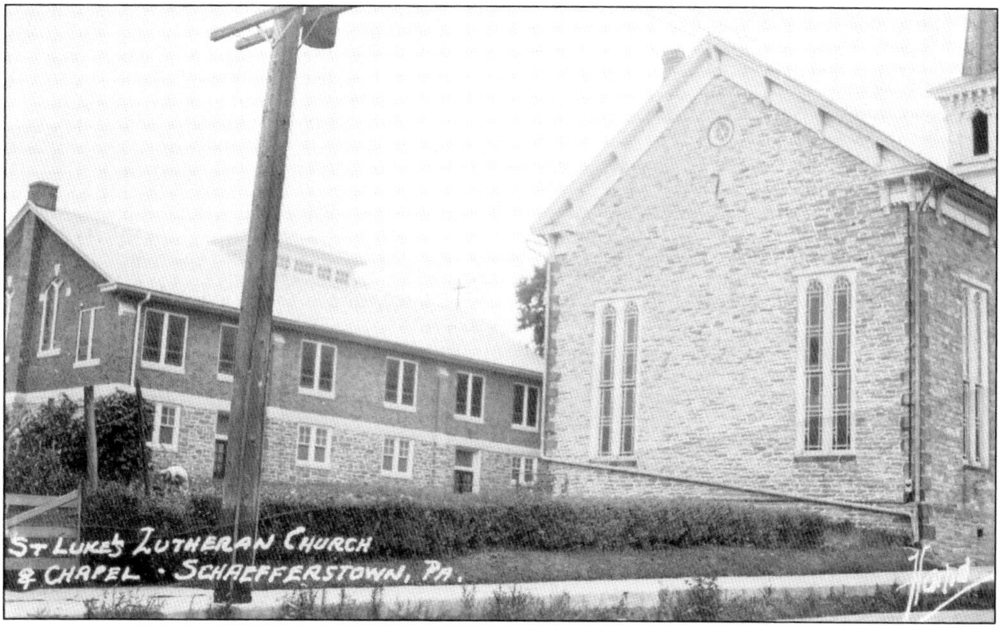

In the 1880s, Schaefferstown Lutherans embarked on an ambitious building campaign; they removed the west end of the church, extended its side walls 16 feet, moved the steeple to the east end, replaced all the windows, and completely modernized the interior. This project, like the renovation of local hotels, highlights the area's prosperity in the late 19th century. Even with the enlarged sanctuary, the congregation soon needed more room. In 1932, it built the two-story brick chapel north of the church. In addition to the space shown here, which was used for Sunday school, the new building had a kitchen and restrooms, conveniences the old church lacked. (Above, courtesy of Mary Smith; below, courtesy of Rita Mock.)

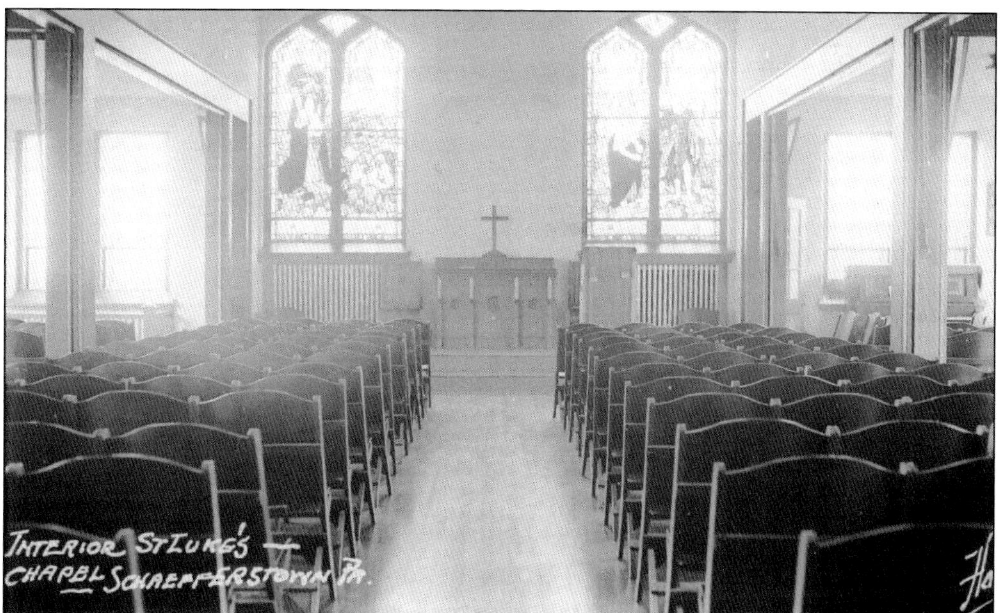

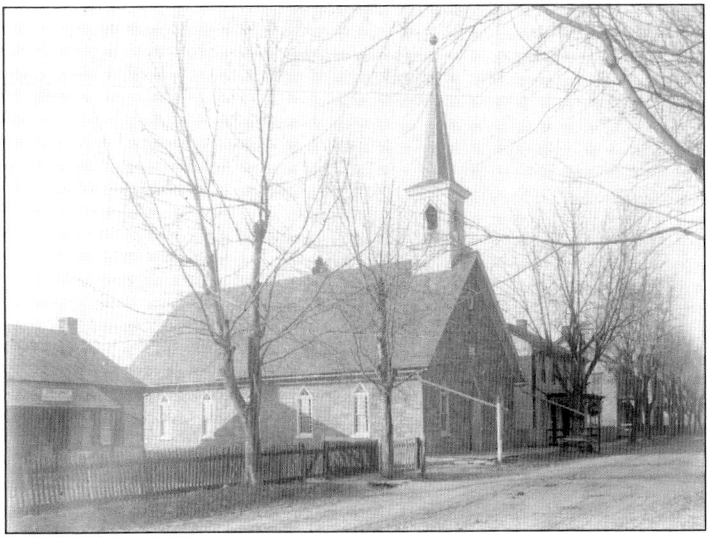

This is the Schaefferstown United Brethren in Christ Church on Main Street as it appeared about 1900. Built in 1851 and enlarged in 1897, this small church served members of an American-born denomination formed in 1767 as a merging of branches of the Mennonite and German Reformed congregations. (Courtesy of Zion United Methodist Church.)

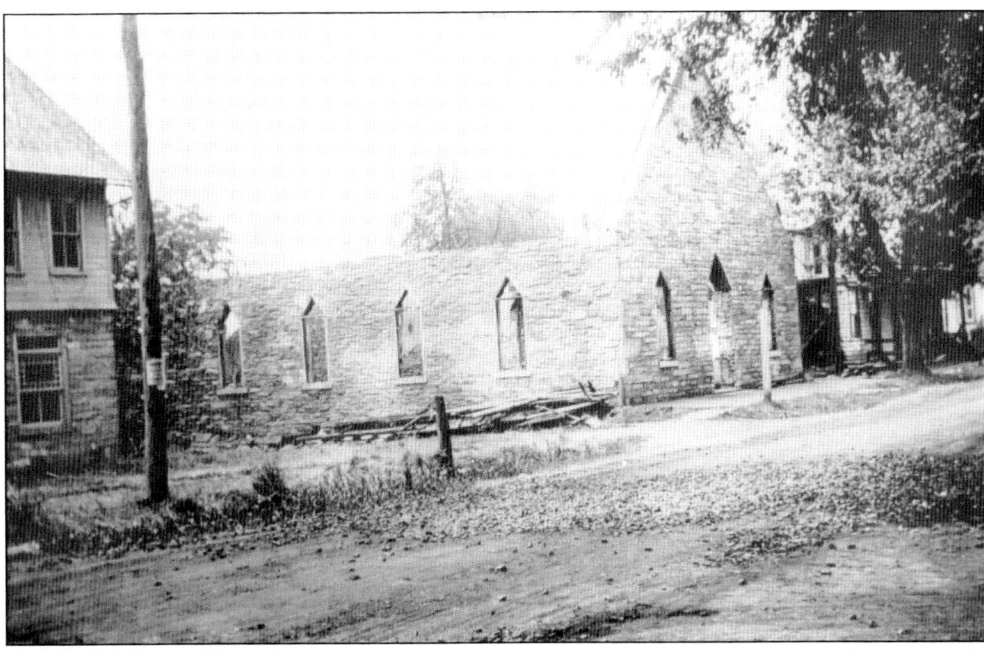

On July 2, 1919, a catastrophic fire destroyed the Schaefferstown United Brethren Church and the Lloyd Hetrick home just west of the church. Schaefferstown's fire protection was in its infancy, and by the time equipment arrived from neighboring towns, the buildings were a total loss. Pictured here from left to right are the Irwin Horst cigar factory, Schaefferstown United Brethren Church ruins, and the remains of the Hetrick home.

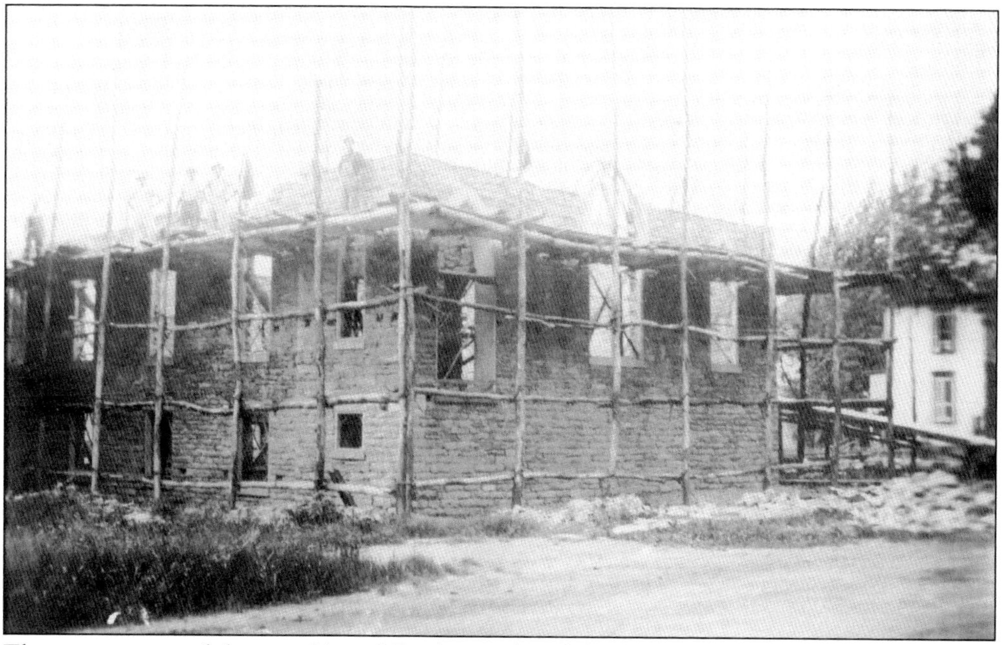

The cornerstone of the new United Brethren Church building was placed on April 25, 1920, and construction progressed rapidly under the direction of Benjamin Hartman. Tree trunks were used as vertical members for scaffolding. Planks were nailed and/or lashed to the uprights, and a ramp was built for trucking stone to the working level. The framed arch for the large stained-glass window is visible in the center of the front facade.

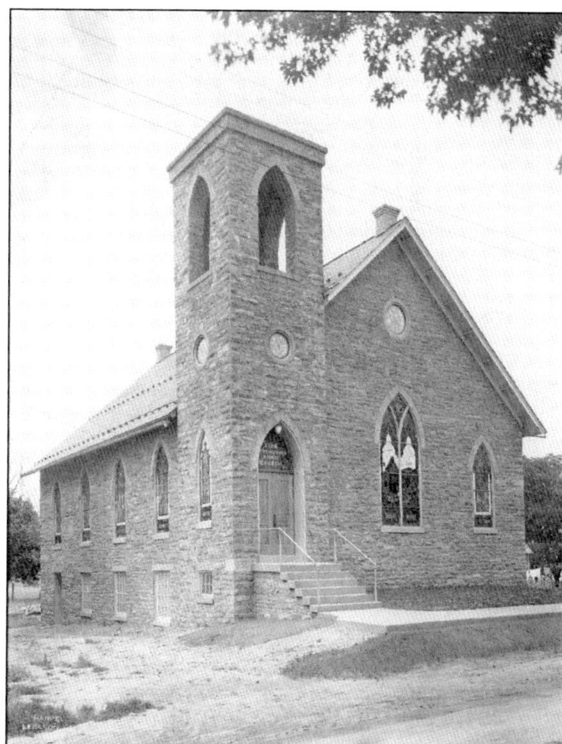

The completed Zion United Brethren in Christ Church was dedicated on August 14, 1921. Today known as Zion United Methodist Church, the church retains its small congregation and old-fashioned charm. Each stained-glass window memorializes congregation members and friends who helped make the reconstruction possible. (Courtesy of Zion United Methodist Church.)

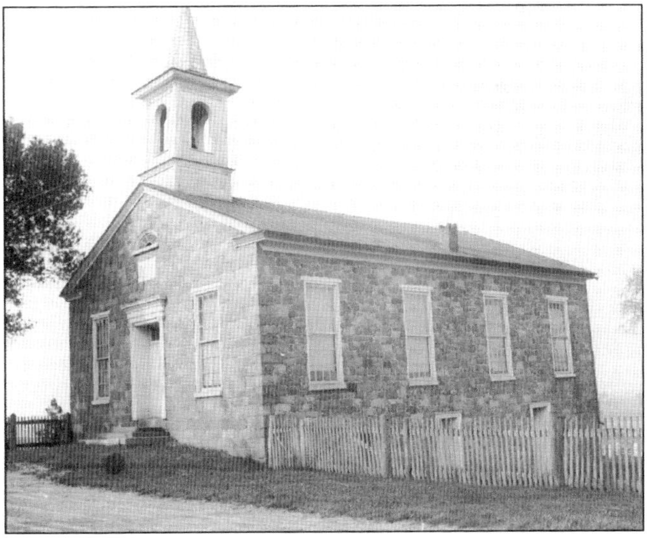

Albright Memorial Chapel was erected in 1850 in memory of Jacob Albright (1759–1808), the founder of the Evangelical Church. The chapel was built next to his burial place in the John George Becker II family cemetery, now the Evangelical Church cemetery. This sandstone chapel developed structural problems and was rebuilt in 1860. This 1911 photograph was taken prior to lightning setting the steeple on fire. It was never rebuilt to the original specifications. (Courtesy of Rita Mock.)

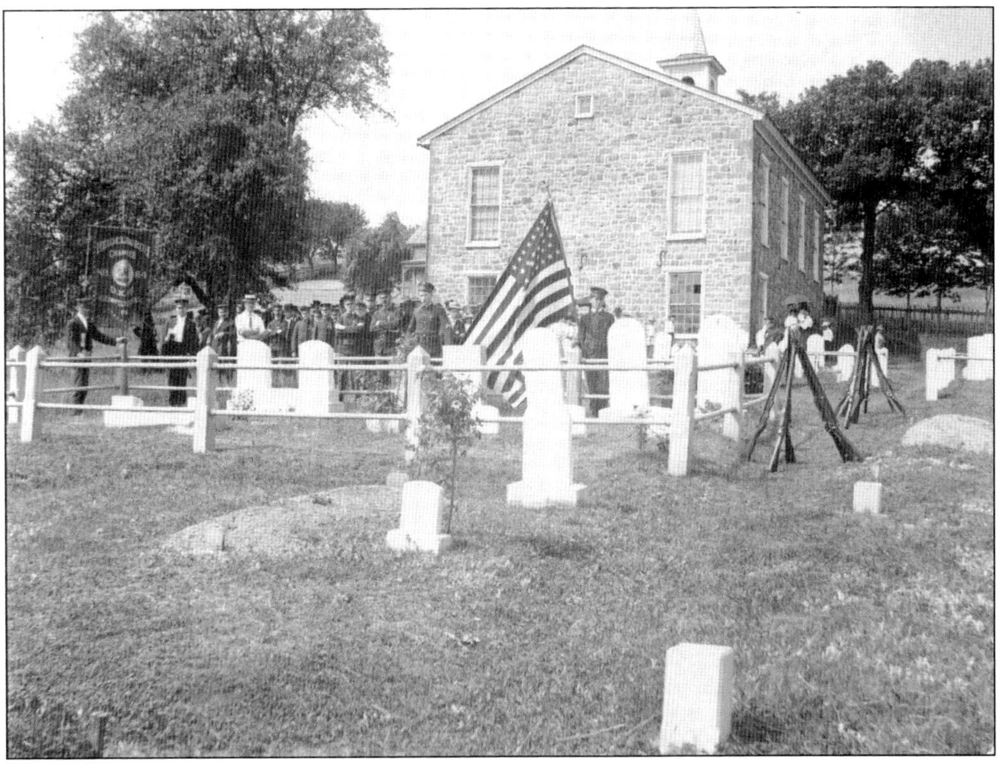

The Heidelburgh Chamber of the Order Knights of Friendship and Kleinfeltersville residents gather in the Evangelical Cemetery behind Albright Memorial Church for Decoration Day. The predecessor to today's Memorial Day, Decoration Day was a time to honor and remember those who died in the Civil War and, then, later wars. This real-photo postcard was made around 1912. (Courtesy of Rita Mock.)

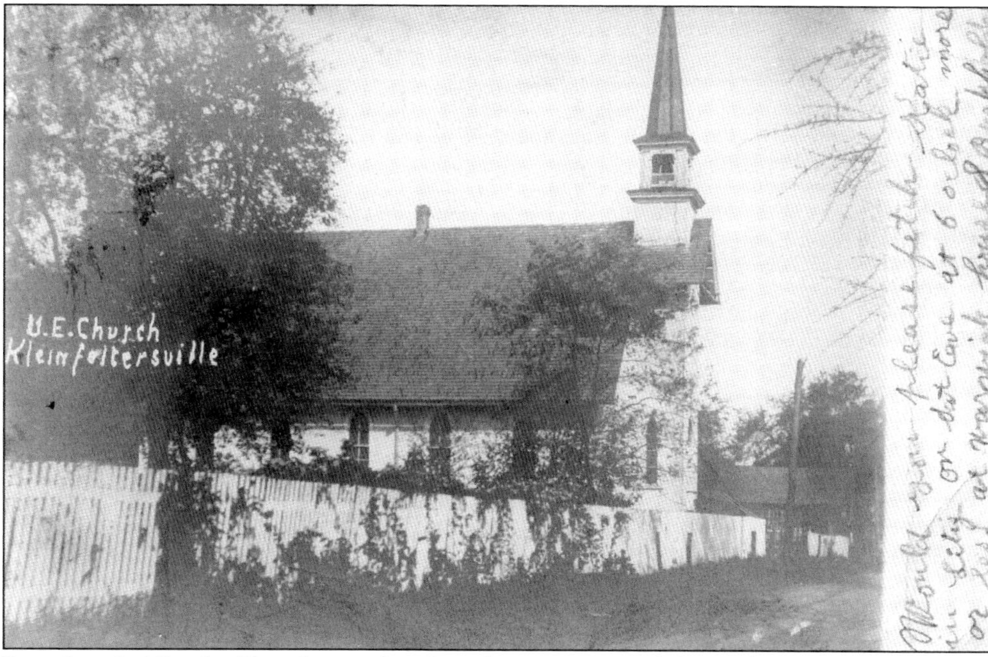

Even though Albright Chapel was only a short distance away, it did not fully meet the needs of the growing Evangelical membership around Kleinfeltersville. So, in 1897, Trinity United Evangelical Church was built on Millbach Road. This real-photo postcard, postmarked 1908, shows the small area available for a message on early postcards. Only the address was permitted on the reverse. (Courtesy Institute of American Deltiology.)

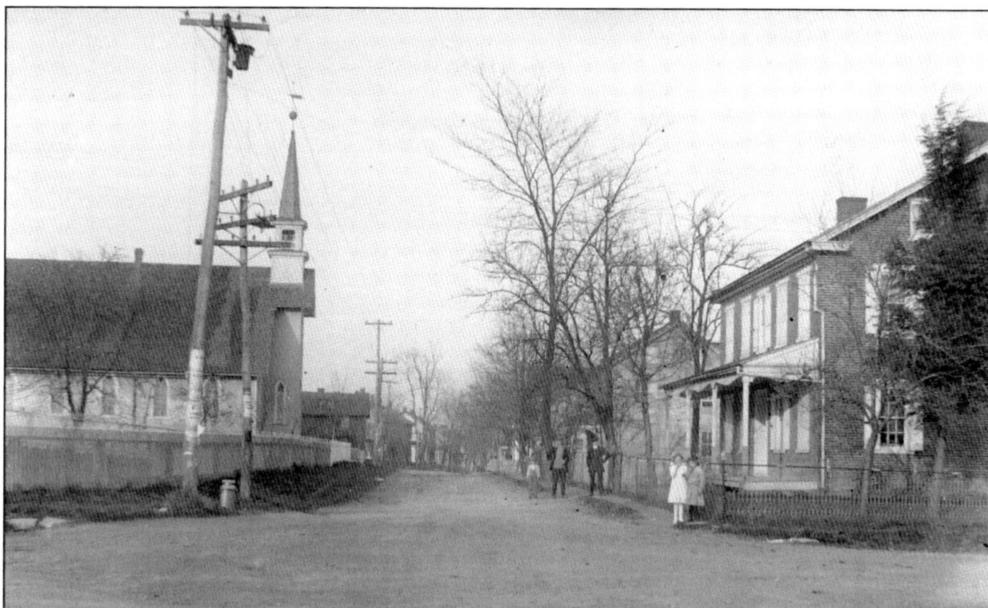

Another postcard view of Kleinfeltersville shows the houses surrounding Trinity Church, including that on the far right identified as "Grandma Lesher's house." In 1915, the church was remodeled and expanded, the steeple was moved to the side, and a large stained-glass window was added. Today, this church is known as Trinity United Methodist Church. (Courtesy of Susan Horst Kershner.)

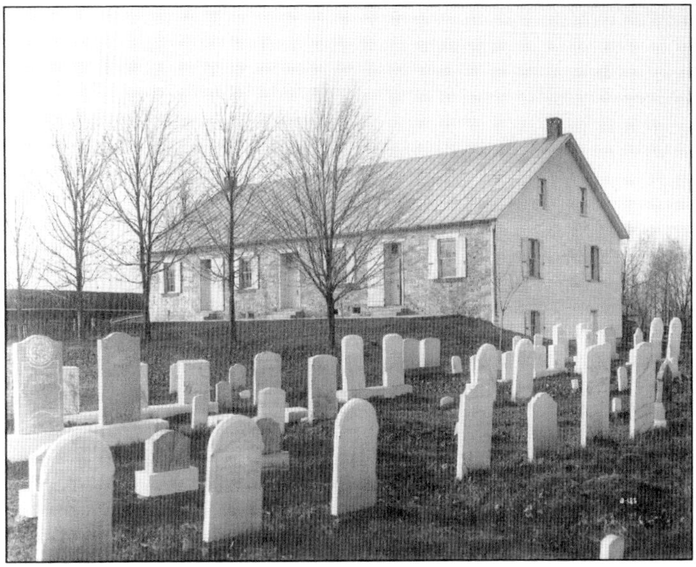

The Church of the Brethren was organized in the Lebanon Valley in 1841. Sharing the beliefs of Anabaptist as well as pietist groups, Brethren seek a life of peaceful action and plain living, following the New Testament. The Heidelberg Meetinghouse, located a half-mile east of Reistville, was built in 1867. This c. 1937 photograph includes a view of the cemetery and former carriage sheds. (Courtesy of Walter Heisey.)

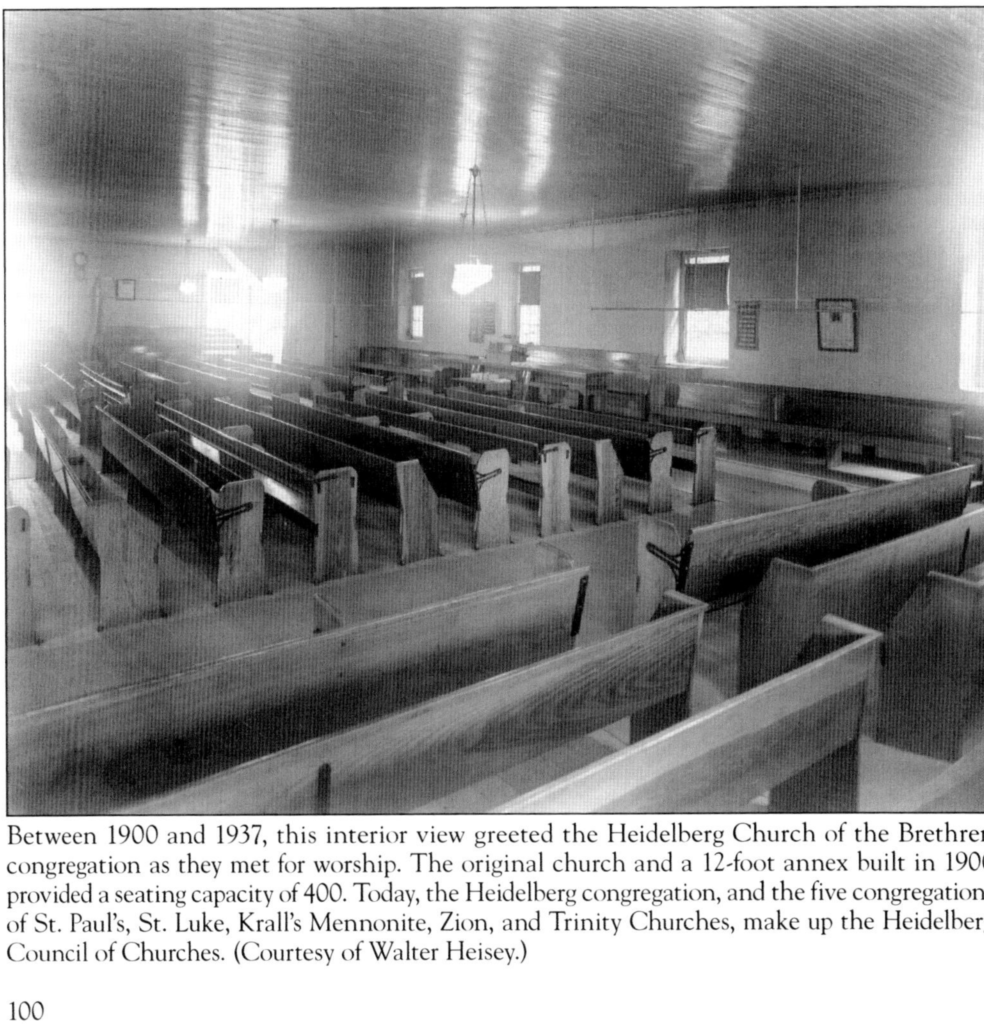

Between 1900 and 1937, this interior view greeted the Heidelberg Church of the Brethren congregation as they met for worship. The original church and a 12-foot annex built in 1900 provided a seating capacity of 400. Today, the Heidelberg congregation, and the five congregations of St. Paul's, St. Luke, Krall's Mennonite, Zion, and Trinity Churches, make up the Heidelberg Council of Churches. (Courtesy of Walter Heisey.)

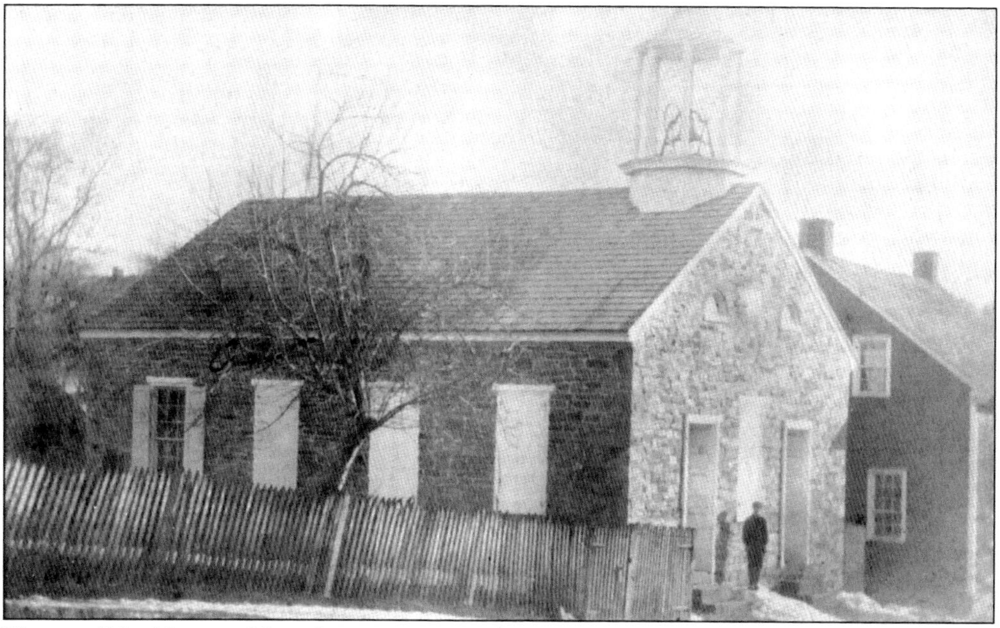

This small building on Main Street was erected in 1847 as an Evangelical church. Throughout the years, it has served many purposes. In 1919, the building was sold to Schaefferstown Volunteer Fire Company for its fire station. When the Schaefferstown Fire Hall was built in the 1960s, this building became the "Scout House," a meeting place for Boy Scout and Girl Scout troops. Today, its future is uncertain.

A tradition that continues to this day, the Palm Sunday Parade in Schaefferstown, complete with donkey, is a celebration by all the community churches. In this early-1960s photograph, James Ginder leads the donkey from the United Brethren and Reformed churches to the Lutheran church, accompanied by his brother Peter Ginder and many others. Rev. Joseph Gyorke of St. Paul's United Church of Christ is at the far left. (Courtesy St. Paul's UCC.)

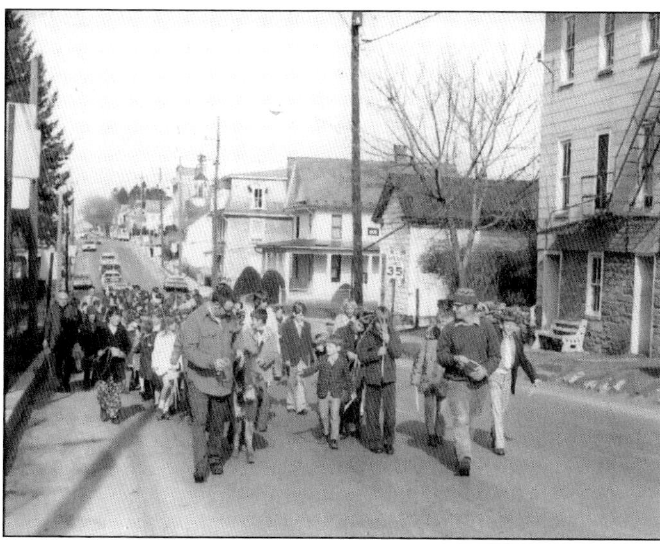

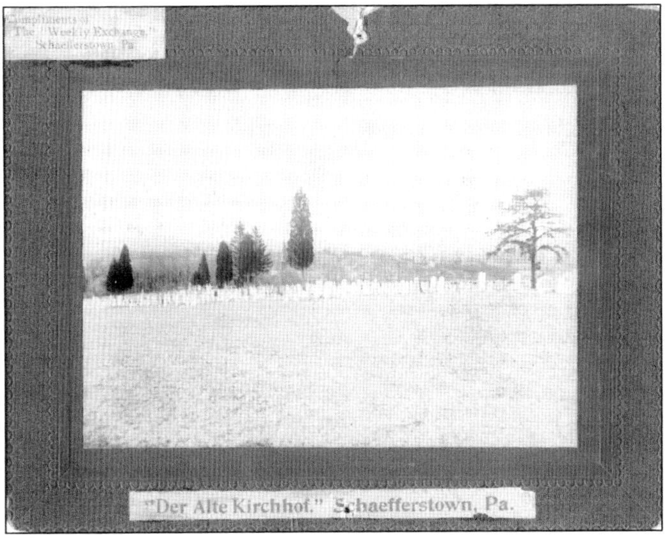

This photograph, published in the 1890s in the *Weekly Exchange*, emphasizes Schaefferstown Cemetery's location on a hill overlooking the town. The earliest part of the cemetery dates to 1763, when town founder Alexander Schaeffer donated a parcel of land to the Lutheran and Reformed congregations for a burial yard. Additional land was added over the years, forming separate but contiguous spaces for other congregations. The cemetery is still in active use.

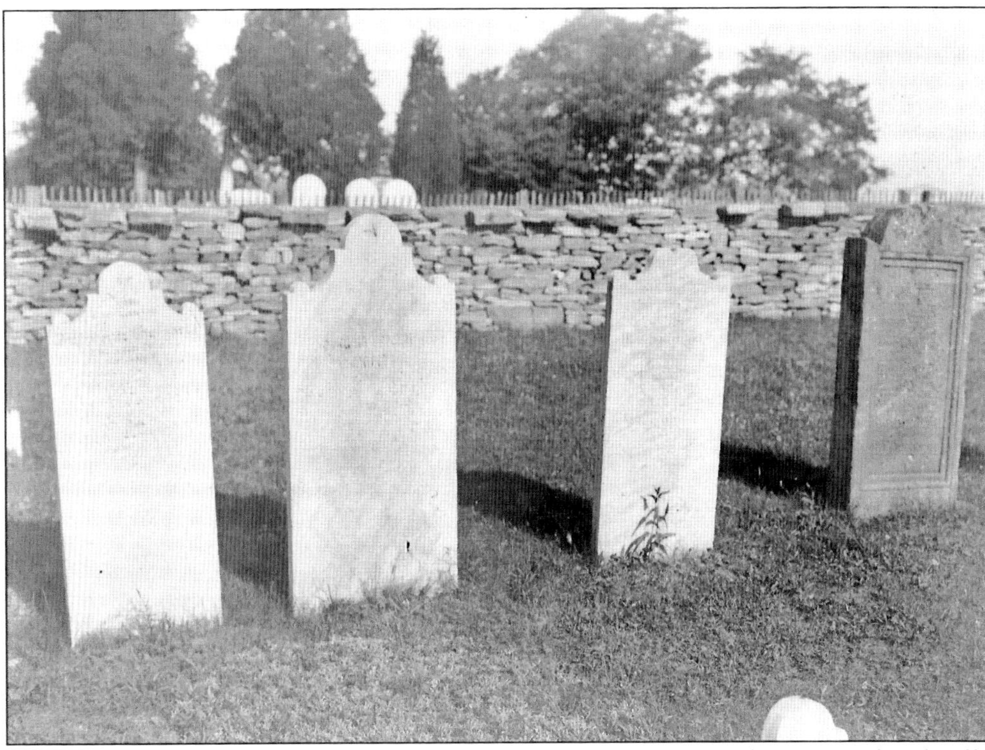

Shown here are the Schaefferstown Cemetery graves of, from left to right, Susannah Schaeffer Goshert, Henry Schaeffer, Alexander Schaeffer, and Anna Engel Schaeffer. Susannah and Henry were children of Alexander and Anna. Like many early stones, these are inscribed in German and are now nearly illegible. Note the stone wall, which once enclosed the various sections of the cemetery. (Courtesy of Diana Wike Castor.)

Seven

Community Activities and Service

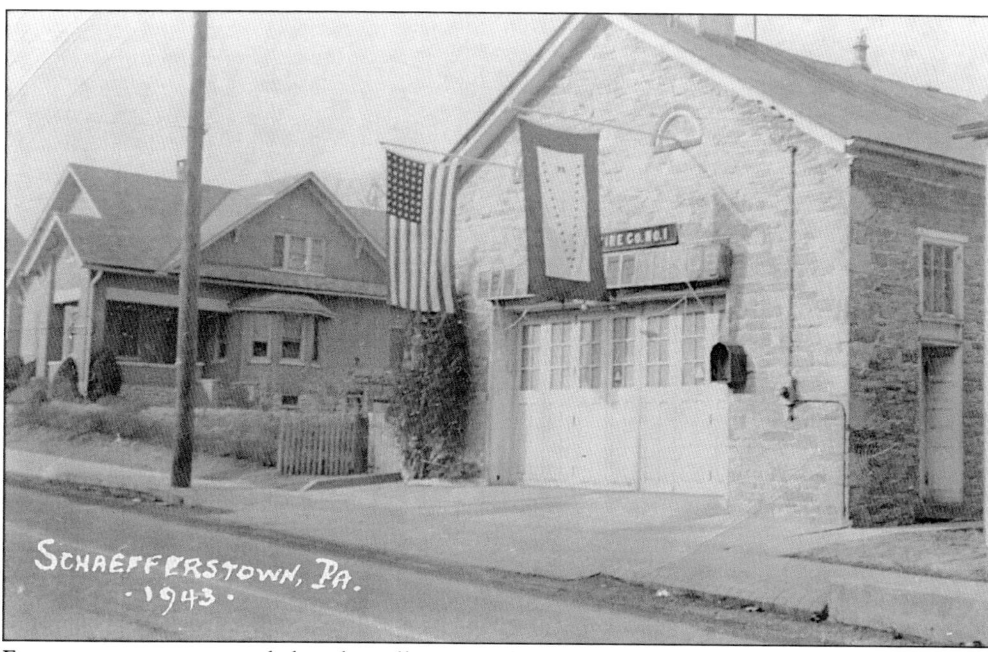

Every community responded to the call to arms during World War II, and Heidelberg Township was no exception. Before the war was over, 222 men and women from the township had served. At home, service flags flown in front of the Schaefferstown firehouse were a constant reminder of this participation. This 1943 service flag has a V, possibly for Victory. (Courtesy of Glenn Wolgemuth.)

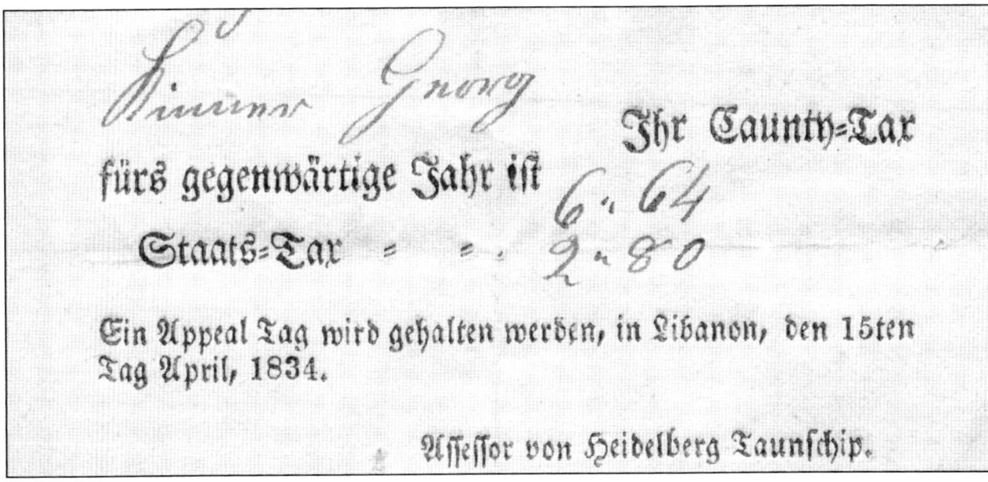

Ihr County-Tax fürs gegenwärtige Jahr ist 6.64

Staats-Tax - - 2.80

Ein Appeal Tag wird gehalten werden, in Libanon, den 15ten Tag April, 1834.

Assessor von Heidelberg Taunschip.

Heidelberg Township in the mid-1800s still had a very heavy German influence, as seen in the 1834 tax bill sent to George Keener (above). The bill is in German, with a German typeface, and Keener's name is in German script. During the intervening years, a gradual transition to the use of English was made, at least for official paperwork. In 1843, George Keener's tax notice was completely in English (below). German-speaking immigrants were not unwilling to learn English as part of their assimilation into their new land. However, use of the spoken dialect in the home and at school continued until rumblings of war with Germany before World War I. Note the opportunity given to taxpayers to appeal the assessed tax at the appointed place and time stated on the bill.

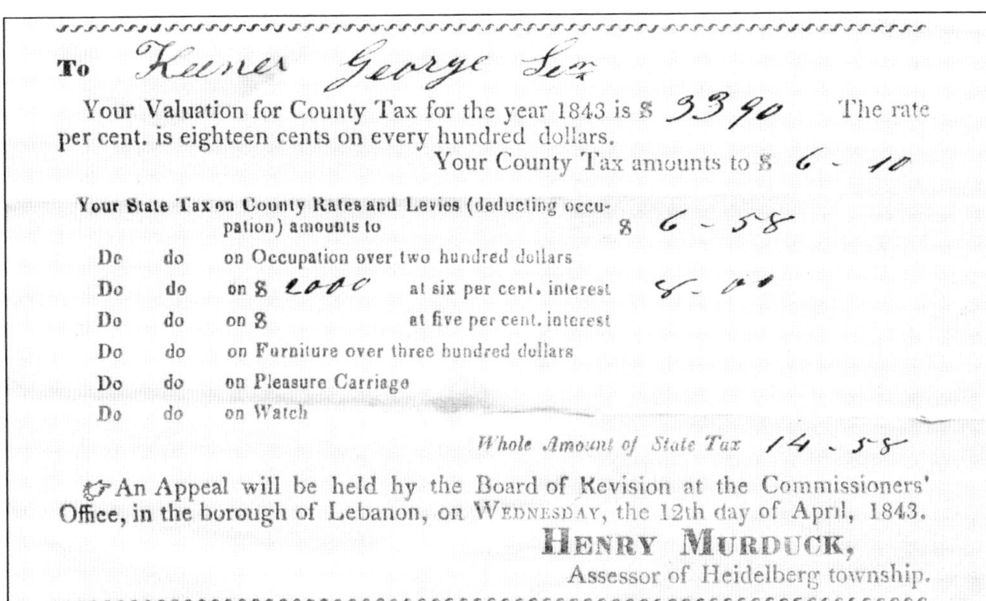

To Keener George Sen

Your Valuation for County Tax for the year 1843 is $ 3390 The rate per cent. is eighteen cents on every hundred dollars.

Your County Tax amounts to $ 6 - 10

Your State Tax on County Rates and Levies (deducting occupation) amounts to $ 6 - 58

Do do on Occupation over two hundred dollars

Do do on $ 2000 at six per cent. interest 8 - 00

Do do on $ at five per cent. interest

Do do on Furniture over three hundred dollars

Do do on Pleasure Carriage

Do do on Watch

Whole Amount of State Tax 14 . 58

☞ An Appeal will be held by the Board of Revision at the Commissioners' Office, in the borough of Lebanon, on WEDNESDAY, the 12th day of April, 1843.

HENRY MURDUCK,

Assessor of Heidelberg township.

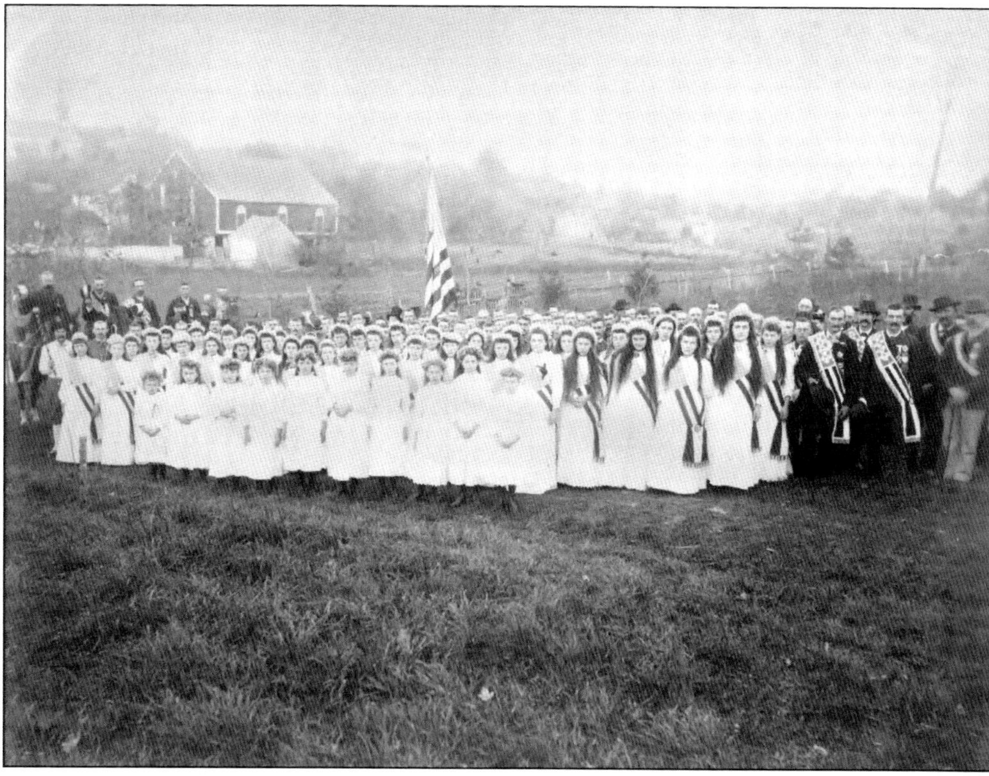

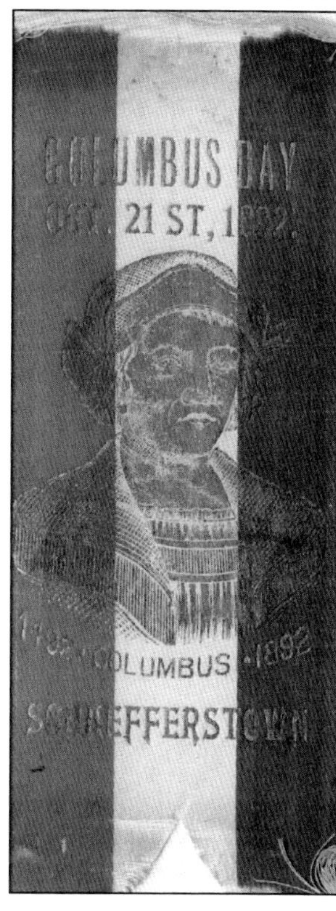

Americans responded enthusiastically to Pres. Benjamin Harrison's call for a celebration of the 400th anniversary of Columbus's discovery of the New World by holding events that highlighted patriotism and national loyalty. The Schaefferstown celebration, on October 21, 1892, was sponsored by Washington Camp No. 256, Patriotic Order Sons of America. Columbus Day festivities included a parade and the coronation of a queen, Isabelle Christ, who was supposedly chosen for her beauty and also because of her name. The above photograph shows parade participants, including the queen and her court and members of the POS of A in their lodge regalia. The photograph to the right shows is a red, white, and blue ribbon honoring the event.

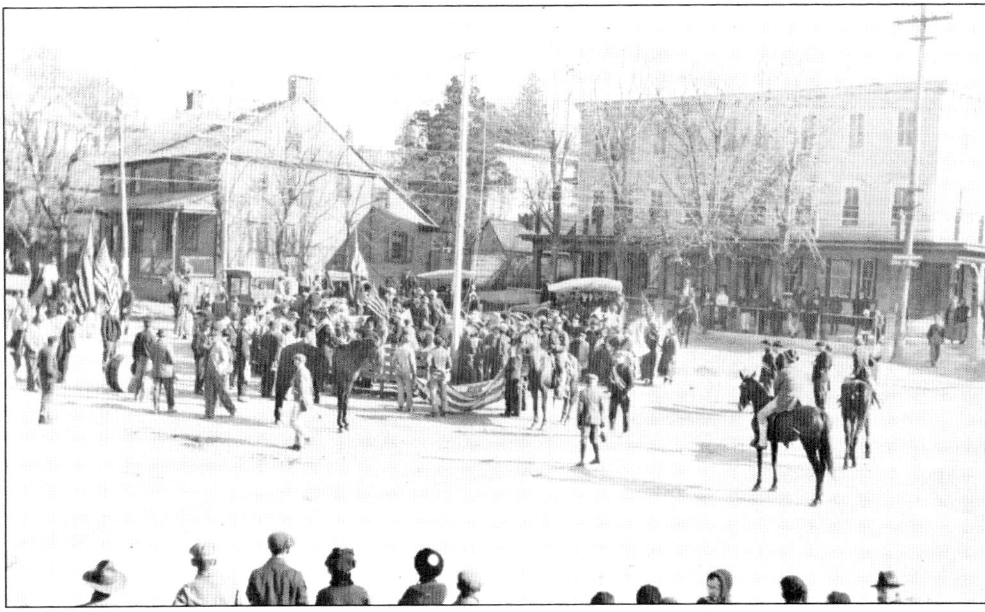

In 1919, Pres. Woodrow Wilson declared November 11 Armistice Day, in honor of those who gave their lives in World War I. Here, Schaefferstown residents commemorate Armistice Day by raising an enormous flag in the town square. In 1954, after two more wars and many more lost lives, Pres. Dwight Eisenhower renamed the holiday Veteran's Day. (Courtesy of Rita Mock.)

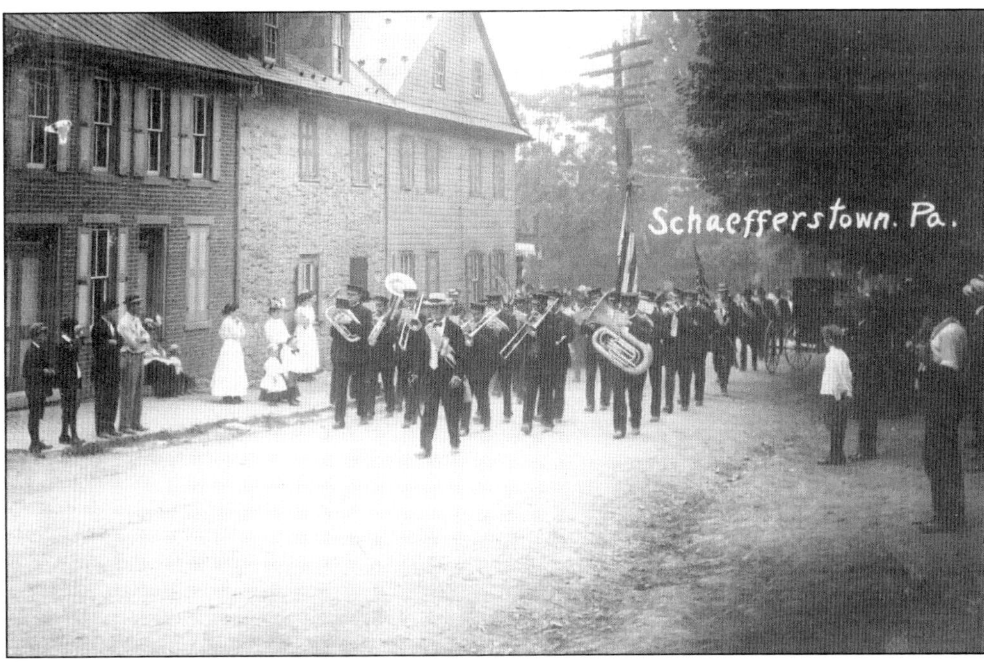

Well into the 20th century, Schaefferstown residents celebrated Memorial Day with a parade, services at the cemetery, and a picnic at Fountain Park. In this photograph, taken before 1914, William M. Smith, of the local POS of A camp, leads the parade, followed by the Silver Cornet Band. They are heading east on Main Street on their way to Front (now Church) Street, which was commonly known as "cemetery lane."

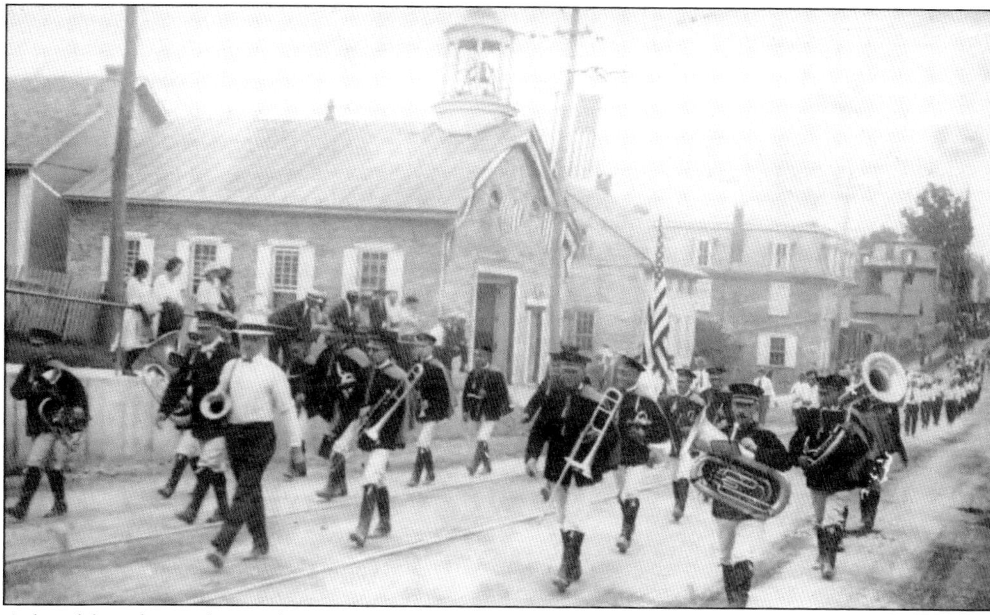

A local band parades in front of Schaefferstown's firehouse, followed by a long line of local patriotic organizations, fire companies, bands, decorated wagons, and automobiles, plus clowns and other costumed folks. The bunting and flags suggest an Independence Day parade, probably in the early 1920s. This photographer had a great vantage point, looking east along Main Street from Carpenter Street.

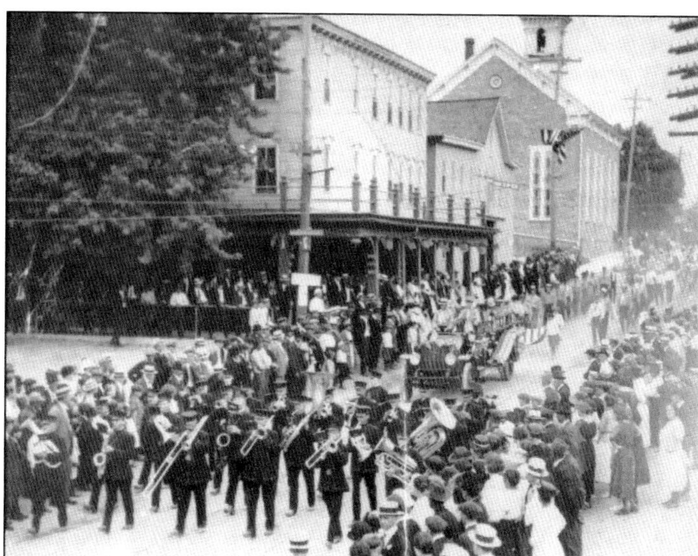

Many people enjoy this Fourth of July parade as it passes through Schaefferstown square sometime in the 1920s. The Central House, livery stable, and Lutheran church line the background. The sign "Cars Stop Here" hangs above the stable doorway, indicating the trolley stop. Most parades in town, with the exception of that on Memorial Day, started east of the Lutheran church and traveled west.

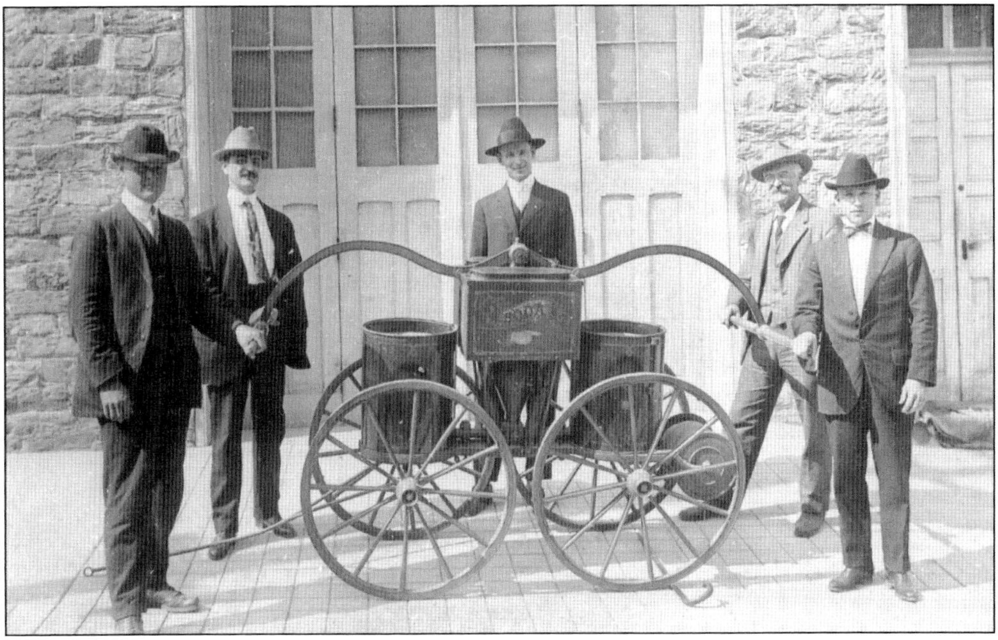

One of the first pieces of fire apparatus in Schaefferstown was this soda acid chemical hand pumper, the "Little Giant," purchased in 1876 and used until 1916. In this c. 1921 photograph, members of Schaefferstown Volunteer Fire Company No. 1 pose in front of the new firehouse. They are, from left to right, Luther Plasterer, William Krieger, Irwin Miller, Thomas Strickler, and Jonathan Corl.

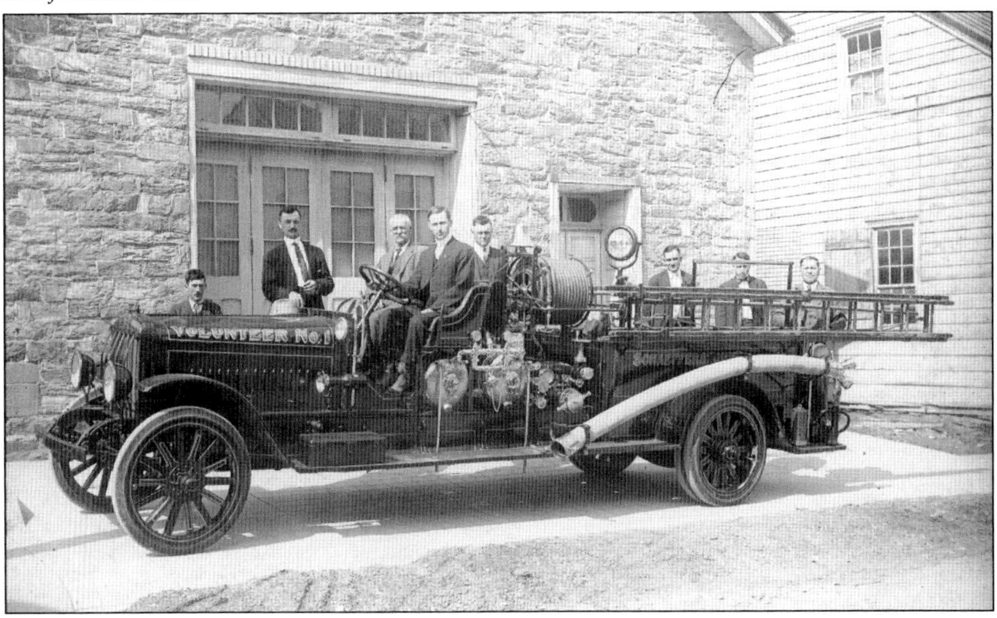

After the severe fire that destroyed the United Brethren Church and Lloyd Hetrick home, Schaefferstown purchased its first fire engine in 1920. The Evangelical church building was purchased and renovated to house the new equipment. Pictured here are, from left to right, Raymond Horst, William Krieger, Thomas Strickler, Irwin Miller, Luther Plasterer, George Hansel, Jonathan Corl, and Morris Boltz.

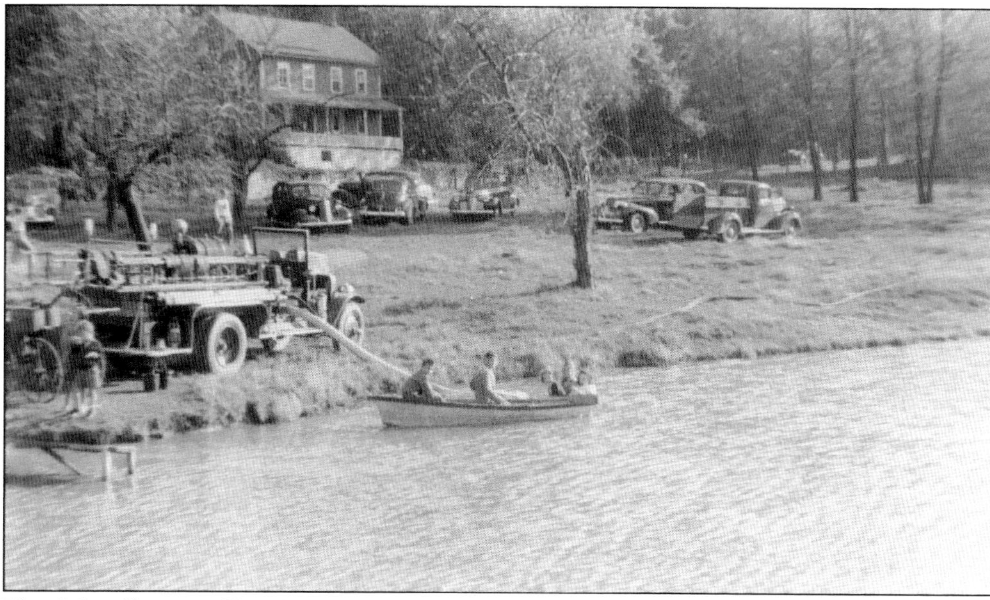

The Schaefferstown Fire Company practices at the Lloyd Horst farm pond on North Market Street while children, possibly of the firemen as well as the Horst family, enjoy the community atmosphere. Note the "Little Giant" pumper and the 1920s fire engine to the left. The 1930s and 1940s vehicles date this photograph to the mid-1940s. The Jonas Ressler house is in the background. (Courtesy of Jan Taylor.)

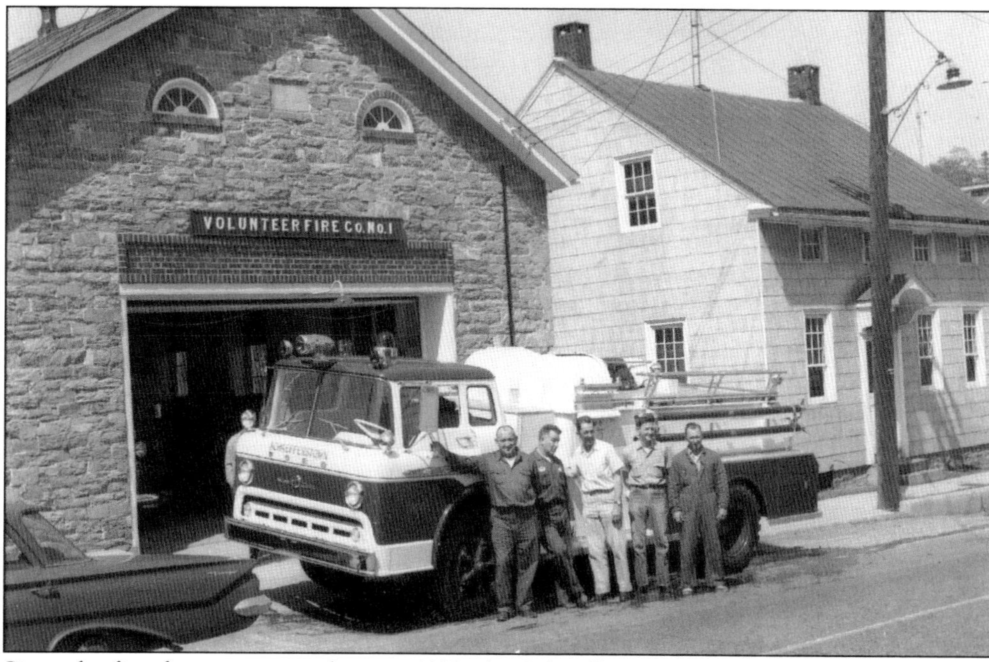

Since the first fire engine purchase in 1920, the Schaefferstown Volunteer Fire Company has kept its equipment current. This high-pressure fog apparatus with 1,000-gallon water tank was purchased in 1961. Seen here from left to right, Ammon Stohler, Metger "Munk" Moore, Lewis Keener, James Keener, and Jacob Netzley show off the new equipment parked in front of the firehouse on Main Street. (Courtesy of Rita Mock.)

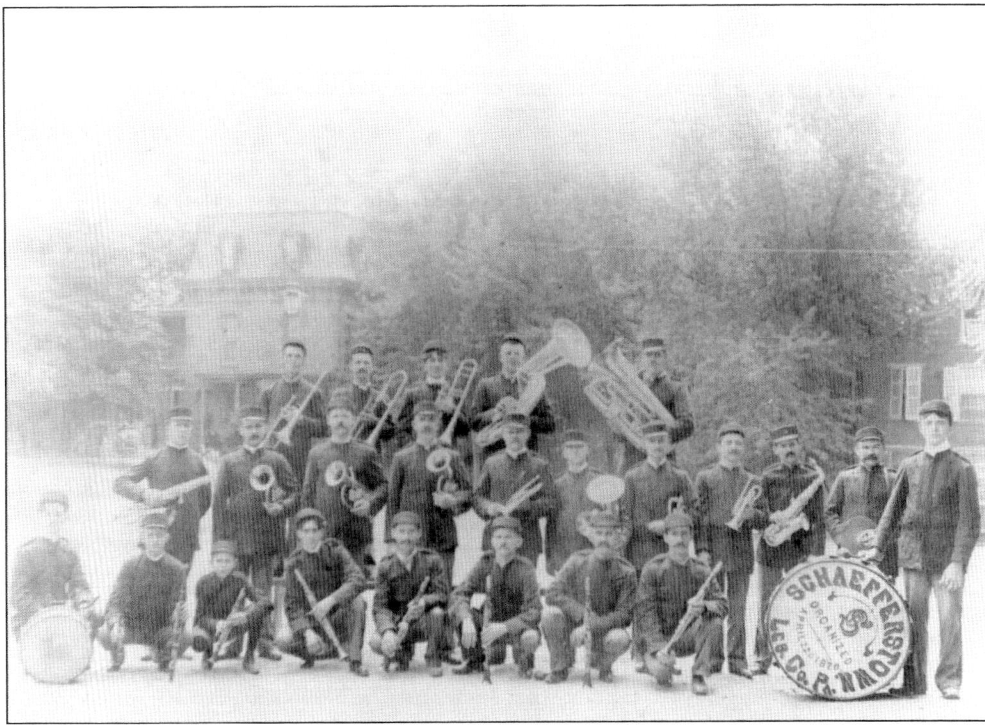

The Schaefferstown Cornet Band, shown here in the town square, was organized in 1870. It exemplifies the patriotic fervor that swept the country as its centennial approached. The third floor of the Franklin House included a large room, accessed directly from the street by its own separate staircase, where the band sometimes rehearsed. The Thomas Brendle Museum's holdings include two of the band's drums and the leader's uniform.

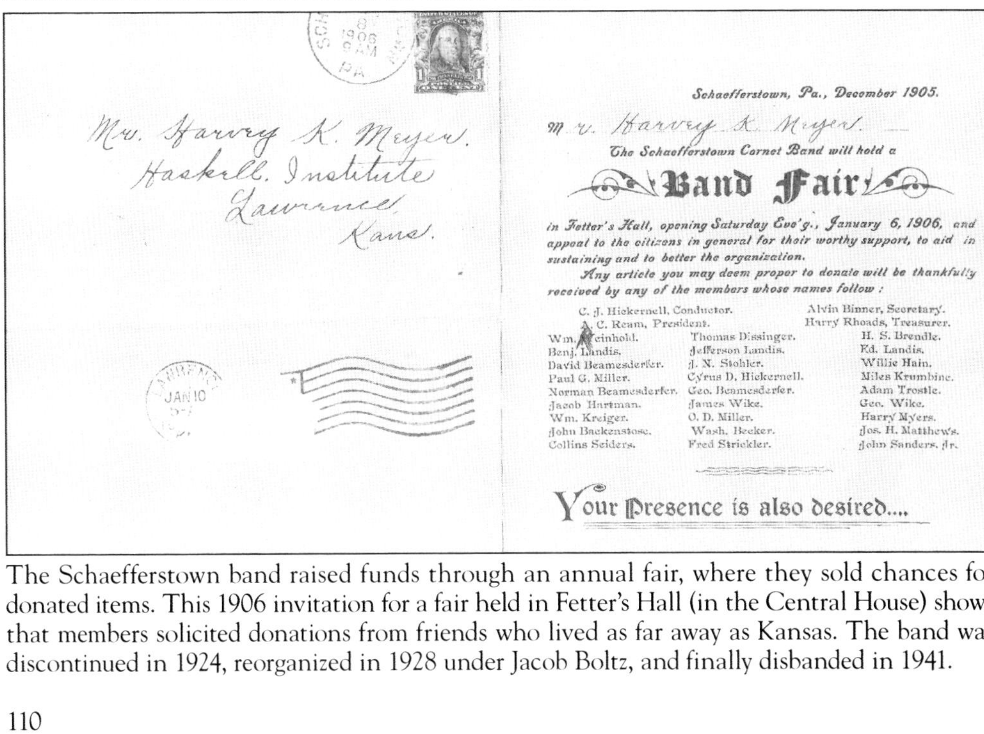

Schaefferstown, Pa., December 1905.

Mr. Harvey K. Meyer.

The Schaefferstown Cornet Band will hold a

Band Fair

in Fetter's Hall, opening Saturday Eve'g., January 6, 1906, and appeal to the citizens in general for their worthy support, to aid in sustaining and to better the organization.

Any article you may deem proper to donate will be thankfully received by any of the members whose names follow :

C. J. Hickernell, Conductor.
A. C. Ream, President.
Alvin Binner, Secretary.
Harry Rhoads, Treasurer.

Wm. [illegible]einhold.
Benj. Landis.
David Beamesderfer.
Paul G. Miller.
Norman Beamesderfer.
Jacob Hartman.
Wm. Kreiger.
John Backenstose.
Collins Seiders.
Thomas Dissinger.
Jefferson Landis.
J. N. Stohler.
Cyrus D. Hickernell.
Geo. Beamesderfer.
James Wike.
O. D. Miller.
Wash. Becker.
Fred Strickler.
H. S. Brendle.
Ed. Landis.
Willie Hain.
Miles Krumbine.
Adam Trostle.
Geo. Wike.
Harry Myers.
Jos. H. Matthews.
John Sanders, Jr.

Your Presence is also desired....

The Schaefferstown band raised funds through an annual fair, where they sold chances for donated items. This 1906 invitation for a fair held in Fetter's Hall (in the Central House) shows that members solicited donations from friends who lived as far away as Kansas. The band was discontinued in 1924, reorganized in 1928 under Jacob Boltz, and finally disbanded in 1941.

C. (Cyrus) J. Hickernell led the Schaefferstown Cornet Band from 1900 to 1922. Hickernell studied music at Albright College in Myerstown. He was a talented cornet player who gave lessons in piano and many other instruments. He was also a composer who specialized in marches, such as his "The Great Reformer March," published in 1911.

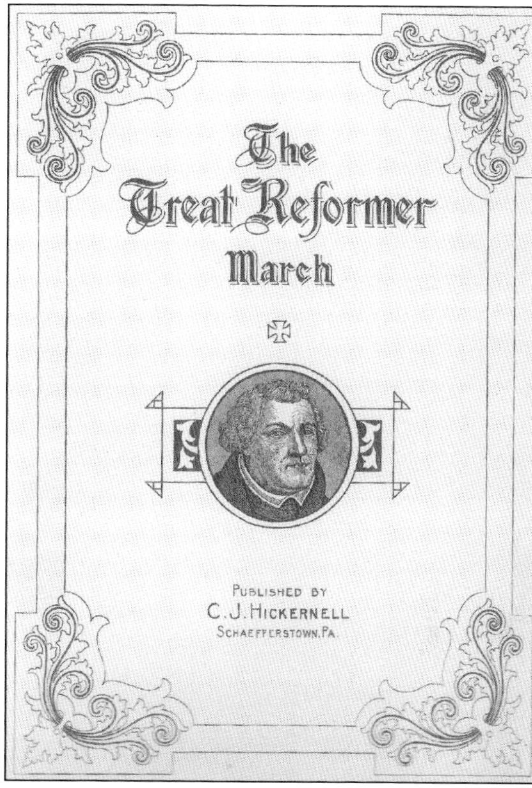

Kleinfeltersville's counterpart to the Patriotic Order Sons of America was the Order Knights of Friendship, a benevolent organization formed in 1904. The Heidelburgh Chamber No. 64 of the Order Knights of Friendship pose with their banner in front of Albright Chapel, probably during Decoration Day activities around 1912. This organization flourished until the Great Depression. It was disbanded in 1955. (Courtesy of Rita Mock.)

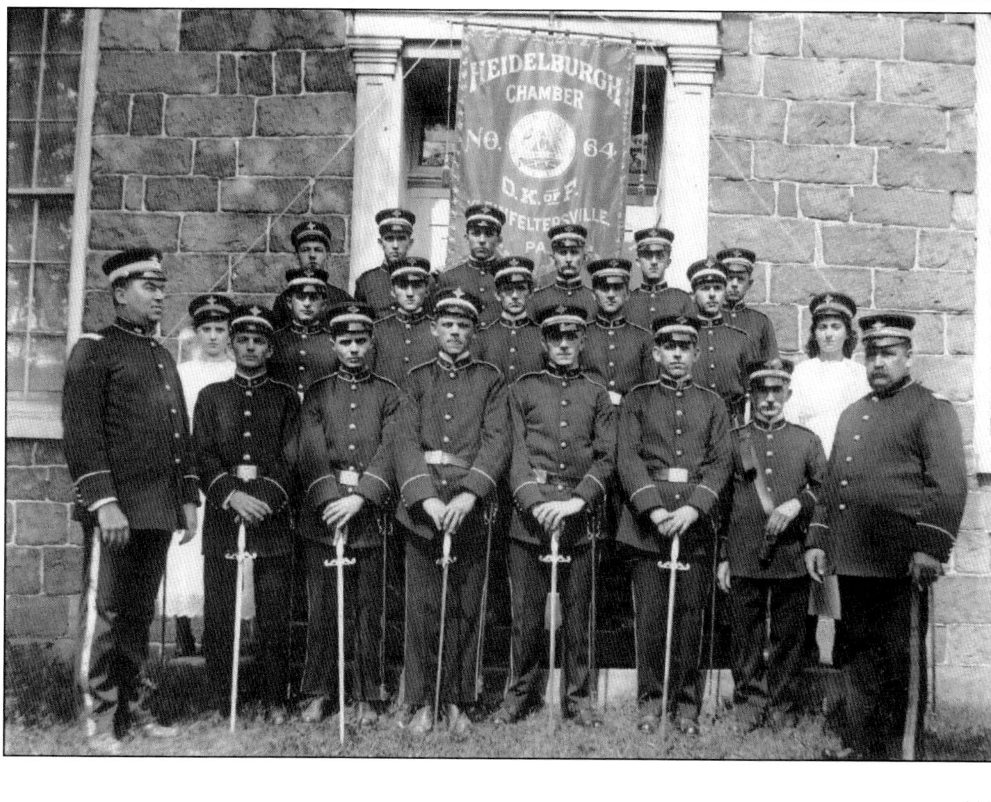

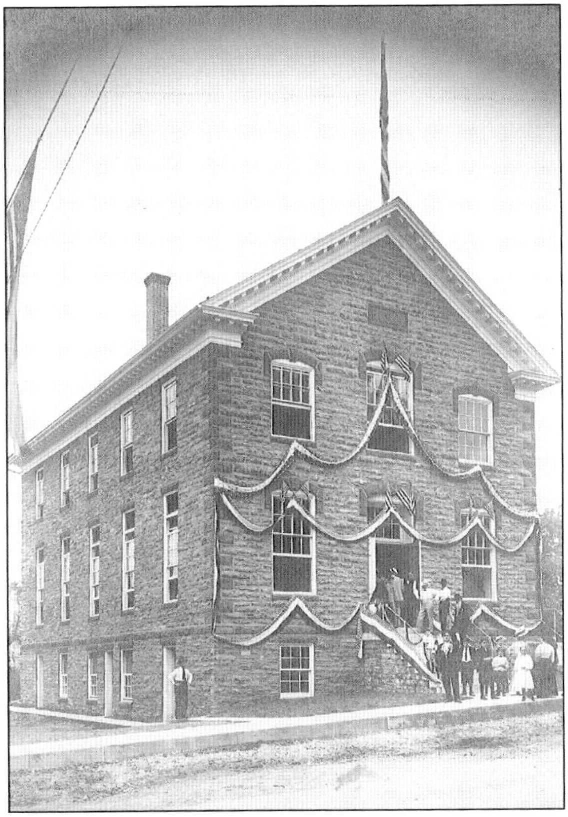

Schaefferstown men established Washington Camp No. 256, Patriotic Order Sons of America, in 1879. By 1910, they erected this building, shown at its dedication on July 2, 1910. A large meeting room on the top floor was used by a number of fraternal groups, and an auditorium with an elevated stage filled the main floor. At various times, the ground level housed a restaurant, barbershop, post office, and laundromat.

The main floor of the Schaefferstown POS of A Hall is shown here decorated for a patriotic occasion. This space, equipped with stage, dressing areas, and ticket booth, was used for fairs, community plays, dances, movies, and concerts. From 1947 to 1948, General Cigar Company used this room for processing tobacco. Today, it houses the Thomas R. Brendle Museum, which still displays the Washington Camp No. 256 charter.

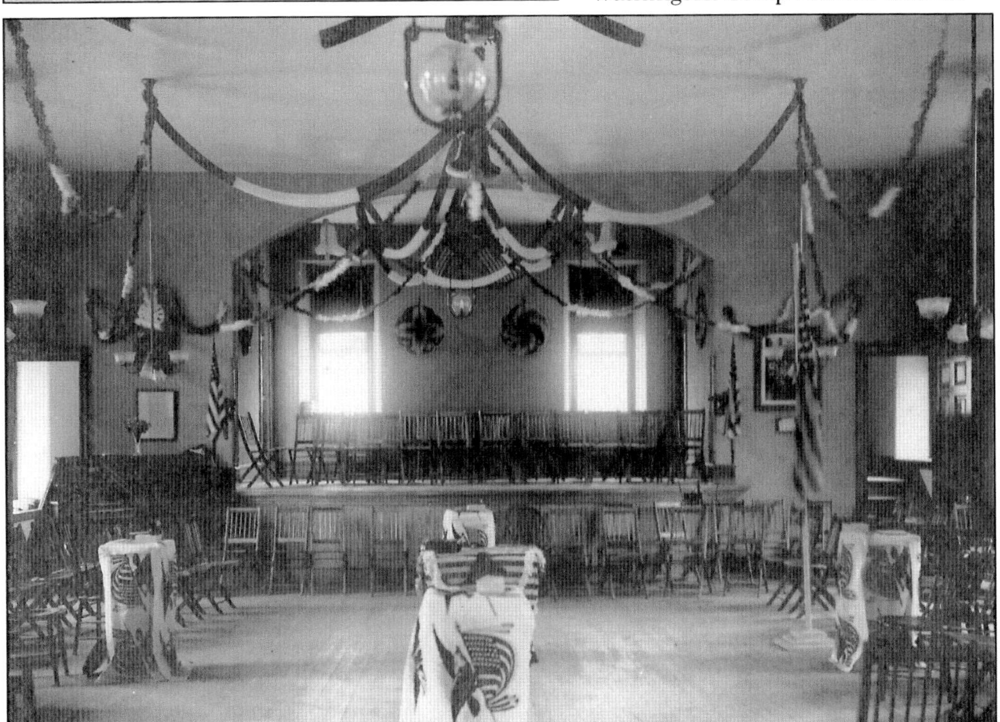

This advertisement for the American Theatre dates from sometime after 1928, when *Hello Cheyenne* was released. Although a specific location for the theater is not given, it likely was in the POS of A Hall, where silent movies, such as *Hello Cheyenne*, were shown by projectionists Rex Weigley, Harry Moyer, and Alvin Binner. Local pianists provided music to accompany the films and to drown out the noise of the projector.

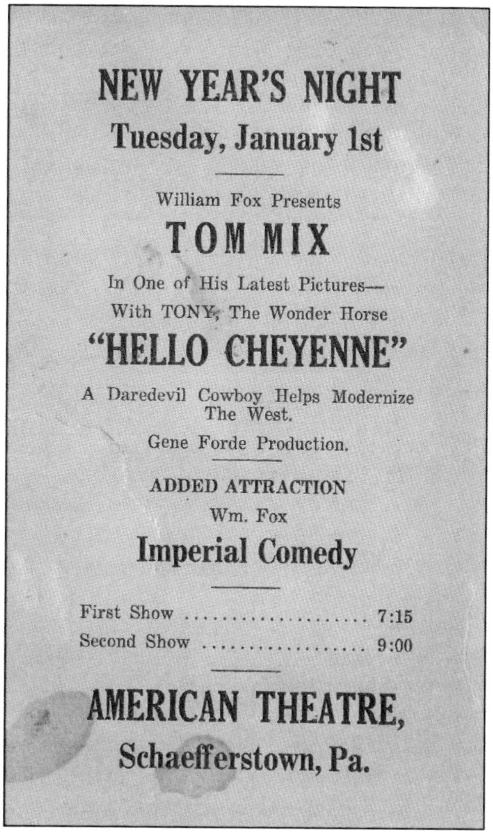

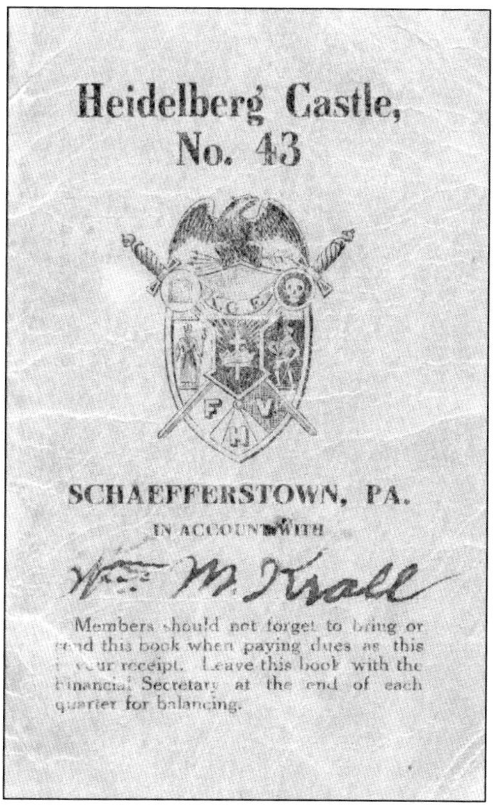

Knights of the Golden Eagle (KGE), Heidelberg Castle No. 43, were among the male fraternal groups that met in the Schaefferstown POS of A Hall. Members such as William Krall, whose book is shown here, progressed through three stages: pilgrim, knight, and crusader. The POS of A and KGE had auxiliaries known as Ladies of the Order and Ladies of the Golden Eagle.

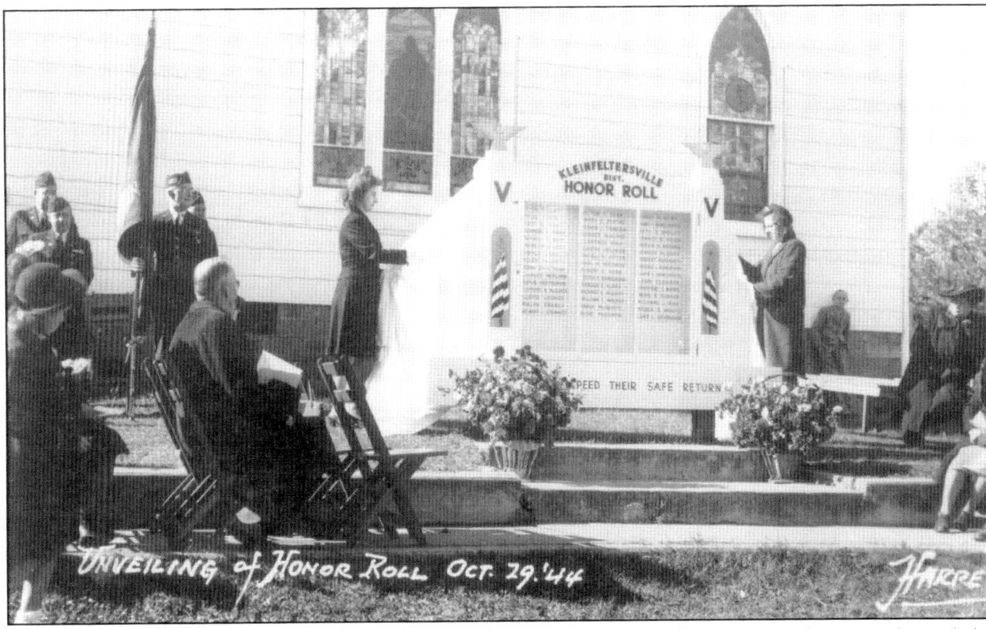

On October 29, 1944, Kleinfeltersville honored its servicemen and women with a parade and the dedication of this honor roll, erected in front of Trinity Evangelical United Brethren Church. The honor roll listed the name of every Kleinfeltersville resident serving in World War II. Heidelberg Township had its own honor roll, which stood in front of the Schaefferstown firehouse. (Courtesy of Rita Mock.)

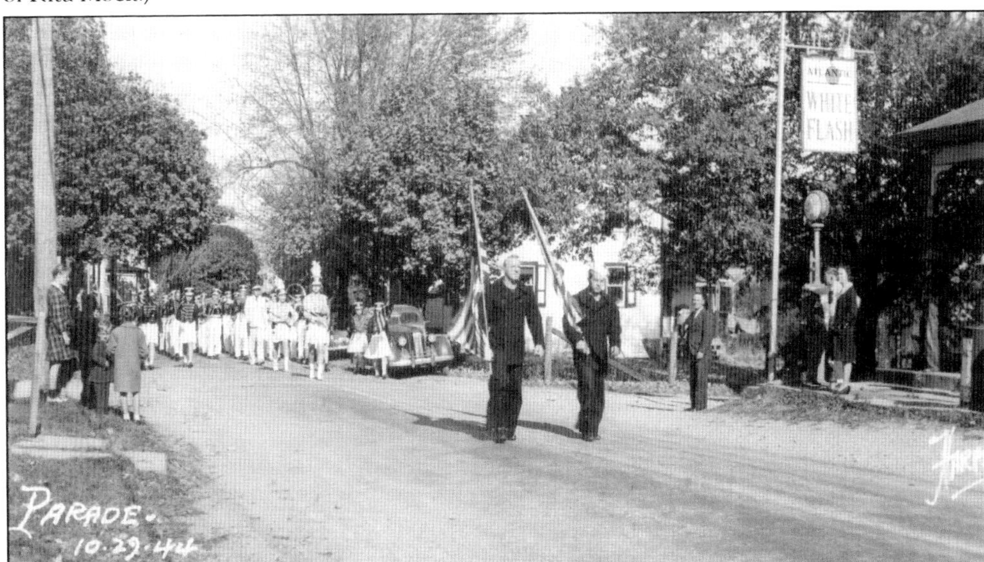

Kleinfeltersville sailors carry the colors at the head of the parade on this beautiful fall day in 1944. The parade passed in front of Doster's Market on Millbach Road and then on to Main Street, heading west. By the end of World War II, three men from the township had given their lives: Russell Weik and Harold Kurtz from Kleinfeltersville and Guy Dulabone from Schaefferstown. (Courtesy of Rita Mock.)

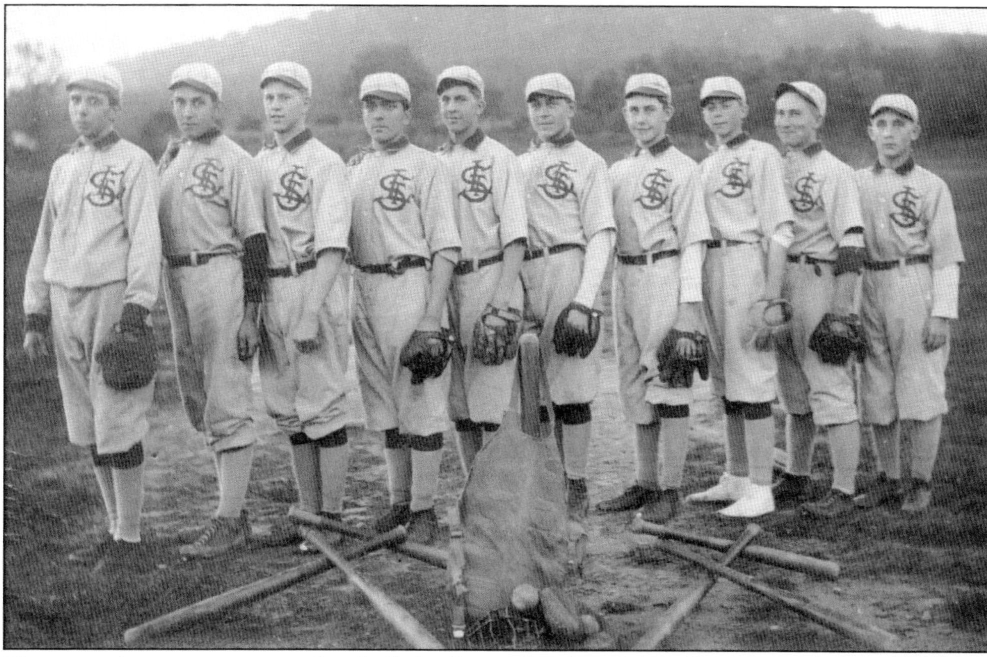

The great American pastime, baseball, has been played in Schaefferstown and the surrounding area since the mid-1800s. The Schaefferstown Baseball Team was organized as early as 1890, and games were played with area towns. Among the places where the team practiced were Zerbe's meadow, Tower Hill, Weigley's lot, Brendle's woods, and Schaefferstown School field. This real-photo postcard dates from around 1908. (Courtesy of Rita Mock.)

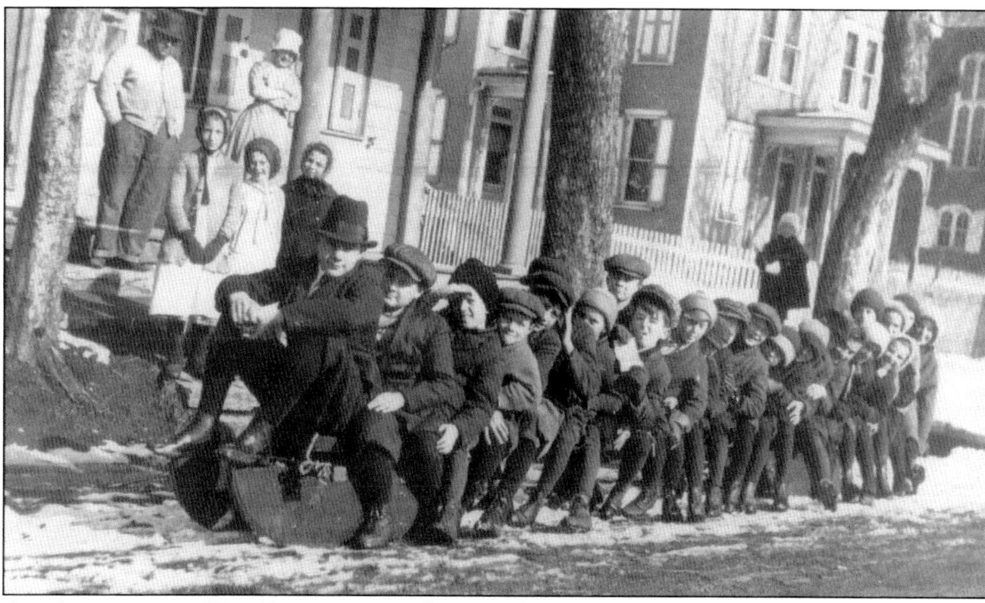

Another creation of Doc Zimmerman I, this town bobsled was enjoyed by all. Pulled to the top of Tower Hill, the bobsled would run downhill, through the square, and up the opposite hill. Then, the direction was reversed, and riders would try to coast back up Tower Hill. Here, children show off the 17-foot bobsled's capacity while Sol and Sallie Beamesderfer observe from their porch. (Courtesy of Betsy Nolt.)

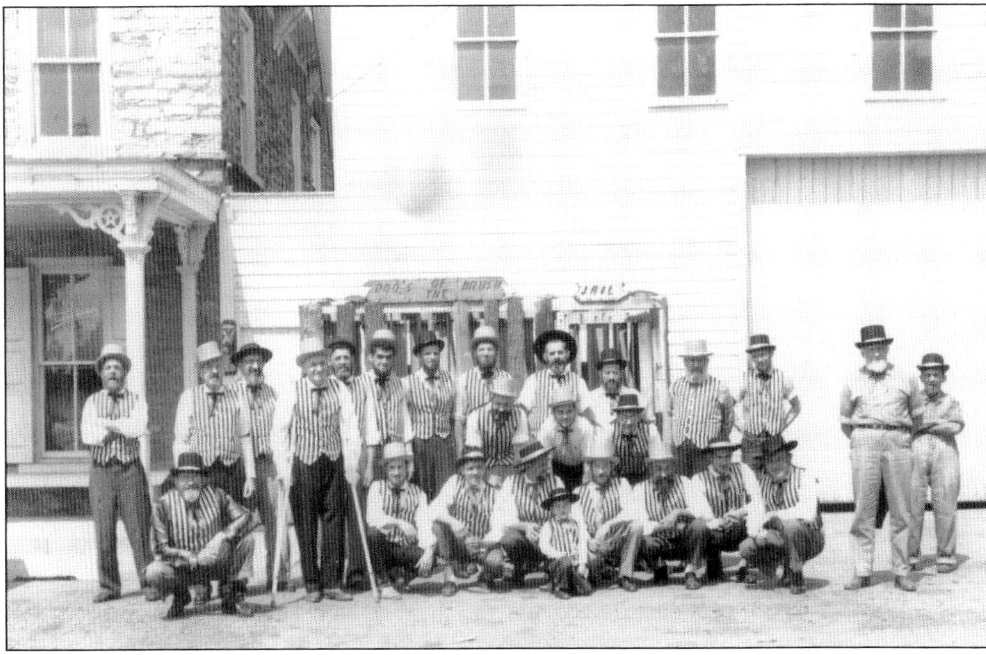

Schaefferstown held a bicentennial celebration on June 16–23, 1963, commemorating, not the founding of the town, which was customary, but the establishment of its water system. Entering into the spirit of fun while also celebrating local history, local men donned top hats and vests, grew beards, and called themselves "Brothers of the Brush." This group posed in front of the temporary "jail" set up at the Franklin House.

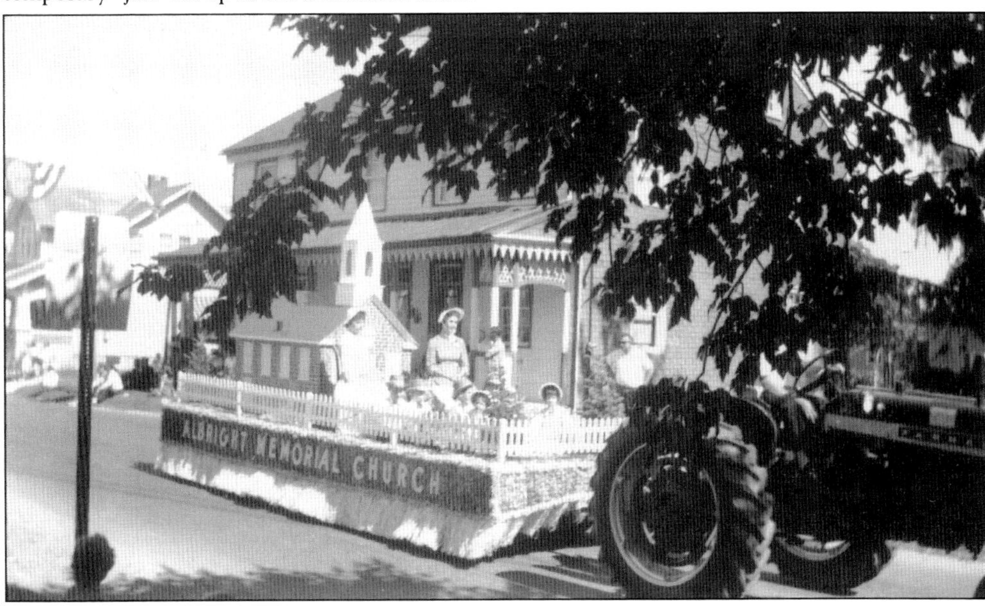

A gala parade featuring local bands, civic groups, and historical-themed floats was a bicentennial highlight. The float pictured here was one of several that displayed models of local churches; this one honored the Albright Chapel in Kleinfeltersville. It is shown passing by the Dierwechter house on West Main Street, Schaefferstown. In 2011, this house was moved to make room for the Route 501 bypass around Schaefferstown. (Courtesy of Walter Heisey.)

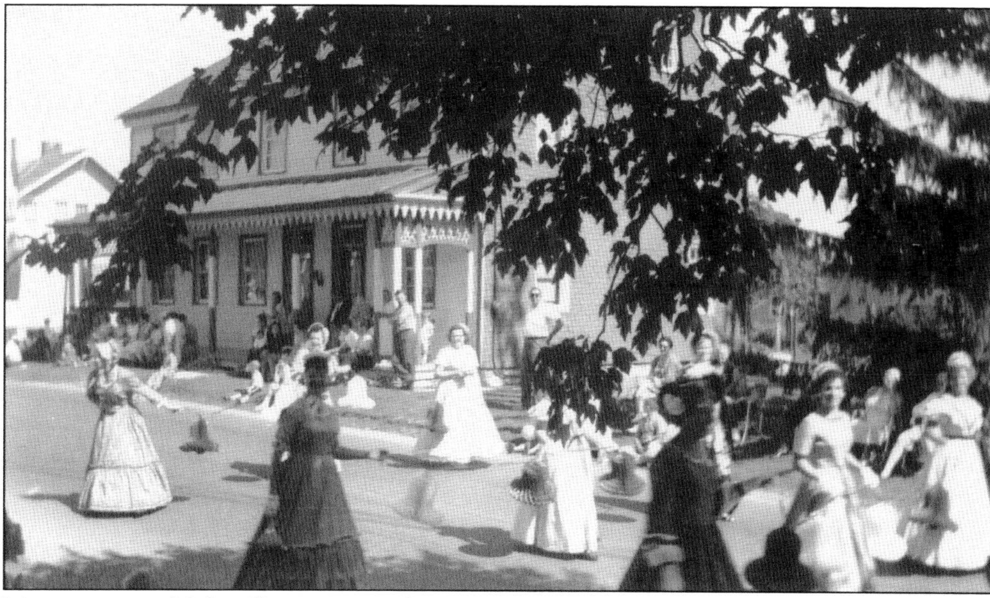

Many women of Schaefferstown sewed costumes and joined one of several Bicentennial Belle groups during the celebration. This group played on the "belle" theme by marching in the parade carrying paper bells. The photograph was taken from the Heisey house, which was demolished in 2011 as part of the Route 501 bypass project. (Courtesy of Walter Heisey.)

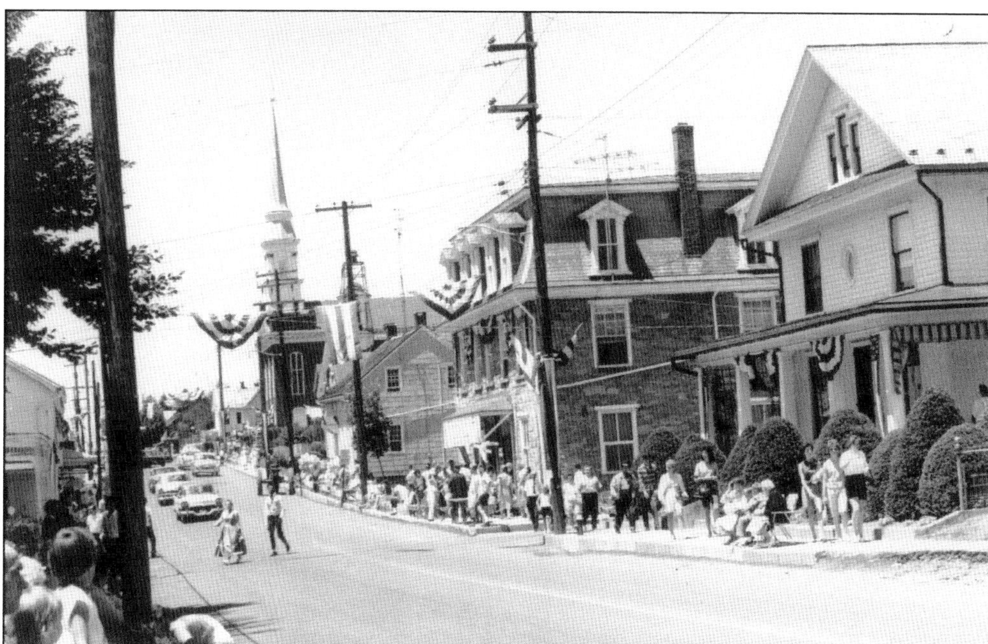

This photograph of Main Street looking northwest was taken as the crowd dispersed after the bicentennial parade. Bicentennial headquarters was in the large limestone building in the center; it once housed the Krall Store and was later a cigar factory. By 1963, Schaefferstown Fire Company owned the building and had converted it into apartments. (Courtesy of Institute of American Deltiology.)

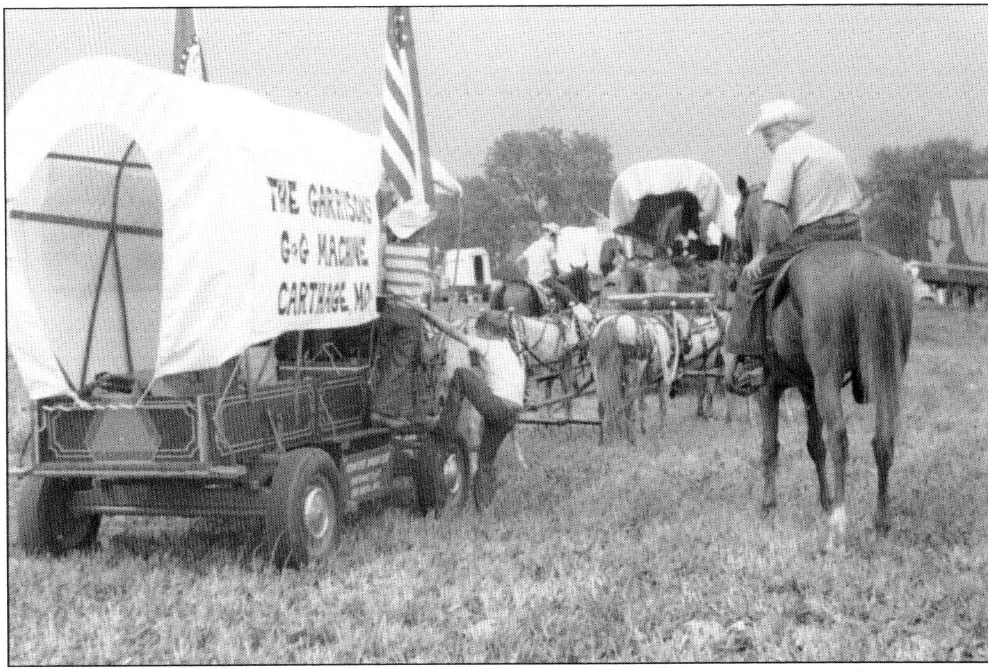

Beginning in June 1975, a number of wagon trains traveled across the country. Starting from points in the north, west, and south, they took seven different routes east, with the goal of arriving in Valley Forge one year later to celebrate the nation's 200th birthday. An initiative of the Pennsylvania Bicentennial Commission, the project involved reproductions of pioneer wagons driven by volunteers; each train was led by a wagon master. The trains made many stops along the way and gathered signatures on "rededication scrolls" that were intended to show Americans' (re)commitment to their country. The trains made 249 encampments, including one at the historic Alexander Schaeffer Farm (above). The photograph below shows wagons heading east on Main Street, passing the Franklin House (on the right) as they leave town.

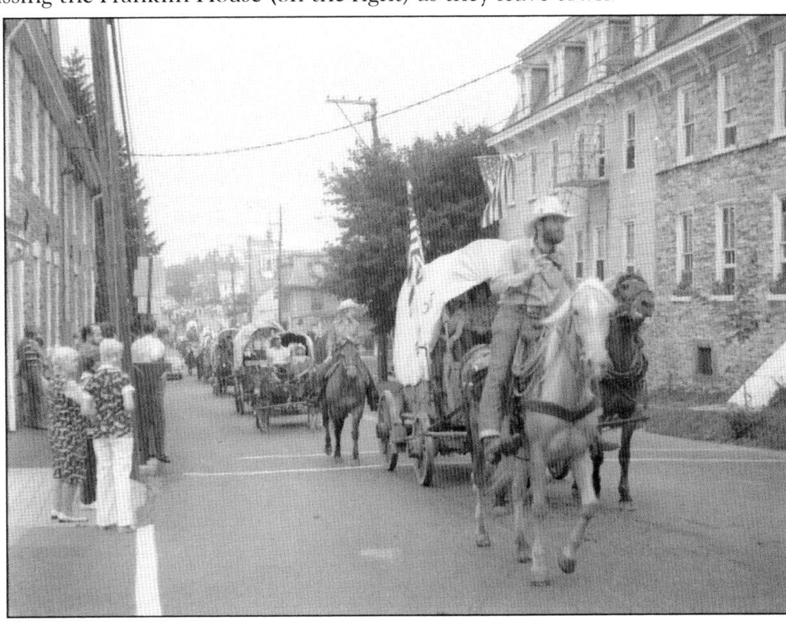

This limestone farmhouse on the Alexander Schaeffer Farm dates from the mid-18th century. It is shown here in a 1930s photograph taken from the meadow, looking northeast. Period records suggest that Schaeffer lived at his tavern (now the Franklin House) rather than on his farm, but he used the resources of the farm, including a still in the basement of this building, to supply his business.

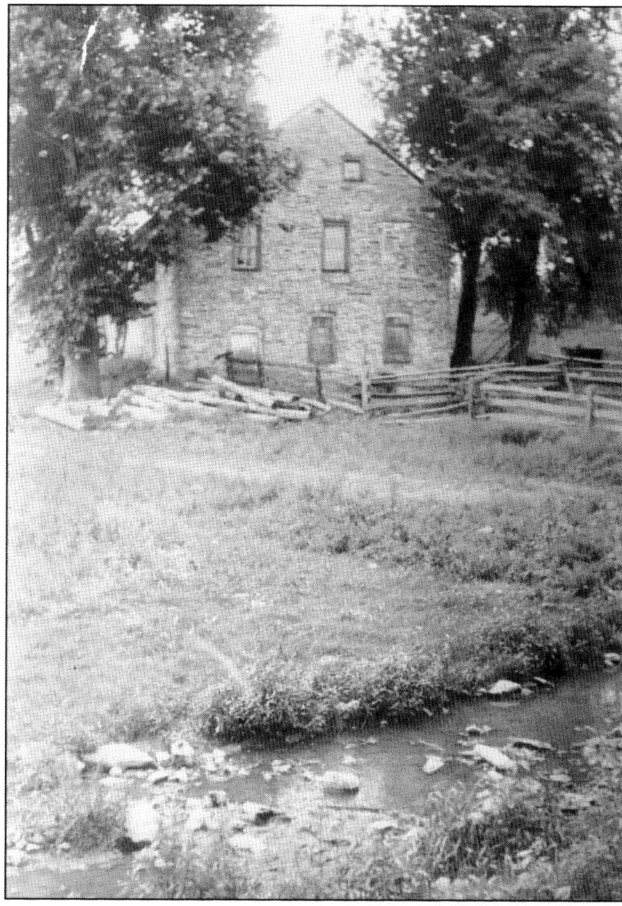

Henry Schaeffer inherited the farm from his father in 1775 and enlarged the house for his family's residence. As part of his alterations, he added a kitchen wing with squirrel-tail bake oven on the north of the house (shown here) and installed a cold cellar and second whiskey still in the basement. Recent archaeological investigations have uncovered the fireboxes for the stills. Architectural investigations of this unusual building are ongoing.

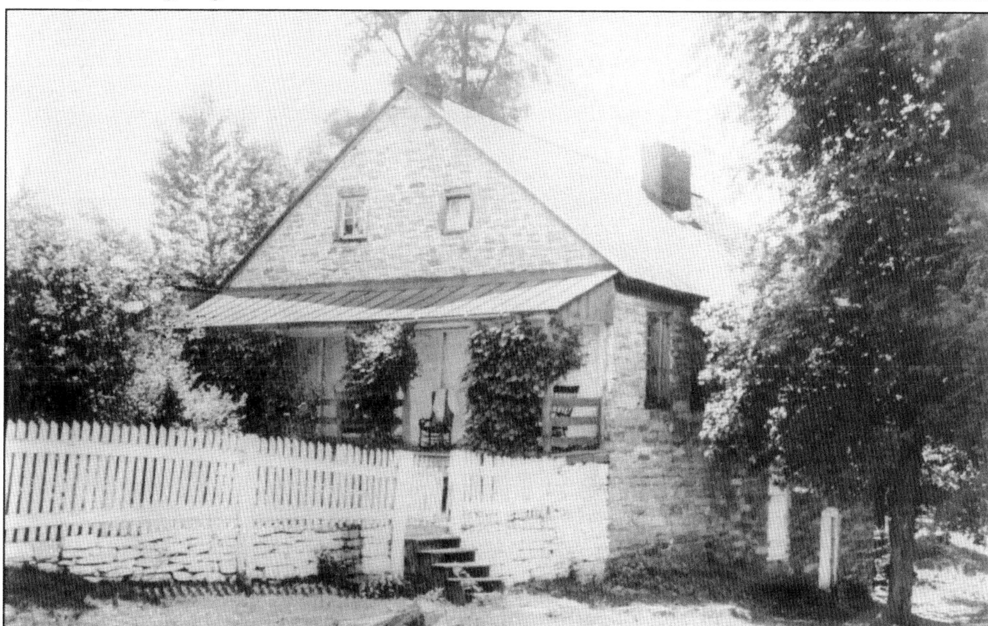

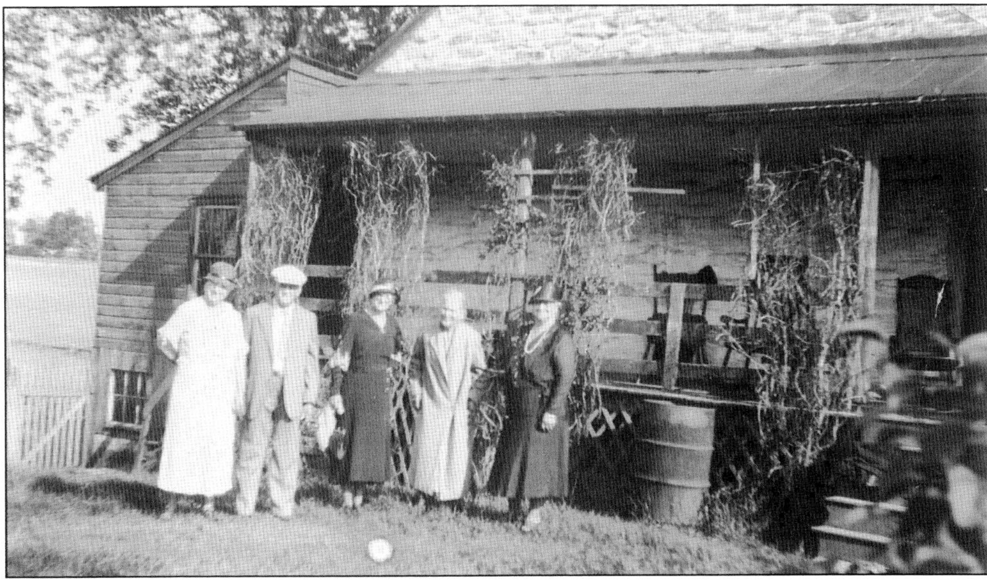

This photograph, taken before 1930, shows the north side of the Schaeffer House as it looked when it was home to Thomas S. and Mary Bomberger Brendle. Shown here are, from left to right, Annie Hains, John and Eliza Light Bomberger, Ella Shiffler, and Mary Bomberger Brendle. The Brendles had four children, including Thomas Royce Brendle, noted Pennsylvania German folklorist, for whom the Brendle Museum is named.

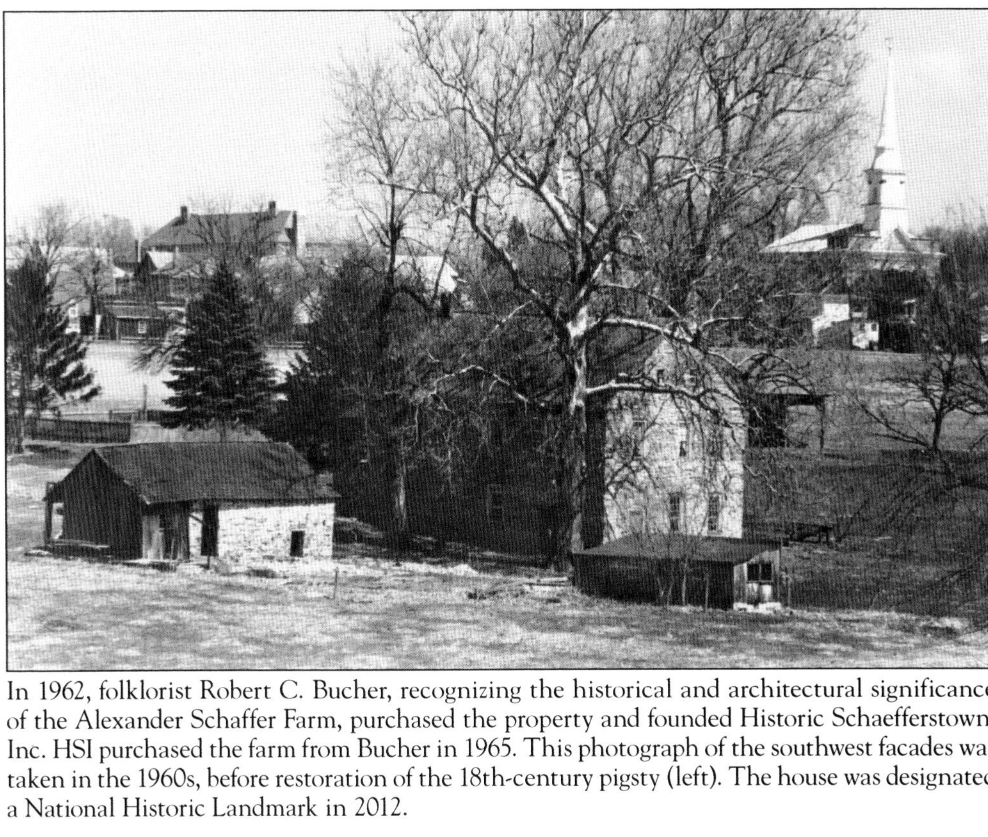

In 1962, folklorist Robert C. Bucher, recognizing the historical and architectural significance of the Alexander Schaffer Farm, purchased the property and founded Historic Schaefferstown, Inc. HSI purchased the farm from Bucher in 1965. This photograph of the southwest facades was taken in the 1960s, before restoration of the 18th-century pigsty (left). The house was designated a National Historic Landmark in 2012.

Dr. Charles D. Spotts (1899–1973) was president of Historic Schaefferstown from 1967 to 1973. Here, he stands in front of the 18th-century smokehouse on the Schaeffer farm displaying tobacco stalks, which have been speared and placed on a wooden lath for drying. Spotts wrote on tobacco culture and frequently lectured on the subject during HSI's early festivals.

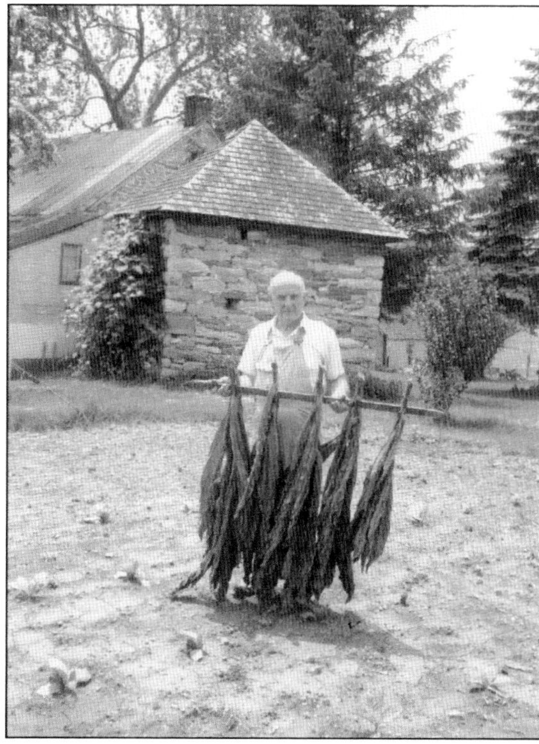

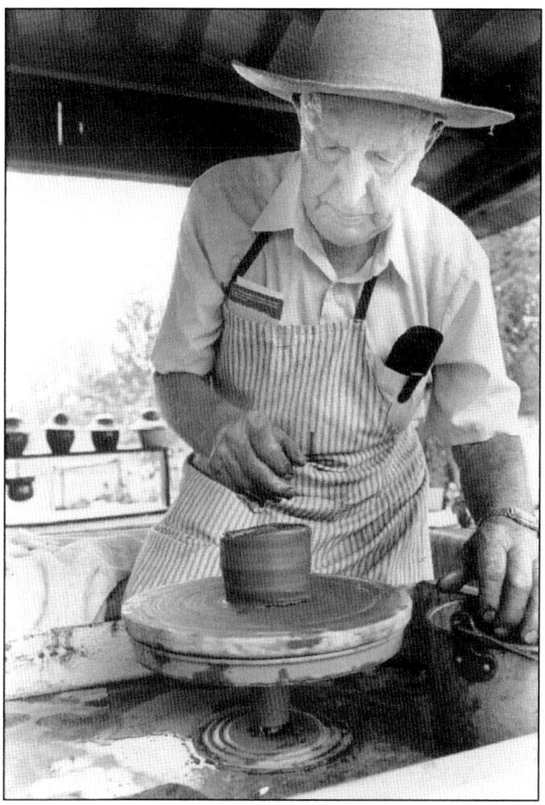

Charles H. Huber (1916–1993) continues a family pottery-making tradition by demonstrating the making of redware pottery at one of Historic Schaefferstown's festivals on the Alexander Schaeffer Farm. An active member of Historic Schaefferstown, Inc., and a historian, Huber compiled *Schaefferstown Bicentennial, 1763–1963.* Huberhaus Pottery is now carried on by Huber's nephew, Steve Huber Horst.

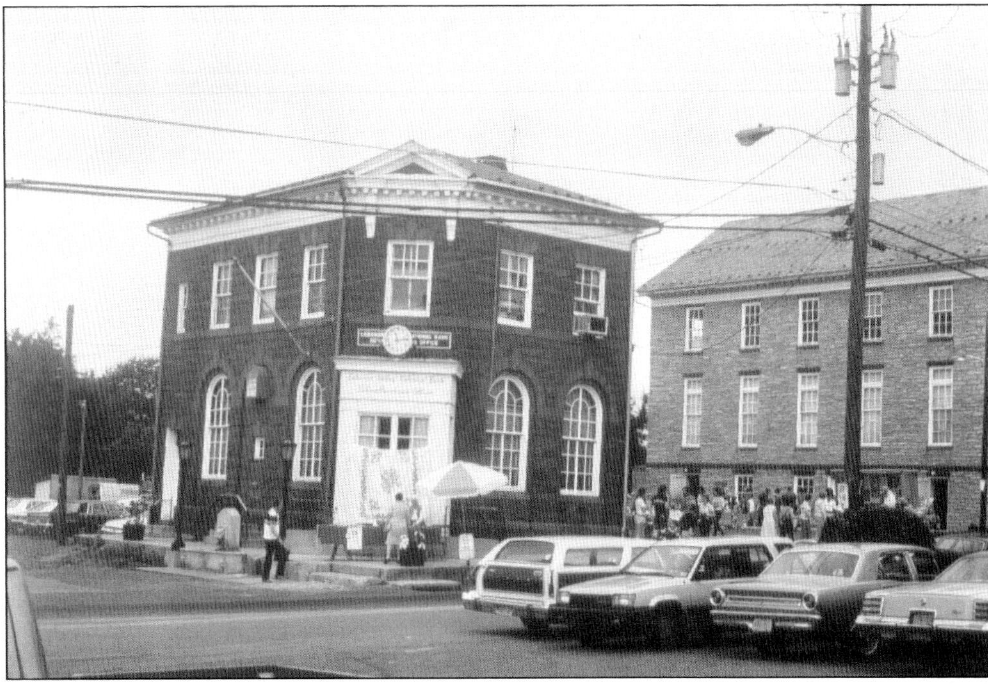

In the 18th and 19th centuries, Schaefferstown was famous for its annual cherry fairs, which drew visitors from a considerable distance. The events lasted several days and featured food, games, dancing, and music. According to A.S. Brendle, the fair was "a promiscuous gathering for merrymaking." The fairs ended when the market house was removed in the mid-19th century. In the 1970s, Historic Schaefferstown revived the tradition by holding a one-day cherry fair on the square and grounds surrounding the Brendle Museum each June. These photographs were taken on the town square in 1984. In recent years, the cherry fairs have been held on the grounds of the Schaeffer farm. (Both, courtesy of Susan Verhoek.)

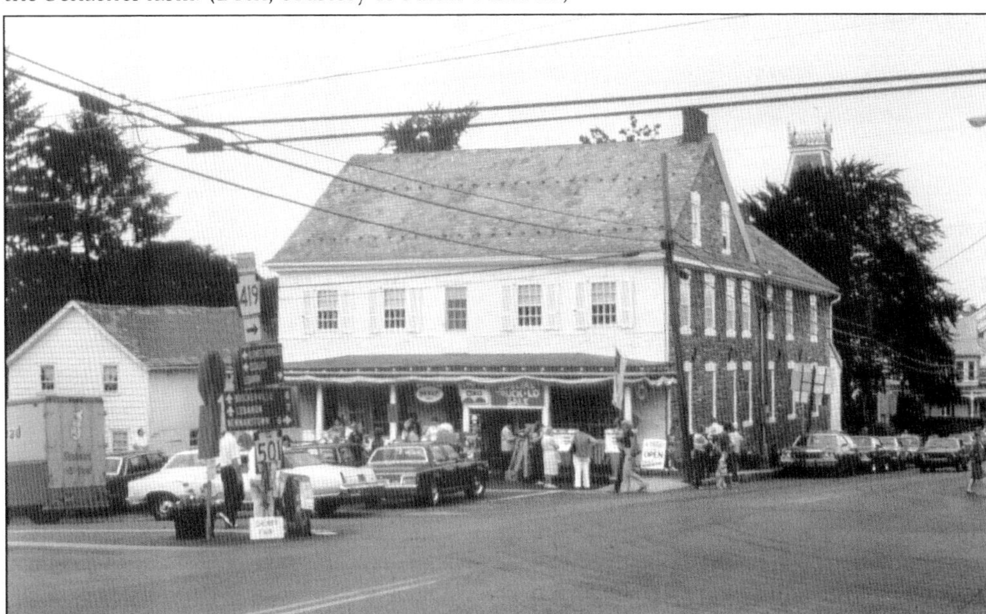

Eight

Schaefferstown and Heidelberg Township Today

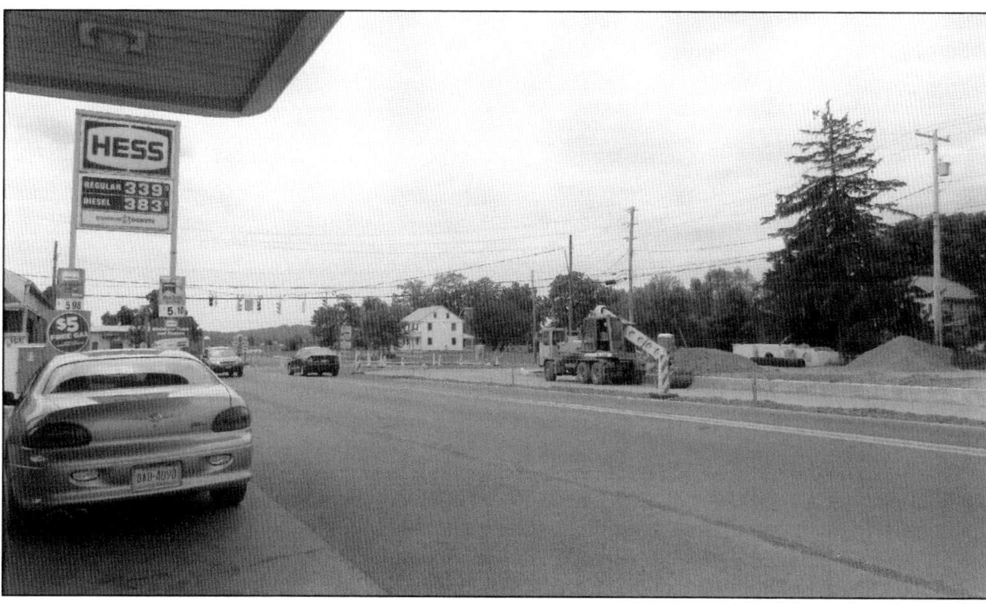

In the spring of 2013, as work continued on the Schaefferstown bypass, this was the view looking south from the intersection of Routes 501, 419, and 897. The two-story Dierwechter family home, visible in the background, was moved 50 feet from its original Main Street location to accommodate the new highway. A large barn associated with the house was demolished. (Courtesy of Diane Wenger.)

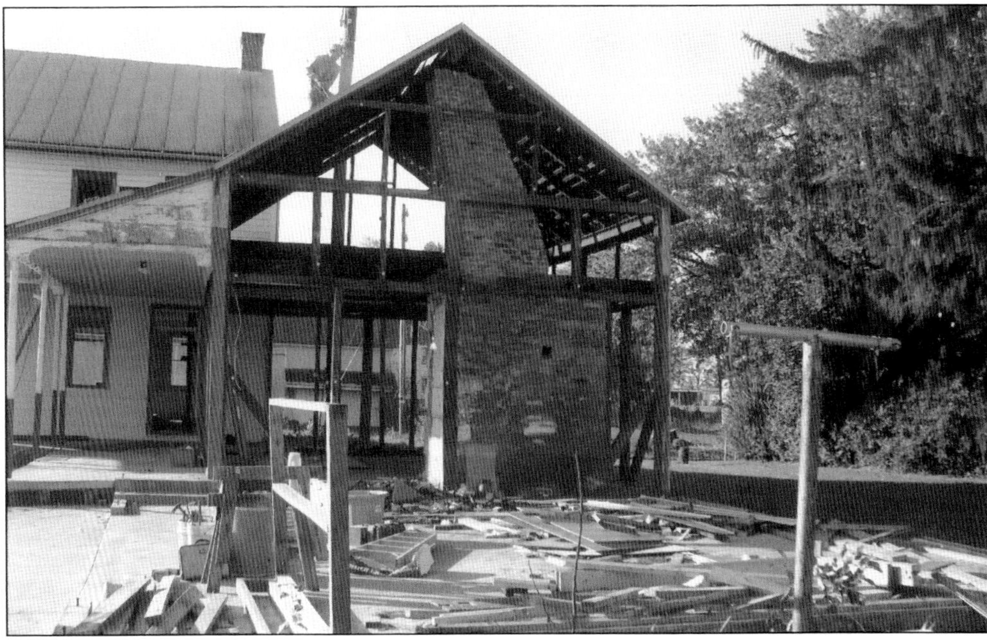

While one house was relocated as a result of the bypass project, the Heisey house, shown here, suffered a different fate. The two-story log building with attached summer house and bake oven once sat on the northwest corner of the intersection. It was razed in October 2011 so that Route 501, now known as Stiegel Pike, could be widened. (Courtesy of Diane Wenger.)

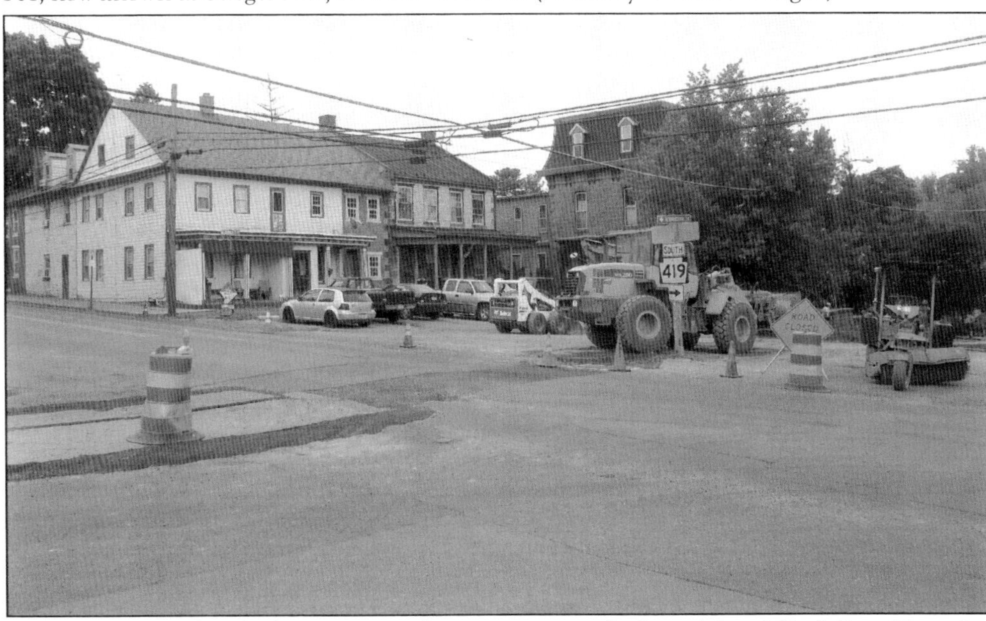

At the same time that the bypass was under construction, the long-delayed Heidelberg Township sewer project began. Sewer lines were installed from the township's western border through Schaefferstown to Kleinfeltersville. Traffic delays due to construction became an everyday occurrence, as four separate contractors and crews tackled different areas of the township, each with different challenges, many times requiring drilling and/or blasting of bedrock. (Courtesy of Jan Taylor.)

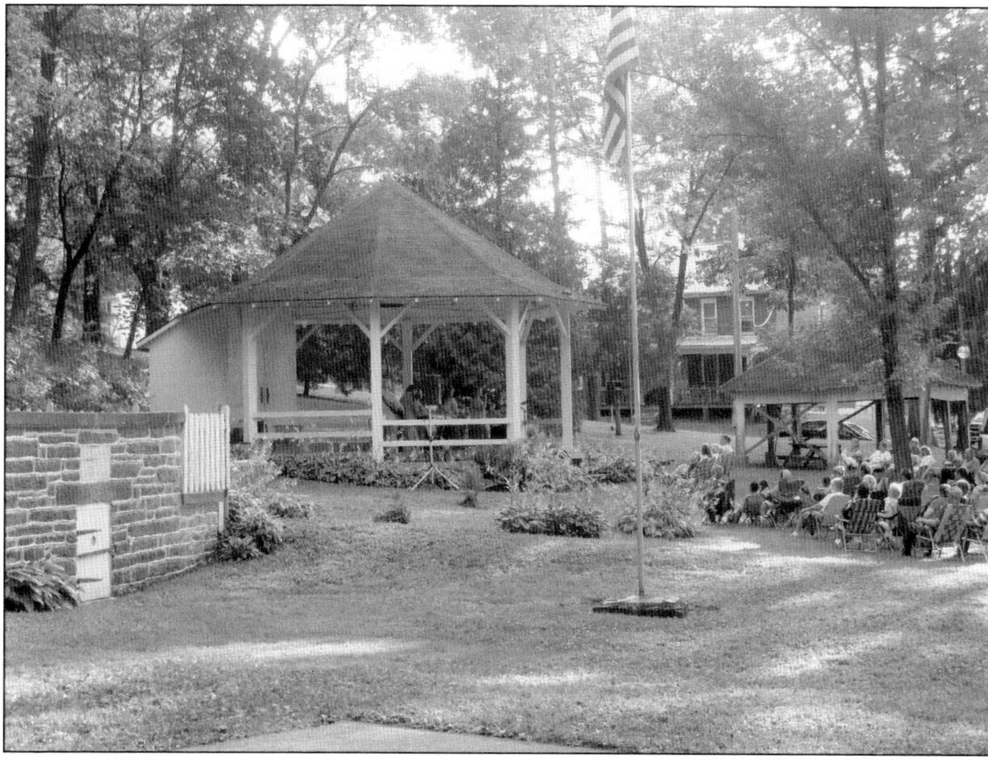

Every year, Fountain Park plays host to family gatherings and picnics. Heidelberg Community Churches sponsor gospel concerts each July, attracting visitors from near and far. Here, the Wehry Family performs at the 2013 Fountain Park Services, the 75th year of vesper services held in the park. In 2013, the town held its 250th anniversary celebration of Schaeffer deeding the water system to Market Street residents. (Courtesy of Jan Taylor.)

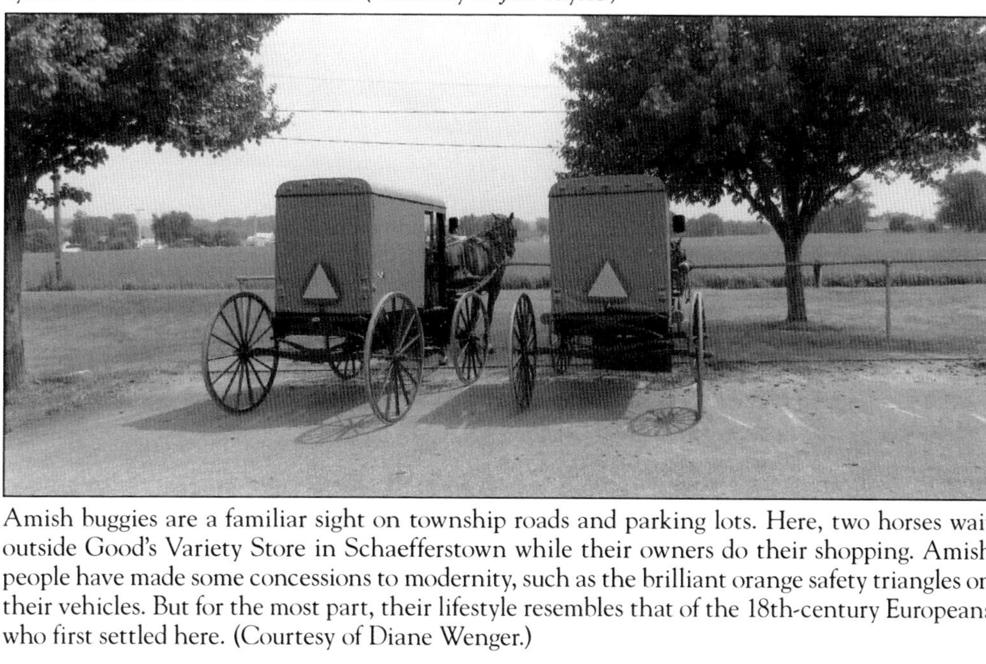

Amish buggies are a familiar sight on township roads and parking lots. Here, two horses wait outside Good's Variety Store in Schaefferstown while their owners do their shopping. Amish people have made some concessions to modernity, such as the brilliant orange safety triangles on their vehicles. But for the most part, their lifestyle resembles that of the 18th-century Europeans who first settled here. (Courtesy of Diane Wenger.)

Bibliography

Beers, F.W. *County Atlas of Lebanon Pennsylvania*. Philadelphia: F.A. Davis, 1875.

Bergengren, Charles Lang. "The Cycle of Transformations in the Houses of Schaefferstown, Pennsylvania." Ph.D. diss. Philadelphia: University of Pennsylvania, 1988.

Brendle, A.S. *A Brief History of Schaefferstown*. 1901. Reprint, with index, Schaefferstown, PA: Historic Schaefferstown, Inc., 1979.

Croll, P.C. *Ancient and Historic Landmarks in the Lebanon Valley*. Philadelphia: Lutheran Publishing Society, 1895.

Dibert, James A. "Changing Historical Interpretations of the Alexander Schaeffer Farm." *Historic Schaefferstown Record* 36 (August 2005): 1–24.

———. "A Chronology of the Alexander Schaeffer Farm." *Historic Schaefferstown Record* 37 (2006).

"Heidelberg Township, Lebanon County, PA." http://heidelbergtownship.com.

History of the Schaefferstown Water Company, Incorporated. Schaefferstown: Schaefferstown Water Company, 1986.

Hoover, E. Eileen. "Questions Regarding the Early History of Schaefferstown." *Historic Schaefferstown Record* 7 (December 1973): 46–53.

Huber, Charles. *Schaefferstown, Pennsylvania, 1763–1963*. Schaefferstown, PA: Schaefferstown Bicentennial Committee, 1963.

Kosack, Joe. "The Middle Creek Story." Pennsylvania Game Commission, 2011.

Kline, Myrle Mann. *Education in Heidelberg Township ? to 1962*. Unpublished manuscript, 1976.

Sachse, Julius Friedrich. *A Photographic Ramble in the Millbach Valley (Lebanon County, Penna.)*. Philadelphia: Alfred J. Ferris, 1896.

Spotts, Charles D. "Tobacco in Lancaster County." *Historic Schaefferstown Record* 18 (July–October 1984): 3–4.

Sullivan, Jack. "The Bombergers: Distilling the Mennonite Way." http://pre-prowhiskeymen.blogspot.com/2011/12/bombergers-distilling-mennonite-way.html.

Wenger, Diane E. *A Country Storekeeper in Pennsylvania: Creating Networks in Early America, 1790–1807*. State College: Pennsylvania State University Press, 2008.

About the Organization

Historic Schaefferstown, Inc.'s (HSI), mission is the collection, preservation, study, and dissemination of the history and folk culture of the Pennsylvania Germans in South Central Pennsylvania, with particular focus on Schaefferstown, Pennsylvania. The organization disseminates information through educational programs for adults and children, tours of its buildings and collections, festivals and special events, and publication of research and promotional materials.

Established in 1965, HSI fulfills this mission in a number of ways. The group operates three museums: the Schaeffer Farm, the 18th-century farmstead once owned by the town's founder; the Thomas R. Brendle Museum, a repository for archival materials and objects related to everyday life in Schaefferstown, particularly in the 19th and early 20th centuries; and the Gemberling-Rex House, an 18th-century tavern and home. These sites are open for tours seasonally and by appointment. Each year, HSI holds a number of historical-themed events to raise funds to help fulfill its mission and maintain its properties. These include, but are not limited to, a harvest fair, cherry fair, holiday Christkindlmarkt, and tavern lunch. The group publishes articles related to Schaefferstown and the surrounding area and Pennsylvania German culture in its annual volume, *Historic Schaefferstown Journal*, and its predecessor, the *Historic Schaefferstown Record*. Members of HSI receive the annual publication and a quarterly newsletter as part of their membership; they also receive free admission to events. Classes in traditional crafts and the Pennsylvania German dialect are also offered annually; children learn old-time skills at the Young Villagers Workshop or by becoming an apprentice to an experienced artisan. Finally, a lecture series offers talks on such topics as archaeology at the Schaeffer Farm, storekeeping in Schaefferstown, painted chests, folk medicine and powwow, and 18th-century distilling.

Information on membership is available at www.hsimuseum.org, by e-mailing HSI at info@hsimuseum.org, or by calling 717-949-2244.

All author royalties from this publication benefit Historic Schaefferstown, Inc.